trust *in* TEXTS

Susan Miller

trust in TEXTS

A DIFFERENT HISTORY OF RHETORIC

Southern Illinois University Press
Carbondale

11 10 09 08   4 3 2 1

Library of Congress Cataloging-in-Publication Data
Miller, Susan, [date]
  Trust in texts : a different history of rhetoric / Susan Miller.
      p. cm.
  Includes bibliographical references and index.
  ISBN-13: 978-0-8093-2788-1 (pbk. : alk. paper)
  ISBN-10: 0-8093-2788-0 (pbk. : alk. paper)
  1. Rhetoric—History. I. Title.

PN183.M55 2007
808.009—dc22   2007013357

Contents

Preface

My mother had ways of describing people that I never hear now. She meant to teach us human standards, an agreed-upon code that everyone already knew. For instance, she would approvingly call someone "personable." Dictionaries define it as "attractive," but I gathered it meant "able to be a person among persons," that is, comfortable with people in an easy, confident, engaging manner she rarely attributed to my high school friends. People might also be "well spoken," which was more than grammatically correct. It included being able to talk at all—an ability most without a finished social education lost in the presence of anyone's parents. But "well spoken" primarily meant ingratiating, always polite and able to hold the floor among equally personable people. It has been much later, from studying writing and teaching it, cultural theory, and strategic modes of persuasion, that I realize how thoroughly this code prescribed an emotional makeup. My mother would say that someone "didn't have much personality," directly naming character as significantly and pleasantly emotional, or not. She approved a "good disposition" and disapproved of its counterparts: "too quiet," "show off," and "not to be trusted."

Most people attach the substance of that list to interior motives within a self composed of genes, family styles, and private traumas. But as its last item most emphatically suggests, the inner sources of these socialized states of feeling were not at issue. From my mother's standpoint, interactions with others equaled a person's identity, no matter what causes or effects determined the interactions. Whatever might determine an "I," this second- and third-person code was neither uniquely individualized nor an official template for types to be diagnosed from elusive motives we glimpse in blurred communications. Yet to characterize the entirety of this model as good manners in public would oversimplify its tacit claim to describe a total character and to reference that character to a scale on which people are intrinsically credible, or not. "To be trusted" was the point of her lesson.

Of course, she never organized this lesson to approve of people who set aside a core self in favor of occupying a role. Her code blended old-fashioned essentialism with authentic but always situated performances. Personable people were fundamentally transactional beings: they might be disapproved as "too quiet" but were never called "shy"—a very differently derived, isolated state. As the items in this list also imply, speaking out and well was the benchmark standard of this code. Unevenly successful uses of language manage this interactive *ethos*. What people said and could not say identified them as trustworthy and responsive interlocutors and thus as a certain quality of person. What they did or did not tell others about how they felt determined how she gauged that quality.

I highlight a system so nearly defunct to focus on historical conditions that have enabled similar evaluations, both commonplace and institutional. This model embodies a different view of educational and political mechanisms that have combined in human dispositions that claim more or less purchase on community standing, both when "standing" itself had tangible results and now, when it does often require quotation marks to convey its situated importance. Thus, the decline of this particular view of the "personable" is also at stake now, as such organized forces are fragmented beyond the capacity of one Western cultural ideal to set normative human standards whose results will at best be mixed.

Nonetheless, even if only within academic disciplines that foster such codes, they deserve new attention. For the purposes of this study, which traces the personable and responses to it through unevenly sized social and intellectual conduits, organized views of trusted character may offer specific if not always obvious alternatives to stale dualist assumptions in both literary and rhetorical studies. In order to preserve rationalist credibility, both still avoid equating identity with feelings. Their credibility is another sort of template for feelings that privileges detachment over interaction—not, as is commonly argued, reason over whim. But here, a different historiographic approach to rhetoric imagines emotion as the content of character, not as its result, and the legibility of feelings as the trust that precedes agreement. This approach suggests that when broadly defined literary, philosophical, and rhetorical discourses are divided from their shared cultural projects, and when this division is made on the basis of separating artistry, craft, and representations of truth, all are reduced. The classifications that allow these discourses to appear to conflict certainly make it impossible to absorb the grounding of my mother's human values. That is, we easily miss the feelings that constitute any moment of trust, the conglomeration of core dispositions and situated responses that allow us to state either absolute or relative truths, to accept our own and others' cases as worth consideration, and to craft the language that is identical to any statement. All of these discursive processes make her values—and of course many other such codes—conventional.

Treating these elements of choice as separate and opposed processes that estrange disciplines also makes it possible to mistreat rhetoric. Especially when it is cast as the functional language skills of persuasion that manipulate equally mistreated feelings, we imagine rhetoric only as results, not causes. We thus disallow consideration of the reverse processes in which trust precedes assent, even if we know that a lack of trust precedes many polite and conflicted silences. We therefore rarely recognize the shared purposes and histories among these disciplines and other metadiscursive explanatory discourses whose cultural work depends on prior trust that results in emotional assent. We instead separate philosophical, if too often only high-minded, resolutions of human uncertainties from rhetorical practices, and both of these official metadiscourses from the modern aesthetics credited with alternative emotional expression in music, dance, visual arts, and literature. Yet philosophy's quest for statements, literary characterizations of feeling and distances from it that personification involves, and rhetoric's discoveries of what might be said in and about discrete puzzles all share means of persuasion. That is, they enculture us emotionally and thereby define successful appeals to various conventional media of interaction.

In that context, my mother's task was easier than the one I undertake here. One of my points is on its face often thought of as at best counterintuitive and at worst a denial of shared humanity: that enculturation into the conditions for assent is historically situated, a result of specific political and material vectors, and that these shifting forces warrant situated revisions of oratorical and other metadiscourses that teach codes like my mother's. This point is in many ways so obvious as to be banal, but its enabling claim that emotion is not an outcome of biological inevitability nor of a universal "human" makeup may not be. Even in the current explosion of academic and popular interest in emotion itself, its uses and status as an acquired human place-keeper remain beyond the edges of new attention to the identity between emotion and specific times and places, with a prominent exception in Daniel Gross's *The Secret History of Emotion*, which firmly supports that view. To note that my mother managed lessons in appropriate emotional codes is also to recall the differences among a privileged Athenian father's duties, those of his child's pedagogue, and the competitive homo-social curriculum that produced favored character then and later. That is, the modern domestic transmission of conduct that my mother undertook obviously stressed other feelings in another historical moment.

It follows that metadiscourses, especially training for oratory, are always and only pedagogies that sustain cultural signatures. Metadiscursive theories usually are composed as ancillae to ordinary lessons and exercises, or as promotions of them, not as detached thought. Those teachings regularly shape and manage, or fail to manage, populations schooled by increasingly inclusive and diffused curricula over time. Thus, emotion needs attention as my mother understood it, as a cultural scene of interaction in which specific groups are bonded and thus found mutually acceptable or not against a standard that is enforced in recurring lessons and remembrance of them.

The primary effect of this different approach to rhetoric as many metadiscursive educations in shared emotional conventions may be uncovering its cultural work largely without revisiting the texts of its canons. The exceptions I make focus on Aristotle's *Rhetoric* and the often-read texts of eighteenth-century Scottish moral philosophers. The latter demonstrate the post-Cartesian, pre-Freudian creation of (universal, gendered, class-coded, race-aware, capitalist) consciousness. Their post-Cartesian work makes normal the continuing view that emotion is a closely held individual property, not a community expectation. But it has not often been noticed as dedicated to that precise project.

Of course, this is not the first study to take this approach or voice my concerns about current traditions in rhetoric studies, although it traces the thematics of trust, character, and textuality across a broader history that is necessarily less detailed than many others. Few at any distance from the specific moments of interest named here take up rhetoric as one of many variously interested sources of trust in discourse. That claim throughout this study portrays persuasion as a result of situated emotional investments in the desires aroused by crafted, and expected, language. As I emphasize, the emotions at stake here are not the internalized versions of *ethos*, *logos*, and *pathos* that twentieth-century human sciences investigate as ego, superego, and id. They are instead conventional responses to events and their representations in many discourses, even when manifest as hysteria or as the pouting that Aristotle associates with injured merit. They constitute communities, not narrated selves, at least not before narrative itself becomes the most trusted source of contemporary argumentation.

I think of the many professional and scholarly conversations that come up to guide and sometimes to oppose these claims as various "rhetorical cultures," a phrase chosen to emphasize the feeling tone of the many works that I simultaneously depend on and critique. Of course, the possibility of disagreement applies whenever we write to say more. But in this case, delicate yet sometimes impermeable boundaries around the research interests that contribute to this study's constitutive ways of thinking and talking about rhetoric may appear to be too closely linked to rest comfortably against each other. I have gleefully seized many obvious opportunities to avoid focusing on conflicts among these conversations and hope to have successfully created more ways of avoiding such disagreements. But I missed many chances to avoid injury out of ignorance and my enduring sense that the future of cultural pedagogies, especially discourse education, needs additional objections to the determinism of its conventional histories. I hope we may together review the operations of language that ground our most basic needs for credibility and acknowledgment in shifting group relationships, a project that Kenneth Burke's work first opened to me in more formalist contexts.

Lollianus, the third-century grammarian who appears soon, could be certain that his appeal to the empire for back pay on the ground of shared devotion to the Muses would elicit imperial trust in a shared *paideia*. But we are now rarely sure we can invoke predispositions to agree in everyday encounters, let alone as scholars and as teachers. When we do invoke them, we may wonder if we have been entirely clear. Yet we notably do share the curiosity that initiated the multiple cases I make here. That energy—which is never merely a cognitive state—is our mutual guarantee of shared, if skeptical, respect.

Acknowledgments

This project has taken much longer to complete than I knew could be the case when I began. A 1997–98 National Endowment for the Humanities Fellowship allowed me to begin substantial research into biological, literary, historical, and philosophical perspectives on emotion. That topic was then a tentatively emerging, still embarrassing scholarly interest, acknowledged most frequently as a way to reconceptualize and popularize rationalism. Consequently, I remain grateful to my friends and former colleagues Kathleen Woodward and Herbert Blau, who were then as always ahead of most academic curves. They were enormously helpful readers of my first attempts to articulate some overlooked complications of attraction and charisma that constitute any history of trusted discourses. Over the time since then, my scattered friends—David Bartholomae, Lynn Bloom, Charles Berger, Stuart Culver, Janet Giltrow, and Gary Olson, with Karl Kageff at Southern Illinois University Press—have offered support that allowed me to continue through a number of forced hiatuses.

I am also especially grateful to an accumulating cohort of students in graduate rhetoric classes that I have taught. Their responses to my increasing unwillingness to accept received histories of one unified rationalist rhetoric and their suggested alternative versions of those narratives were the best tests of my formation of a different plausible case and the best sources of conservative good sense. Among many, I am variously indebted to Suellyn Duffy, Chris Diller, Doug Downs, Shaleane Gee, Gaelynn Henderson, Octavio Pimentel, Brian Rajeski, Kelly Ziegler, Sam Wakefield, and Michael Wright.

I am also indebted to 2004–2005 sabbatical support from the University of Utah's College of Humanities, which allowed me to complete this book as I began another project. Invitations to try out portions of my case among its most stringent critics occasioned the book's first tentative participation in academic conversations, so I also thank the Modern Language Association, Utah's Tanner Humanities Center, the Rhetoric Society of America, Drake University, Northern Illinois University, Iowa's Project on the Rhetoric of Inquiry, and the American Society for the History of Rhetoric for providing the best possible audiences. In those and other settings, Susan Jarratt, Janet Atwill, Patricia Bizzell, Jackie Royster, Michael Leff, Larry Green, Ralph Cintron, Steve Mailloux, Victor Vitanza, and Lynn Worsham were wonderful conversants. Daniel Gross's *The Secret History of Emotion* appeared just as this study was completed, so our brief conversations cannot adequately recognize his work as the secret sharer of my claims.

I also thank my Utah colleagues for direct interventions in the completion of the manuscript. They have been kind and patient and have served as sources of variously crucial corrections and equally crucial approval. Scott Black, Richard Preiss, Tom Stillinger, and Barry Weller, colleagues in the Department of English, read sections of the manuscript to check its accuracy and to comment on the chapters that take up early modern and eighteenth-century rhetorics. Len Hawes and Daniel Emory in the Department of Communication welcomed this project with details of professional interactions that equally forewarn and comfort me. Raul Sanchez in the University Writing Program was this study's faithful friend and constant critic. Barry Weller's editing was crucial.

I would not have undertaken nor completed this work without Carol Poster's generous support at every step. Our frequent conversations and shared discoveries across obvious intellectual borders inform many of my statements. She and the final reviewers of the manuscript, Greg Clark and Patty Harkin, are this book's latest protection from not writing, as here, to say more.

trust in
TEXTS

Introduction: Rhetoric, Emotion, and Places of Persuasion

> If names are not properly defined and used, the speech can never sound
> agreeable. If the speech jars, nothing can be accomplished. This means that
> there would be no proper observance of ritual and ceremonial activities, the
> legal system would collapse, and people would no longer know how correctly
> to behave themselves.
>
> —*Zhu Zi Ji Cheng*

Rhetorics, Pedagogies, and Methods

It is obvious to many who focus on rhetoric's history that there is no longer
one entity that fits that term, and some think that there never was, that no
unified rhetorical tradition ever existed. The ways we refer to rhetoric make
it for once easy to agree with Gorgias that nothing exists that this word refers
to. One frequent response to this situation is to claim that the way I use the
term *rhetoric* is right and that others' uses are wrong. But outside an interplay
of definitions, which postpones some discussions forever, we might turn
to different historical methods and consider emphases in various schools
outside the still active view of rhetoric as types of Aristotelian argument.
Rather than define it, we might ask, "What versions of rhetoric are going to
be of use to us in particular situations?"

Answering that question may allow us to uncover a history of choice itself. At the least, it would create an overview of many culturally constitutive
discourses among which shared definitions are but one condition of trust.
There are, we quickly see, others.

My use of the word *rhetoric* thus understands it as a plurality—multiple
metadiscourses derived from ritual, imaginative, and affiliative discursive

1

practices that we trust for their well-supported and reasoned statements, but also because they participate in infrastructures of trustworthiness we are schooled to recognize, sometimes by lessons and habits we cannot name. Those infrastructures vary according to the time when a specialized plane of understanding and its consequences emerges in specific cultures—political, religious, social, technological, even meteorological impact on what we know and how we can know it. But the purpose of these prescriptive networks remains constant: to endow a discursive practice with precedent trustworthiness. These rhetorics organize our emotional receptivity to statements on which we can depend for answers to speculative questions. They thereby guide us to choices that may not produce the best outcome but that we trust to be the "right thing," not in a shallow morality but because we are persuaded of their source's share in our best interests.

From the discrete perspective on discourse that modern intertextuality permits, we feel that way because we recognize various hierarchies that more than one oratorical rhetoric contains. We base this disposition to trust on what Mary Hamilton in *Situated Literacies: Readings and Writing in Context* calls "structured routines and pathways that facilitate and regulate actions, the rules of appropriateness and eligibility" (17). Those rules differ markedly among discourses that unevenly change over time. Contemporary cultures, for instance, have medical and epistolary discourses whose phenomenologies of trust determine how any interaction with them may succeed, or not, depending on their interlocutors' schooled view of "appropriateness and eligibility." Thus, we accept a letter as authentic automatically, or reject it with equal speed, because we have at least tacit training to sense its relation to a long history of forgeries, as M. T. Clanchy explains in *From Memory to Written Record: England 1066–1307*.[1] We learn epistolary rhetoric, as we do routines of medical communication, as cultural pedagogies under one rubric: they are metadiscourses that organize persuasion around specific conditions of trust.

Pedagogy is of course yet another term we think of as having a discrete tradition. It is rarely recognized as the name of historically diffused formal schooling and self-instruction in temporally, regionally, and otherwise situated conditions of trust in language itself. From infancy, we learn an absolute difference between words that are "right" and "wrong." But we are then differentially encultured to identify reliable ways of thinking and talking, especially those organized around imaginary, speculative, yet crucial decisions. Such discourses emerge from antique civilizations and their precedents, offering separately framed ways to consider choices we make despite our ignorance of the knowledge on which they must be based within areas we have neither mastered nor enact, and often that no one has. That is, we trust discourse we perceive to contain unknowns—undisclosed if not secret content that inevitably intimates that more than we know might be known. Such persuasion tells us as well that we already know more because we learn by precept and example about a metadiscourse whose very formulation promises that the unknown is not unknowable. This is to say that many mechanisms around uncertainty function symbolically and charismatically, not logically or analytically.

A chief benefit of this approach to rhetoric is to highlight its culturally constitutive nature and thereby to set aside arguments about its conceptual definitions. Conceptual definitions never connect ideas to the circumstances that produce them; their treatments most often downplay the interested uses to which they have been put; and they by nature separate one metadiscourse from another. They do not link their inevitably overlapped results for people, for sociability, and ultimately for institutions. But a pedagogic definition of rhetoric also renovates the historiography usually applied to it, well after we jettison Hegelian chronologies of canons formed around concepts rather than situated uses. Obviously, we add content to rhetoric's history by emphasizing that its multiple forms constitute a plurality of instructive, variously situated lessons in language and in aesthetic, formal, and ordinary discourses that create contexts for choice.

But this awareness also allows us to rethink methods after the telling anecdotes of New History, which reverts to traditional omniscience about progress; after Sponge-Histories, which absorb overlooked, marginal participants into dominant discourses they rightfully have had doubts about joining; and after myriad other ways of manipulating time, which portray it as a product of totalizing concepts. As research about multiplicities of literacies has done, this emphasis also uncovers the egoism of rhetoric's own "autonomous model," the essentialist view of literacy that New Literacy Studies critiques for its abstractions of civilized smartness. That criticism thus shows that New History reproduces formal categories despite its narrations of "actual" moments. It especially admits that neither discourse practices nor speaking subjects are singular, logical, or consistent. As Albert Einstein reminds historians, time itself is multiple interrelated levels, not neat past/ present/future categories. We can only construct and control the past and the future in an emergent present. Thus, another benefit of making cultural teachings the shared purpose of many rhetorics is that doing so insists that a multiplicity of lessons will change relative to the view of its observers as a present emerges.

Of course, it is also obvious that an autonomous model of rhetoric treated as a singular, historical oratory imagines it as a conceptual tradition constituted by carefully formulated teachings. But that model also transmits an abstract if always locally exemplified code. In this context, variations in lessons about public speech are taken to fragment a unified whole, not to demonstrate that oratory appears, is superseded, and is finally de-emphasized in relation to other rhetorics that have been recruited to build a particular cultural imaginary. Nonetheless, the forms and genres most closely associated with oratory all stimulate admirable imitation exercises, but never only admiration. That is, handbooks, style guides, transferred instructions in preaching, ongoing declamatory performances, treatises that define universal taste as a quality of readers, and Aristotle's and Early Modern French poetics all realize discrete metadiscourses as direct instruction in named techniques. We might generalize John Ward's comment on later uses of classical rhetoric in epistolography to that instruction: "Classical rhetorical theory, prose composition and epistolography responded to distinct market niches which appeared from time to time in different places as a consequence of social and political changes" (175).

These instructions all describe processes that determine credibility and more—the infrastructures of our choices to believe. We remember Peter Ramus for textbooks and Augustine and Richard Whately for lessons in preaching and even Socrates for worry over how to create the best speech. But we may nonetheless fit each figure and treatise into conceptual histories whose methods lift their skirts at the thought of real teaching.

Yet variations within these lessons fit more than "market niches." For instance, Renaissance English style guides participate in attempts to create a vernacular as authoritative and as trustworthy as Latin in an emergent post-Latinate literacy, not in the fragmentation of a never unified rhetoric. And considering that Book III of Aristotle's *Rhetoric* may have been a transposed work from his early teaching—and that scholars continue to disagree about the dates and sources of the composition of parts of the whole as we have it (Kennedy, *Aristotle* 304)—it is likely that its third chapter about style is part of an attempt to bring disparate elements of composition together, not part of a unified theory that falls apart toward the end. But in any case, Renaissance style handbooks and a new philology devoted to vocabulary respond to new, national interests.

These examples also point out the ambiguity of naming rhetorical "theory" of any sort, historically and now. With few but quickly canonized exceptions, the most commonly conceptualized rhetoric is a practice, specifically a teaching practice. Thus, much we call rhetorical theory presents how-to's of production. They might be interpreted as how-to's of textual analysis but are not intended to be so, at least in their composition before the twentieth century. In almost all cases, the work we call rhetorical theory is not so effective a meta-analysis of practice as the *Symposium*'s critique of poetic representation. Apart from that persuasive Realist dissection of how a poet's mediated imitations cannot convey universal truths, theories of metadiscourse are thin on the ground before the eighteenth century and remain relatively rare outside literary theory.

However, when we treat rhetorics as pedagogies, we more easily notice how they form, inflect, and disseminate their content in ways that connect it to local circumstance. For instance, Jay Fliegelman's *Declaring Independence: Jefferson, Natural Language, and the Culture of Performance*, which analyzes both American nationalist language and rhetorically performed political aims, notes John Witherspoon's late-eighteenth-century "great rule of sincerity." Witherspoon recommends self-revelation in speeches aimed to dismantle ranked hierarchy in new democracies, a suggestion that captures the spirit of American rebellion against monarchic control and aristocratic ranks (Fliegelman 119). Later, after the American Civil War, school rhetorics pointedly perform what Jean Ferguson Carr, Stephen L. Carr, and Lucille M. Schultz's *Archives of Instruction: Nineteenth-Century Rhetorics, Readers, and Composition Books in the United States* calls a "subversive reverence." That is, they gather the discrete, detailed prescriptions of earlier rhetorics into general principles that smooth over their distinctness from each other. The resulting simplified systems teach new mass education's enlarged student population, who are hereby trained to trust and to aim for a national character, to replace divisive regionalism (47). Through this work, American rhetorics also promote idealized life-narratives of citizenship, a plot of participation by fundamentally Calvinist, self-monitorial actors who learn from these modified lessons in rhetoric to avoid further civic disorder.

To respond effectively to various cultural exigencies requires that such pressures also remain familiar. Their frameworks must assure the continuing legibility and status of a discursive response to shifting cultural needs in literary, religious, dramatic, poetic, political, and other discourses whose practices merge in systematic lessons. Repetitive exercises that require using conventional figures and naming taxonomies of argumentation certainly inculcate rhetoric's Hudibrastic "tools."[2] But repetition also characterizes histories of a unified rhetoric's recurring novel debuts. That is, even a limited history of metadiscursive teaching practices compressed into one oratorical tradition shows how those practices circulate and recirculate across cultures. They deliver seemingly pure prescriptions for appropriate motives, speakable topics, and a conventional range of discursive actions in various present circumstances. But such repetition is also crucial to monitoring, reprocessing, and delivering the lineaments of trust.

This is obviously to say that multiple dull lessons alter historically to conserve dominant social structures and cooperation with them in fresh circumstances. These unfamiliar conditions sometimes include war, new forms of government, challenges to economic relations, inventions that disturb established social relations and patterns of communication, and other events perceived to require rearticulating principles and thus also require revising linguistic and discursive conventions that sustain their credibility. This process shifts spoken and graphic conventions, rewrites the implications of specific words, and highlights new or newly elastic genres. A variety of metadiscursive lessons reorganize trust in religious, philosophical, political, aesthetic, and practical reconstructions of reality.

In such moments of cultural slippage, interruption, and self-interrogation, shifted circumstances also turn up discourse pedagogy's extremely durable power to recuperate limits on what may be said. Roland Barthes calls those limits our "Aristotelian vulgate."[3] Paolo Valesio argues that "the content of man's vision has always been expressible only through a set of ready-made simplifying forms whose recognition . . . requires only a long, cold look at the underlying similarity of all acts of human communication, where it is always the same mechanisms, always the same frames that keep reappearing" (31–34). Insofar as both critics willingly privilege conventional expression in these ways, they imply that the metadiscursive teachings that become prominent in any era will be rewritten explanations of discursive processes that nonetheless immediately become authoritative. We accept them even as they are recomposed because they conform to structures they may otherwise be expected to replace. This is also to note again that even oblique historical claims that the authority of rhetoric derives from conceptual alliances with philosophy efface the powers of discourse networks. Metadiscourses control what to say and how to say it, not knowing what it is or how it came to be.

Thus, with Gorgias again in mind, we might note that critics invested in language, literature, and philosophy prefer interpretation along hermeneutic lines to analyses of how discourse is produced and deployed in material circumstances. That preferred focus on singular texts also ignores how these discourses and theories of their production accomplish the power of cultural reproduction. But not even an interpretative turn in rhetoric—much less the cultural and linguistic turns that have followed it—has forestalled the need for detailed discussions of that production in the protected third space that postcolonial critics name as a way to suspend fixed, often stereotyped identity. By extension, third spaces also remove professional conversations from fixed methods and worn paradigms for understanding their appropriate objects of study. Yet the freedoms of spaces that suspend surety also allow us to be deserted by once comforting traditions. In this rhetorical case, without foundational certainty that speakers and writers interchangeably control the meanings that emerge from interpretive technologies, we already wander into ambivalence. Rhetoricians are simultaneously strategically essentialized scholars and critics who know not only what they mean but what Cicero surely did, and also new media participants in a linguistic turn in which *meaning*, now a word *only* in quotation marks, depends on operations within language.

In this rhetorical culture, as always, what we do not see and cannot know attracts and repels us in almost identical measure. The ways of thinking and talking that mediate between apprehension about the unknown and attraction to it always require creating trust, a nonce confidence that unevenly collapses troublesome distances between a symptom and a diagnosis, death and its aftermath, heroes and their destinies, and especially our likely control of responses to community puzzles. Insofar as cultures school their constituents to rely on community experience and individual perceptions more than they do on guesses, fantasy, self-interested advice, and even the combined data and enchantment that constitute supposedly rational argumentation, those cultures define insight as *emotional* agreement, no matter how provisional or temporary.

These propositions are not meant to suggest that one original, archetypical, explanatory discourse first combined with a hardwired trusting human response to allay unevolved human insecurity. Nor do they indicate that systematic address to such uncertainties inevitably fragments into the disseminated conventions of such an impossible archetype. Neither do these hypotheses involve more or less enduring trust in the original purposes of those conventions. Narratives of progress that tell how developed rationalist minds eventually forgo primitive magic to become "scientific" are certainly belied by current political decision-making, as they are by the operatic if fulfilling results of romance. Yet historical accounts of discourse production easily produce such narratives when they turn up progress and decline or imagine time itself as series of this-then-that absolute changes. The result is to apply the same explanatory metaphors to any materialized social process, to thereby foster the view that cultures can erase or irrevocably transform any such process. Such method totalizes even the most particular local views and circumstances into one abstraction—The State, The Speech, The Speaker. These constructs are not only theoretical, for the State, Speech, and Speaker they produce behave precisely as they are hereby taught, as totally impenetrable performances, not responses to exigent circumstances.

Such models in common histories of rhetoric overwhelm the possibility that the discourse of "history" could narrate accumulating options—in this case, accrued ways to address fairly stable human and social discourses that will be redeployed in new models in recurring human situations. That is, in this alternative to a historiography built from concepts, competitions, and belief in absolute change, one or more common discourses of intercession that address a specific community vexation may become the most prominent model for addressing that collective issue. But obviously, other models will also supply conventional ways to contain anxiety and inspire useful responses to experience. Such means remain differently active and multiply differentially, largely in thrall to material and political possibilities for their production and reproduction. For instance, we now invite representatives of religious discourses to preside at weddings and at many state events. But their modern presence collects other mythic representatives of solemn surety in many rituals; it neither critiques nor obliterates them.

Retained historical models also can disallow interest in the relative credibility of mediating discourses, at least apart from their embedment in uneven power relations. That is, when specific ways of forming, talking about, and performing linguistic conventions are imagined to result from contests of social strength, but not actually to constitute those contests, their relative credibility and thus their uses appear to be enforced in absolute ways. The loss is that they are not then treated as acceptable or not in proportion to their fit to a specific conventional audience's responses. Nonetheless, relations of power never *essentially* define a discourse of mediation, nor do they evenly sustain its perceived place among others. For instance, drama, oratory, medical persuasion, and other trusted interpretations in specific cultures may become less easily staged and less willingly received at any time. They will thus disproportionately contribute to conventional subject positions that are trusted as "normal." But obstacles to their production, dissemination, or reception never entirely erase their persuasive force nor our shared willingness to use these agreed-upon frameworks to make experience available to memory and reflection. Despite claims to the contrary, e-mail never replaces what appear in its wake to be cumbersome handwritten notes. Electronic writing allows us to contrast still active ways of writing in terms of available time and different expectations of temporary immediacy in relationships.

My claims that persuasion is always a matter of trust that precedes any form of its expression and that its worthiness for that trust will be verified against multiple discursive conventions obviously revise the possibility of one rhetorical tradition. Like many other historiographies, this view questions the reliability of origin stories—here, an Athena-like birth of oratory in classical Greece. It also moots the possibility that systematic rhetoric is or may be made obsolete by forces outside it. No abstracted "philosophy" can dismantle multiply realized lessons about discourse production, no matter how poor their reputation among Idealistic essentialists. Outside patriarchal histories, which insist on dialectically enacted wins, losses, and syntheses, rhetorical performance is only one among many systematic ways of encouraging comfort with uncertainty. Defined here as one discourse about discourse, rhetoric is identified with the singular spirit claimed by sophistic Socrates, with the orator who embodies conventional responses to events that assure emotional assent to any well-argued position, with the scribe who transmits documents to renew the displaced authority of these early cultural icons, with the vernacular stylist, and, in recent circumstances, with the circulated postprint text whose source is impossible to distinguish from its publicity. In this current case, rhetoric portrays credibility as a reputation without exemplary cases.

Topics: Simultaneous and Consecutive

To make these suggestions at all credible and thematically manageable from the specific angles of incidence I sketch below, this study describes a decentered, always mobile relation between texts and their acceptance as trusted cultural resources. To do so, it simultaneously follows the chronological canon that constitutes one familiar rhetorical tradition and injects into it topics and perspectives rarely used to qualify its singularity. Classical oratory occupies chapter 1, "Decentering Rhetoric," as the master text of rhetoric studies now under revision by new political and social histories of antique worlds, especially by relatively recent discoveries of sophisticated uses of texts that occur millennia before the invention of the alphabet. My critical return to commonly accepted wisdoms about Athenian oratory does not question the superiority of the classical Greek texts that we do have as against others that we cannot know of. But it does refer to work that reveals, for instance, highly specialized and sometimes secreted writing systems used only within discrete vocations, as impressed stamps were used on small clay envelopes that contained cargo records read by merchant ship captains along the Mediterranean coast. In addition to using this information to suggest that neither the media nor the messages of oratory are likely to have been singular, the chapter takes up the extraordinary sophistication of ancient links among character, convention, and style.

The chapters that follow in turn address early modern technologies of trust in print, rhetorics, and texts, especially the emblematic phenomenology of uncertainty that enables epistolary rhetorics and that underlies the standardized language and consciousness sought in eighteenth-century moral philosophy (see chapter 3). The conclusion returns to the antique bifurcation of selves identified as "real" versus "emotional." This last chapter provides a retrospective context for the earlier propositions of the book, an ending that results from wanting to show that linear chronologies inevitably downplay how ever-emerging futures will reinvent any enduring tension in a new emergent present.

Chapter 2, "Trusting Texts," revisits the suppositions of many histories of classical rhetoric to show that print, often glorified as another alphabet, caused neither cultural revolutions nor a very direct intervention in common communicative practices. That is, overlaid print/manuscript practices result in print imitations of existing literacies. Coteries shared manuscript poetry; rural communities received holographic newsletters reporting royal acts and important legislation. Thus, handwritten texts stimulated the invention of print by exposing its potential economic advantages to literary and political cultures.

But print documents also imitate the manuscripts they transcribe. For instance, early printed plays might be authored by typesetters who, like medieval scribes, capture many versions of one text and introduce to it variations and errors as they edit to accommodate the space, time, and political danger attached to language. Across these traditionally demarcated eras, and still today, the letter and its treatments in various epistolary rhetorics also access the phenomenology of trust that may or may not attach to any written text. I suggest that such assent is always at stake in letters, which mediate between experience and unknowable circumstances around them, between a supposed direct statement and its absent source. Correspondence is thus a theoretical touchstone for issues around the multiplicity of rhetorics: the genre comments on the medieval theoretical sophistication that required minuscule details about how to fictionalize textual authenticity. And unlike other preprint genres, it cannot be thought of as an imitation of somehow direct spoken communication. Nonetheless, discrete epistolary rhetorics prescribe how to maintain the illusion of a writer's physical presence to verify the intentions of unavailable individuals and offices.

Chapter 3, "The Mobility of Trust," argues that eighteenth-century European postrevolutionary cultures rework much of the metadiscursive grounding of trusted texts. The period's rhetorical treatises articulate a Lockean version of the Cartesian individual, whose consciousness becomes the source of credible perception in the period's novels, political sermons, scientific papers, and other emergent genres. This consciousness is partially constructed from classical literary actors and philosophical characters in highly stylized public self-presentations. In toto, this move to consciousness requires a general reconception of trust, just when status and ecclesiastical probity are made broadly available, even to women, insofar as both of those human markers emerge from control of particular styles.

This is to say that conventional language had earlier indicated prior entitlements, indications that gradually become valued for their own sake, apart from their actual signification of class standing, high or low. Particular preferences are labeled "Taste," which becomes more abstract than an individual's preferred objects, acts, and surroundings as it is increasingly used to designate a standard applied to individual understanding. Just when differential access to truth and tradition in these societies becomes a secular social problem, not a result of God-given ranks, that standing is also devalued in favor of the standard of thoughtful, thus trusted, deliberation. The newly interiorized identities of republican citizens render ancient oratorical conventions less persuasive as sensitivity and sincerity come to certify authors. They become self-supported writers, members of a demarcated profession, just as they more often advertise their access to secrets of the heart by staged withdrawals from society. Shakespeare's sociability, which Samuel Johnson stresses in the preface to his edition of Shakespeare's plays, becomes less a marker of poets' perceptivity than is the unfortunate self-absorption displayed in Johnson's biography of Richard Savage. Savage is one of the first widely known nonfictional English characters who attributes the cause of events to psychological trauma he shares with his family.

Chapter 3 ends by arguing that eighteenth-century political and social changes have discursive results in the trans-European revival of elocutionary rhetoric. That topic, eagerly avoided in most rhetoric studies communities, centers the chapter's consideration of nationalism and language standardization. These lessons contribute to the longer, ongoing project of creating stable and publishable vernaculars precisely by articulating—if in two senses—a linguistic and vocal norm meant to replace both local dialects and Latin as the medium of consequential discourses. Its teaching also enacts a symbolic oligarchy insofar as elocutionary precision excludes most speakers and those with no elementary education in writing or only rudimentary practice.

This survey is not meant to predict a progressive chronology. As the title of the conclusion suggests ("Centering Rhetoric—The Psychology of Anxious Moments and Solemn Occasions"), the book ends by returning to questions raised at least tacitly here and in the first chapter. The conclusion addresses the human character again, especially its constructed historical division into opposed rational and irrational/emotional forces. This section's brief picture of antique practices of the self in Mediterranean prehistory explains the creation of the rational/irrational self along the lines of E. R. Dodds's *The Greeks and the Irrational*. He describes shamanistic customs that entered Mediterranean cultures and were incorporated into human identities as sources of the impulses of a split individual. That split, identified on notice of different perceptions in waking and sleeping states, defines the Greek word *thumos* not as "anger" but as "spirit," the force of intrinsic emotion that causes energized human acts and insights that were privileged over experience.

This source helps frame the principal thematic of this study, the significance in the West of conflicts between the seen and the unseen, the known and the unknowable. These antique practices help explain how it becomes normal to imagine that "mind" is a reality rather than a metaphor equivalent to the mathematical equations that constitute almost all we know of wormholes. Their persistence asserts that mind is not feeling, that material realities are ontologically different from their transcendent counterparts, and that the human body contains a hidden interior spirit. The concrete historical intervention of shamanism closes the theoretical circle of this book's topics by returning to their first focus on the tentative yet always hopeful trust with which we endow any site of crafted explanation. But this assertion is not exactly equal to providing access to the thinking and sources that support it, which I sketch below.

The Trouble with Emotion, and Rhetoric

We all claim expertise about the feelings that we have, or do not have, and about our reasons for expressing them, or not. We own feelings as properties that constitute our images of a self and, in particular, easily assert that we feel ourselves and others trustworthy, or not, depending on an exchanged "I know how you feel." Despite competition with supposedly primal tendencies, we most frequently experience trust or its absence as an often preconscious dis/comfort with ourselves, our circumstances, and others. As a verb, it is often understood without an object; some of us are by nature "trusting." Yet this and other emotional dispositions have until recently been unmentionable topics in positivist knowledge-making. As recently as the 1950s and 1960s, scientist Michael Polanyi's differences with positivism were circulated with cultlike enthusiasm as a surrogate for many scholars' irritation about the scientism that recognized neither the uses of his unarticulated "tacit knowledge" nor his view that human creativity creates science. In the humanities, his *Personal Knowledge: Towards a Post-Critical Philosophy* allowed the word "personal" some respectability and with it a wary possibility that (a feeling of) satisfaction creates assent.

Of course, Polanyi is one of many such place-markers. But it is still likely that we may be very well schooled without thinking emotion is a plausible topic for investigation. With the exception of various studies of particular, usually unpleasant and sinful emotions (envy, anger, humiliation, and the like), emotion has been acknowledged as a universal human attribute, sometimes an attribute of animals that are equally endowed with feeling or at least with the evolutionary sources of our sophisticated expressions. Since the philosophical phenomenon "Descartes," emotion is a collectible we all keep without pride, an indiscreet counterpart to valued reason. Within a long antique medical history, we usually treat *pathos* as the unfortunate third persuasive appeal in Aristotle's *Rhetoric*, subordinate to reason in explanations of ancient rhetorical schemata. As Donald Bryant puts it in a seminal article calling for further research to distinguish rhetoric, "Rhetoric is thus closely involved with logical and psychological studies [and] employs imagination and emotion not to supplant but to support reason" (420). Here and elsewhere after Homer's more realistic understanding of motives, emotion comes in last, at its best a (gendered) handmaid of reason.

Until recently, praise from psychologists for Book II of Aristotle's *Rhetoric* as their discipline's founding document has not meant that they take emotion to be an appropriate object of study. As Magda B. Arnold's preface to *Feelings and Emotions: The Loyola Symposium* says, "Before 1927 [at the first Wittenburg Symposium on the topic], emotion was viewed with suspicion because its value for scientific psychology appeared doubtful" (x). In his study *Emotion: A Comprehensive Phenomenology of Theories and Their Meaning for Therapy*, James Hillman notes the 1955 *Encyclopedia Britannica* entry on this topic: "Our knowledge of the topic emotion is much less complete than our knowledge of the other topics in the field of psychology." Hillman is exasperated about this gap: "When we come home to systematic (academic or theoretical) psychology to inquire quite naively: 'What is emotion, how is it defined, what is its origin, nature, purpose, what are its properties and laws, everyone uses this concept "emotion"—what are we speaking about?,' we find a curious and overwhelming confusion" (7). Hillman recruits René Descartes as well, citing, "'There is nothing in which the defective nature of the sciences which we have received from the ancients appears more clearly than in what they have written on the passions'" (7). The same might be said of the topic in later social-scientific approaches to rhetoric.

Of course, histories of rhetoric include excellent studies of the appeal to emotion as pathos, often in attention to Aristotle's treatment of it, and writing studies has focused attention on its pedagogic relation to composing. Examples include W. W. Fortenbaugh's comprehensive *Aristotle on Emotion: A Contribution to Philosophical Psychology, Rhetoric, Poetics, Politics, and Ethics*;[4] Jakob Wisse's *Ethos and Pathos from Aristotle to Cicero*; William Grimaldi's exposition in *Aristotle,* Rhetoric II: *A Commentary*; Douglas N. Walton's *The Place of Emotion in Argument*; Elizabeth Belfiore's *Tragic Pleasures: Aristotle on Plot and Emotion*; Lawrence D. Greene's "Aristotle's *Rhetoric* and Renaissance Views of the Emotions"; and two essays by Lynn Worsham: "Going Postal: Pedagogic Violence and the Schooling of Emotion" and "Eating History, Purging Memory, Killing Rhetoric," the latter of which appears in *Writing Histories of Rhetoric*. That collection also includes

Takis Poulakos's "Human Agency in the History of Rhetoric: Gorgias's Encomium of Helen," which equates emotion with the power of language over Helen and her appropriate, a-rational response. Unpublished papers include Lance Stockwell's "Appealing through Logic and Emotion: Logos, Pathos, and OJ [Simpson]"; Grant Boswell's "Language and Emotion in 17th-Century Rhetorics"; Laura Micciche's "Emoting for a Change: Feminism and the Rhetoric of Anger," which became (with co-author Dale Jacobs) *A Way to Move: Rhetorics of Emotion and Composition Studies*; and John Heil's "The 'Appearance' of Emotion in *Republic*."

Increasing numbers of theorists in writing studies take up the place of emotion in composing, as does Alice G. Brand in "The Why of Cognition: Emotion and the Writing Process" and "Social Cognition, Emotions, and the Psychology of Writing," and Cynthia Haynes in "pathos@play.prosthetic.emotion." Kia Jane Richmond's "Repositioning Emotions in Composition Studies" notes Susan McLeod's *Notes on the Heart: Affective Issues in the Writing Classroom* and Bruce McPhearson and Nancy Fowler's "Making Connections: Writing and Emotion." Jennifer Edbauer's "(Meta)Physical Graffiti: 'Getting Up' as Affective Writing Model" exemplifies more recent work that links writing and emotion outside the academy. It cites similar approaches to emotion and writing by Worsham (above), Christa Albrecht-Crane, Anna Gibbs, Fred Kemp, Nedra Reynolds, and cultural critics Eve Sedgwick and Lawrence Grossberg.

Treatises that link emotional "suasion" to "moral philosophy" are legion, as are references to emotion training in vast numbers of educational programs, from sophistic philosophy through the very different aims and audiences of mass education. Copious attention to emotion by contemporary philosophers is represented in relatively recent collections like Amélie Oksenberg Rorty's *Essays on Aristotle's* Rhetoric; Juha Sihvola and Troels Engberg-Pedersen's *The Emotions in Hellenistic Philosophy*; Martha Nussbaum's *Love's Knowledge: Essays on Philosophy and Literature, The Therapy of Desire: Theory and Practice in Hellenistic Ethics*, and other studies; and Paul E. Griffiths's *What Emotions Really Are: The Problem of Psychological Categories*. Nonetheless, insiders in rhetoric have generally set this topic aside. It is taken up elsewhere more frequently, especially by those who turn to emotion to guide academic composition studies from its current focus on epistemology or to guide rhetoric from its parallel emphasis on hermeneutics. Perhaps most important in relation to this study is Daniel Gross's 2006 *The Secret History of Emotion: From Aristotle's* Rhetoric *to Modern Brain Science*, which critiques "a generalized psychology . . . and passions that were once overtly rhetorical . . . [that] now quietly gird the Western . . . belief that emotion is hardwired to the human nature we all share equally" (8). His is the landmark study of rhetoric and emotion from a contemporary perspective.

Of course, myriad accepted sources in countless forms link the definition of rhetoric with emotion itself. Some include "emotional appeal" among logical fallacies; some are media and political descriptions of lies, of obfuscation, and of "what I do not agree with" as "just a lot of rhetoric." Exemplary interdisciplinary approaches that theorize the diverse historical activities contained in the word "rhetoric" still appear squeamish about emotion as an important topic. Brian Vickers's earlier belief that to revitalize rhetoric studies "we must first re-think our conception of the relation between language, feelings, and the codes of expression" has not been realized in work that might claim to support it (16). For instance, Walton's *The Place of Emotion in Argument* clings to the view that logic is equal to valid persuasion, not a part of it. It concedes that emotion can supply "good and reasonable argument [if it] contributes to the proper goals of the dialogue" (29), which it firmly qualifies by making a "problem" of emotions' positive valence. They must "be treated with caution because they can also be used fallaciously. . . . [C]ertain types of emotional appeals are very powerful as arguments in themselves, and they may have a much greater impact on an audience than is warranted" (3).

A subtler, more disappointing yet informative example is an outline of the "Rhetoric Culture" project, a collection of essays edited and written by an international group of anthropologists. It acknowledges a "very real turn towards rhetoric in almost all the human sciences." It includes topics in general and basic anthropology, linguistics, rhetoric, literature, psychology, and philosophy. Its editors plan to gloss "the interaction of rhetoric and culture." They list seven categories of diversely addressed topics, which I arrange in order of the number of essays devoted to them: general theory (18); linguistics (17); social relations (12); religion (10); economics, law, and politics (11); creativity (9); and emotion (5). As the least frequently addressed topic, emotion receives less attention than the similarly "soft" creativity.[5]

This example invites appropriate complaints from two groups of theorists. Many historians of rhetoric emphasize emotion as a feature of pedagogic history in studies of individual rhetoricians (for example, Augustine) or imagined groups (for example, the Sophists). And many cited here and later give painstaking attention to emotion in ways that might have already renewed rhetoric's typical historiography. But avoiding the topic of emotion is more likely, for compelling reasons we see in the relative dispositions of interests of the "Rhetoric Culture" project. Thus, precisely named "rationalizations" of rhetoric respond to its generally poor reputation and its intensification by a perceived early modern turn to strictly demarcated categories of learning. Despite their habitual vehemence, Sir Francis Bacon and Peter Ramus do not befriend the topic. Among rhetoricians, no matter how differently situated, emotion may be a specifically unpleasant topic with a specific bad reputation that is fully articulated in post-Cartesian claims for reason over emotion, for mind over matter, for substance over style. In our time, for instance, this feeling is still frequently expressed—in subtle reversals that assert that "reason is rhetorical" or that demur by saying the rhetoric of inquiry is not "unreasonable or unempirical."[6]

As Gross and others also note, Descartes' focus in *The Passions of the Soul* (1649) itself may best exemplify the contests portrayed in these pairs. *The Passions* follows many earlier associations between the body and feelings, a common trope that varies across historical definitions of "science," which then still needed quotation marks. But Descartes also unfolds a prescient description that links formerly separated elements of human nature. Unlike earlier physical science that argues that human "faculties" occupy places in the brain, stomach, heart, and bowels, *The Passions* connects feeling to the body through a "little gland" (the pineal gland) in the middle of the brain, supposed to orient "animal spirits" through nerves to muscles (xxii). This description imagines a physical circuit that contemporary brain science now also identifies as the almond-shaped amygdala, a twentieth-century discovery of a part of the human limbic system in the brain's temporal lobe. This site of affective response and memory is said to stimulate fear and probably most purely negative and positive feelings, which after their formation continue to generate messages to the body throughout life.[7] Mind and body interact under secular auspices, then and now.

Post-Renaissance theories hereby remedy emotional disturbances through the mind, not the spirit. Descartes does so with confidence, believing that those mired in emotion can be helped to "transcend their bodily disposi- tions" to "achieve the conquest of the 'habitus' which defines virtue" (xxiv). More than a century later in new rhetorics of consciousness, Bishop Richard Whately describes the logic of religion by bracketing feeling as "faith" in it; Hugh Blair connects feeling to the Taste of the universal individual's prefer- ences; David Hume and Henry Home, Lord Kames, obliquely remind us that Aristotle's treatment of style is a consequential entrée to affect, a perception that I rely on as well. George Campbell, the hero of this quick survey, follows John Locke in his assertion that descriptive images stimulate imagination, a recipient's involvement in persuasion. Conviction is thus a matter of feeling. In Locke's words:

> To conclude[:] when persuasion is the end, passion also must be en- gaged. If it is fancy which bestows brilliancy on our ideas, if it is memory which gives them stability, passion doth more, it images them. Hence they derive spirit and energy. . . . So far therefore it is from being an unfair method of persuasion to move the passions, that

there is no persuasion without moving them. (VII.IV, qtd. in Campbell, *Philosophy* 77)

Casting persuasion as a result of individual consciousness thus becomes the remedy for emotional errors, for it brings Mind to bear on feeling. But a general devaluation of the body includes a distaste for feeling that still allows arguments to be made and accepted as conceptual projects, apart from their always local, situated, and material content. That is, the rationalist critique of rhetoric is not precisely the conventional criticism of Plato's *Symposium*. There, epistemology is at stake for a cultural figure, a poet, who is cast as unable to translate perceptual experience of an object, whether actual or imagined, into its Form. Insight overcomes a poet's experience. However, Socrates' critique of rhetoric in the *Gorgias* and *Phaedrus* differently pits the pedagogic performance habits of philosophy against those of oratory in a directly opposing view of how we come to Knowledge and Enlightenment through interactive experience. These dialogues stage contests that importantly enact Socrates' objections to any persuasion that does not result from interlocutory exchanges. As G. B. Hereford's *The Sophistic Movement* says, Socrates rejects any conventional discourse that does not examine a conversant (33).[8] Both dialogues thus dramatize how a soul apprehends Truth through interactions that change perceptions *by virtue of* relationships. Enlightenment, which is not always limited to a knowledge of facts, results from cooperative, face-to-face interactions, however strictly Socrates manages them. As both dialogues also emphasize, neither passive, immobile auditors nor isolated composers of oratorical set speeches can reach Truth. Its apprehension results from the interplay of conversation, which in the Aristotelian sense of "discovery" invents situated ideas, not Ideas. Thus, the long speeches Socrates ridicules in the *Gorgias* and the scroll of Lysias's speech under Phaedrus's robe are unreliable guides, orphaned "writing" that is made meaningless by its fixity, as many have noted. But when we focus on the epistemological faults of rhetoric rather than its erroneous polemical methods, we see a critique of writing enacted, not merely stated, in these texts. That is, writing represses emotional relationships that Socrates' gradual dissections of fixed opinion do enact—young lover and mentor, youth and tutor, fan and performer, acolyte and priest.

The trouble with rhetoric is not that it is "emotional," not "relational," insofar as emotions are not evaluations but experiences in the relationships needed to reach Truth. Instead, the trouble is that oratorical realizations of rhetoric are not so effective as vehicles for that journey as the myths, conversations, friendly if bickering exchanges, and love of chic alternative rhetorics. Oratory, Plato claims, becomes trivial *doxa*, what everyone knows yet knows apart from the relational context needed to verify anyone's logic. No matter how ironically engaging Socrates' tone, the dialogues express ancient fear of losing control of discourse precisely by imposing on it the "due process" of a system—a writing system—that can produce unsituated performances.

Thus ancient, early modern, and later fears of emotion are not precisely the continuing philosophical problem with rhetoric as oratory, nor precisely equal to each other. Especially early treatments outside the often unnoticed but absolute influence of later Stoicism treat emotion as a process, not as a series of named moods, and do so in more positive light than current rhetoric studies takes note of. Thus, Athenian worry about losing elite control of a mob of impassioned citizens is also distinct from the early modern fear that an individualized, upstart "self" will disorient the established social force of convention. This post-Cartesian and postrevolutionary fear has more to do with the possibility that social secularization will unloose the chaos of equity as it provides unmediated access both to spiritualism and to education. In addition, print conduct books teach both discursive conventions and successfully moral character habits apart from traditionally sanctioned formal and informal education. They allow anyone to acquire an individually earned property right in otherwise hierarchically distributed salvation, status, and wealth. The emotion portrayed negatively in ancient renditions and later Augustinian and other Christian views, while severely tainted in all settings, is not impossible in rational beings. Emotion is capable of a positive value in itself, well beyond its recaptured worth in reevaluations of positivism in many human sciences.

Such reevaluations of emotion now also take place in cultural studies. Once recognized by psychology, the positive valence of emotion as a social practice has been taken up in work that acknowledges its situated nature, often in the interest of defining how Western and Eastern expressions of emotion differ and thus impinge on business interactions. But a survey of this work might note how its own constitutive emotional tenor sustains nineteenth-century attitudes expressed as ranked categories of human and extra-human behaviors. With at least financially ecumenicist purposes, many evaluative studies of emotion undertaken in the 1980s and 1990s acknowledge that discussions *of* emotion are also "socially and culturally embedded" (Irvine 252).

For instance, in "The Cultural Construction of Self and Emotion: Implications for Social Behavior," Hazel Rose Markus and Shinobu Kitayama assert that "[b]y definition, an emotional event requires another person for its evocation, experience, and expression" (103). However, when this constitutive interaction crosses cultures, misunderstandings result. Like many others who ignore class differences in describing emotion, these authors argue that (the display of?) anger is more acceptable in the West than in Japan because it reveals valued Western independence (101). That contrast is extended in their view that Chinese children are encouraged to see the world as a "network of relationships of which they are a part." "Chinese mothers explicitly stress fostering a happy, close, harmonious relationship with the child, as opposed to [the evidently Western value of] building self-esteem, as a goal of child-rearing" (103). Anna Wierzbicka, in "Everyday Conceptions of Emotion: A Semantic Perspective," describes "universal conceptual primitives" that are retained and placed in discourse differently from place to place, even within supposedly total "Western" or "European" cultures. For instance, in Russia, "the absence of 'emotions' indicates a deadening of a person's *dusa* (heart/soul)" (22). Alan Macfarlane, in "Individualism and the Ideology of Romantic Love," takes issue with social historians who identify companionate marriages as relatively recent results of early modern economies, arguing that the biology of sexuality, if not necessarily expressed, is encouraged in societies whose kinship systems are weakened for various situated reasons (129). This view also appears in Victor S. Johnston's *Why We Feel: The Science of Human Emotion*, which argues that "blocks of meaning can arise only from learned associations between environmental events and the evolved emergent feeling states of conscious biological organisms. A child's developing semantic memory depends upon learning the relationship between those feelings, its behavior, and the world around it" (99).

These views tacitly define emotion as individually evaluative, intentional, and self-interested. Robert C. Solomon's "The Politics of Emotion," an account of gendered manipulative behaviors, notes that "many emotions are about power, persuasion, manipulation, and intimidation" (11). Keith Tester agrees with Hannah Arendt that "compassion is an emotional extension of the individual into the world" and claims that without its better work, people may feel "deeply" without attending to the needs or situations of those who have stimulated that deep feeling (68). In a useful summary, Dinesh Sharma and Kurt W. Fischer portray culturally aware views of such individualized emotion as follows: "From a cultural standpoint, even the most basic emotions and certainly self-conscious emotions can be seen as related to complex clusters of culturally meaningful behaviors and meanings, a 'flow of emotion' . . . consisting of culture-specific embodiments, symbolic meaning, display rules, and interpersonal scripts" (9–10).

Of course, liberally intended cultural studies of emotion in the later twentieth century may also trace the colonizing relation of Western to other cultures. They embed a desire for economic cooperation to occur under Western auspices in normalizing studies that suggest a payoff for cross-culturalism. For instance, one study identifies a different and supposedly only Japanese male emotion, *amae*, a strong desire to be petted and otherwise allowed to be dependent on others. Apart from the obvious universality of this feeling among Westerners across sexes and equal entitlements to express it, the study makes clear my point that cultural studies of emotion unintentionally display chauvinism. This one closes its description with the claim that Western men, who are more "independent" and "manly," could "bring themselves to *amaeru* more if they wanted to" (Morsbach and Tyler 141, 144).

This research paradigm has been significantly altered immediately following worldwide awareness of Mid-Eastern motives to intervene in Western and Far Eastern economic and religious traditions. What was taken to be a previously unexpressed primitivism created anxiety about emotion that had been infrequently expressed in research contexts after the late nineteenth century except as Orientalism.[9]

But recent comments make explicit two agendas that require further qualification of this paradigm's directive tendencies. First, some recent commentary emphasizes that Islamic, Jewish, and other Mid-Eastern populations actually *have* emotions, much as nineteenth-century abolitionists used that claim to win sympathy for African American slaves. A review cited in advertising a documentary account of Palestinian/Israeli conflict in the Gaza Strip, the 2002 Ram Loevy film *Close, Closed, Closure*, claims that "a wide range of views . . . stresses the importance of reminding the world that the Palestinians are not merely casualties, . . . but *human beings* with *dreams, emotions, and a persevering sense of humor.* The film contributes to our understanding of *the average Palestinian family*" (Rogers 4, emphasis added). Assigning emotion and family life to a highlighted Other perhaps is here less a result of colonialism than of a worldwide anxiety about motives unfamiliar in idealized Western experience.

Thus, a second desire assimilates what are cast as impenetrable motives, specifically of terrorists. In particular, recent Western schooling omits Judeo-Christian idealizations of martyrdom and thus offers no preparation that sanctions aggressive, religiously justified suicide. Terri Toles Patkin's 2004 article "Explosive Baggage: Female Palestinian Suicide Bombers and the Rhetoric of Emotion" critiques Western media for concerted efforts to mystify the feelings of female suicide bombers while accepting that their male counterparts act out of what are taken to be comprehensible ideological motives. Yet she also says it is impossible to know these women's "emotional and cognitive responses to engaging in terror" (80).

Of course, it is also universally ordinary to portray female motives as beyond the male pale. In this unfortunately familiar instance, their sacrifice is less honored than accused—as extreme feminism, as a product of relationships with male terrorists, as mental ineptitude, as lack of femininity, and as any other quality that excludes women from being "political animals," which is Patkin's telling alternative (82). Male terrorists are called "living weapons," a label that divorces their ideological constitution from a female emotional makeup, evidently to find a "comprehensible explanation" in the purity attributed to doctrinaire male political actors (85). Summarizing this prejudicial interpretative framework, Patkin says that despite its opacity to most, the actual motive is found in "the lessons of the Palestinian culture of martyrdom that both sexes absorb. . . . [M]artyrs attain the status of celebrities," religious leaders justify martyrdom in elaborate theological interpretations, and "young people, female and male, eagerly line up for a one-way ticket to Paradise" (87).

My point is not to belabor the gender-coding that dogs descriptions of both male and female emotions, motives, and susceptibilities and thus writes tediously predictable scripts like this one within a larger stereotyping crusade. But here, this extremely consequential emotional opacity verifies that feeling arises from cultural scripts that are never entirely outside the ken of others, as male and female Christian martyrs might remind Westerners, but that are nonetheless invisible to those unschooled to trust them.

Emotional Educations

Paideia, a formal curriculum in liberal arts, has since classical Greece tied its usually male recipients to history, to each other, and, if less often noted, to a particular range of emotional responses. Werner Jaeger's *Paideia: The Ideals of Greek Culture* calls these connections "one unbroken line of thought from early critics of Homer's heaven to the Christian fathers" (213). But paideia is more importantly the standard example of a broadly conceived emotional education that is woven from shared sessions of rigorous attention to oral and written texts. This is primarily a literary education. Its graduates internalize guidance from heavenly Muses and a shared spirituality, a tacit power most visible in its uses as a socializing imprimatur. Theologian Diana Swancutt explains this circuit:

> *Paideia* was simultaneously the type or system of primary education in the Hellenistic and Roman periods and a civilizing influence that provided national stability throughout the Greek and Roman empires by educating their citizens and subjects about the virtues of their cultures. In other words, *paideia* was an education in civilization that taught as virtuous the societal standards of empire. The "system" of primary education (called *enkyklios paideia*) supported those standards in part by embracing its own set of traditional texts. Dominated . . . by the poetic epics of Homer, young boys—Greek and non-Greek alike—came to

identify with Greek heroes and ideals as they recited, learned, and occasionally wrote lines from the stories of the *Iliad* and *Odyssey*. (n.p.)

Thus, as a civilizing force, paideia is a conceptual frame around the lessons
it teaches its elite recipients about a shared emotional code. It bonds them
as a class demarcated because it shares the emotional range demonstrated
in the texts its members have parsed, read, recited, and taken as models for
their compositions. They hereby also share this education's ideas about standards of credible behavior, a mobile judgment of fitting responses to specific
situations and appropriate ways of talking about them. In archaic Greece,
Christian Rome, and later, the result is a sense of belonging among those
who have been supervised together in physical, linguistic, compositional,
and interpersonal exercises.

One hero of this educational process is Lollianus the grammarian, whose
third-century petition from Egypt to Rome asking emperors Gallenus and
Valerian for his back pay is exemplary. In it, he evokes precisely this thread
of trust. He appeals to both their "heavenly magnanimity" and "your *fellowship* with the Muses (for *Paideia* sits beside you on the throne)" (Brown 35,
emphasis added). As Peter Robert Lamont Brown's *Power and Persuasion in
Late Antiquity: Towards a Christian Empire* says of Lollianus and indirectly
of legions of others, many hope "to cling to the great through the delicate
osmosis of shared culture" (35). And as this petition demonstrates, that literary culture's heroic ideals result not only from actual friendships that are
cemented by shared physical and academic performances in classes but also
by justifiably assumed trust among any whose similar experience is known. Of
course, Greek athletic and military contests forge links to differently stringent
drill and practice in grammar and rhetorical exercises. From this combination, a certain disposition also emerges, one whose education is well worth its
length and expense. But insofar as the method of this curriculum is primarily
repetition and imitation, another paideia is available outside elite groups. Since
the standard of manly and gentlemanly behaviors is displayed, observed, and
regularly emulated, dedicated onlookers can assimilate it—women, slaves,
the poor, and unsophisticated rural groups are also its common foils. With
varying entitlement across that range, it is a cultural signature.

To demonstrate the powers of that signatory experience, Brown takes expressions of anger as an example. But the feeling he discusses is not a primal,
biologically encoded anger portrayed as a product of the brain's renamed "little
gland" of the limbic system. Nor is it a psychological response derived from
a negative rationalist evaluation of feelings. Among late-empire politicians
who share this education, anger is less personal than either of those views
imagines. It is constituted by decorous mediations of literary allusions like

those Lollianus writes, which convey that writer and reader share values about the proper response, paying what is due.

Yet this anger is also potentially much more dangerous than its explosions in psychologized counterparts who are differently educated. That is, among the educated elite of the Christian empire, anger and political power relations are identical; this anger *is* power. The cultural glue of training in the Muses manufactures shared attitudes toward the *uses* of anger, not a refined conceptual fit of degree to cause. Thus, if anger is inappropriately demonstrated, it of and in itself destroys the social place of those it thereby marks as unacceptable. Modern analyses of anger, whether scientific and behavioral, philosophical, or psychological, all fall far short of explaining this emotion as it was understood as an action, not a cause.

As Brown explains, the empire's far-flung educational identity politics could bring down the imperial governor of a city or province who might unfortunately exercise anger in a violent prerogative of publicly flogging a member of a local elite. To do so was taken to show disdain for class friendship, to reject the bonds that otherwise maintained a shared interest in orderly governance.[10] As Brown says:

> "Anger" was the antithesis to a harmonious and controlled mode of public action. Anger, indeed, emerged as a central component in the language of late Roman politics. It meant . . . the sudden, shameful collapse of self-restraint, associated with a public outburst of rage. But it more usually denoted the morose resentment of a man who would not allow the claims of friendship and esteem, [which] linked one "servant of the Muses" to another, to take effect. Either form of anger was held to constitute a serious breach of decorum. (54)

Brown also realigns the modern assumption that regretting one's anger results from a psychologically motivated change of heart, or that second thoughts and "working through" an outburst lead to interpersonal resolutions. He stresses that in the emotional tuition of a preconsciousness world, anger that breached decorum was in some measure a reversible act. Men of paideia could repent: a governor or emperor might treat breaking the bonds of shared paideia as a normal human lapse. "In this way, emphasis on anger formed part of the late Roman language of amnesty. The counterpart of anger was clemency" (55). There, anger is a matter of persuasion. It is based on mutual trust derived from a shared code, and its restraint, expression, or repentance maintains that code as well. This is to say that it is neither individual emotional property nor reacted to as though it were. Any form of its manifestation—public expression or repentance—launches a public transaction that is visible as violent action or as the "resentment" Brown acutely notes. In such frameworks, plainly repressed anger might be a strategic way to maintain a bargaining position, not a different psychological repression.

Despite the cultural differences I emphasize, contemporary students are not without such uses of feeling. For instance, we read of the righteous wrath of Achilles, or of Superman, which results from an enduring honor code that equalizes rewards to successful warriors. In the *Iliad*, uneven rewards evoke direct action, create and undo alliances, and reshape a world—all after an obviously staged oratorical debate. And as Bryan Register demonstrates, in Gorgias's *Encomium to Helen* a generalized manly lust for Helen creates the circumstance of Achilles' wrath. The insult to his honor and his responding wrath are nonetheless political communications among men, as the *Iliad*'s public debate about it demonstrates. In addition, Gorgias defends Helen's susceptibility to language with a relevant pun: "With a single body she brought together many bodies of men who had great pride for great reasons . . . and they all came because of a love which wished to conquer" (Register 4).[11] That is, anger and lust are both consequential acts whose social and political motives and results have quite ironically become invisible to many who claim for the post-Freudian individual an acute consciousness of feelings and of how they work.

The equivalences among emotion, a literary education, and persuasion thus explain more than the results of calling some ancient literary and legal behaviors "irrational." That equality also uncovers a more textured rhetorical history. For instance, well apart from formal and theoretical treatment of emotional appropriateness in Book II of Aristotle's *Rhetoric* and elsewhere, the instrumentality of *philia* in Athenian society grounds exemplary legal narratives about trust from speakers like Demosthenes (48.14–15) and Lysias (1: 6–7). In Demosthenes, a trusted slave is blamed for cheating a household advisor, a deed especially unacceptable because their positions imply their friendship. In Lysias, a wife who betrays her husband had been thought to be trustworthy—affiliated to her husband's interests—through affection for her new child. Both cases illustrate what Lin Foxhall's study of the Athenian "politics of affection" calls a dubious yet expected "generalized reciprocity" (55). Thus, these examples of unexpected individual limits on that reciprocity occasion significant anxieties among a class trained to expectations of trust.[12] Lynette G. M. Mitchell's *Greeks Bearing Gifts: The Public Use of Private Relationships in the Greek World, 435–323 B.C.* emphasizes Foxhall's points on affection. For instance, Mitchell there argues that ancient affiliations depended primarily on exchanges among personal friends in Athens whose relationships supported the *polis*. Philia, she says, expressed the relation between an individual and society and thus was "a series of complex obligations, duties and claims" larger than interpersonal affection (7).

This view of friendship as a social exchange, not interpersonal goodwill, follows Aristotle's philia of "utility" (*Nicomachean Ethics [NE]* 8, II56aI4–30). He says, "The *philiai* of citizens and tribesmen and fellow-sailors" is like the *"philiai* between associates . . . 'according to some agreement'" (*NE* 8, II6IbII). In all these accounts, friendship involves a more or less regulated association (*NE* II6IbII and II59b31–2). It is always conventional, either by virtue of a formal agreement or "naturally," as an expectation of family, kin, and lovers whose social bonds exist in relation to long histories of law and custom. Thus, trust, gifting, expectations of friendship, and biological relationships all make primarily rhetorical statements. As with the third-century empire's anger, unconventional means of handling such expectations occasion consequential social anxiety but, so far as we know, especially for Achilles, not low self-esteem.

These sources are not, however, origin stories. Antique emotional pedagogies are so commonplace as to be invisible after a long history of equally prepsychological definitions of appropriate relationships in which feeling is a transaction, specifically an action that indicates standing among others. For instance, the thirteenth-century BCE Ten Commandments not only address a specific community but also define its sins as offenses to social order. The commandments in turn prescribe the appropriate relationship to God (acknowledging primacy, speaking respectfully, worshiping with devotion), then how to regulate the conduct of the primary family unit and five additional ways to maintain order by avoiding specific disruptive acts: murder, adultery, theft, false accusations, and covetousness. We might assume the last item on this list controls a private, ultimately self-critical passion—envy. But covetousness here implies scheming to acquire items that the commandments portray as belonging to a neighbor.[13] Many foundational lists of commandments, rules, and strictures predate and follow the Decalogue that establishes this one community's relation to God as a matter of its mutuality.

In his "Story—List—Sanction: A Cross-Cultural Strategy of Ancient Persuasion," James W. Watts points out that ancient Near East and eastern Mediterranean royal inscriptions form similar three-part lists that "specify the contents of [the king's] decrees" (199). Recovered from several Kassite kings of Babylon who ruled in the middle of the second millennium BCE, these lists show congruence among such social rules. Athenian Solon's sixth-century BCE commandments include "Honor the gods," "Have regard for your parents," and, in first place, "Trust good character more than promises." These prescriptive codes guide the emotional tone of credible interactions, as in Solon's "When giving advice, do not recommend what is most pleasing, but what is most useful." But well before Solon legislates exile as punishment for murder, that deed evokes the same penalty in numerous epochs: "Homicide disturbs civic or community order, and this threat is addressed by sending the murderer directly into exile. . . . The time frame and the route of exile were carefully prescribed; even the unintentional killer must keep out of Attica and away from games and festivals attended by all Greeks. If he returned, he could be killed" (Dougherty 33).

Later forms of punishment suggest even more frightening narratives that disallow the possibility that crimes against a community's peace are consequential only to their perpetrators and victims. For instance, as Pope Gregory the Great's sixth-century version of the Seven Deadly Sins enumerates, they disrupt relations to God and to others, not a flow of interiorized probity. Pre-Reformation Christianity judges pride, avarice (greed), envy, wrath, lust, gluttony, and sloth to damage the body of the church, not the psyche of their sources. Thus, in addition to the obviously transactional nature of sins against God and neighbors, gluttony implies taking more than one's share. Sloth, first defined as laziness in regard to spiritual work, also bespeaks failure to provide for one's dependents. Later sixteenth-century punishments for these sins are appropriate metaphorical responses to consequential damage to Christian relationships.

But schooled literary sensibility is also at work in these responses to sin: pride evokes torture on a stone wheel; greed is repaid with boiling in oil; envy results in immersion in freezing water; anger is repaid with dismemberment; lust matches being burned alive; gluttony requires eating rats, toads, and snakes; and sloth is tossed into a snake pit. Commandments, transgressions, corresponding virtues, and similar lists across Western cultures share a socializing purpose in concert with ancient ethical philosophy and the well-wrought rhetoric of Pauline epistolary sermons. All prescribe and prohibit implied emotional environments. All assume that feeling is a behavior toward others, a sustaining force that motivates, controls, and evaluates community interactions.

Of course, emotional education is also the obvious goal in much of Aristotle and Plato. They disagree in some measure about whether schooling can overcome, develop, or actually erase an already inherited disposition, the chemistry that later is individualized to one psycho-logic. The *Nicomachean Ethics* explains why private schooling is superior in shaping character: "For as in cities, laws and *prevailing types of character* have force, so in households do the injunctions and *the habits of the father*" (10.9, emphasis added). Among later philosophers, Galen, Seneca, and others treat education as a way to infuse passion with rational controls.[14] It is obvious as well that when the Roman Empire is dismantled, Christian Augustine's *De Doctrina* teaches a rhetoric to preachers that stresses clear speaking to uneducated converts. But it also stresses the exercise of compassion, the disposition that becomes the overriding emotional tenor of pastoral care before and well after fearsome Puritanism.

Brown argues that the early Christian church's success was also largely a rhetorical production of its character, which depended in great measure on attaching this constructed compassion to one trope, paradox. That is, the obvious wealth of the earliest church leaders and the poverty of their followers are absorbed into the paradox of *sacrifice*: gain requires a loss that is impossible without possessing something to lose. Brown says of wealthy bishops and cooperative local notables that "the theme of 'love of the poor' exercised a gravitational pull [to join the church] quite disproportionate to the actual working of Christian charity . . . [drawing] into its orbit the two closely related issues of who, in fact, were the most effective protectors . . . of the lower classes of the cities and of how wealth was best spent by the rich" (78). Compassion vies with the strength of empire. In contradiction to traditional Christian care of only its own indigent newcomers, widows, and orphans, fourth-century Christianity expands charity to create a dedicated emotional politics. Supplementing the traditional elite paideia, this Christian bonding derives from a different entitlement in which members of the early Christian church programmatically identify with a massive constituency of non-elites. The unentitled are to be included in a religious access to shared love and compassion, the emotional/political expression of the Christian establishment's identification with their circumstances. Much later, a similarly strategic promise of freedom allows emergent republican "citizens" without material resources to identify with power on the basis of a secular equality among "all men [who] are created equal." Submitting to the paradox of democratic governance by elites in the early American colonies and other revolutionary states, republican citizens are included in a precisely named identity politics. Its founding dynamics are repeated as they spawn state institutions of many sorts—and, of course, in many repetitions of its founding dynamics, in a precisely named identity politics.

The Trouble with Rhetoric, and Emotion

The different history of rhetoric implied by these and other examples of how emotions constitute cultures is of little value without evidence that many discrete discourses about discourse signal their recognition of such agendas. It is easily said that emotion is a still denigrated topic, one associated with either hidden human motives or transparent results of clearly moral, chemical, or judgmental forces. It is also arguable that rhetoric studies has already evinced many of the theoretical and disciplinary troubles that regularly come up throughout this study, for instance, questionable Hegelian historical models and the American compression of many rhetorics into one oratorical origin that is mistaken for universal access to equitable political participation. As the synapse of culture, metadiscursive education sensitively but unobtrusively responds to changing circumstance. It makes needed repairs to the emotional infrastructures that permit such misrecognitions, to maintain legible interactions within interested groups. But in these cases, the interests served by upholding transhistorical spins on history need reevaluation in light of their continuing resonance across classes and discrete yet globally interactive cultures.

That project of reevaluation is not accomplished by changes in the methods of any branch of discourse theory, nor by applying already worn approaches to overlooked texts. The issue at stake is emotional and thus a matter of redefining the project to hand. For instance, as Seth L. Schein describes the need to introduce cultural circumstances into that project, he outlines the construction needed to imagine one classical rhetoric as follows:

> The most important lesson Classics can learn from Cultural Studies is that cultures, including classical cultures, consist not of a single, authoritative tradition but of multiple, competing discourses, practices, and values. . . . The construction of a classical tradition is not only a matter of simplistically misreading or decontextualizing complex, historically conditioned texts. It involves a kind of censorship, whether inadvertent or deliberate, that includes some works in a canon and excludes others, or else deflects attention from admittedly canonical works that seem methodologically or ideologically problematic. (294).

Obviously, I would take his suggestions beyond "works" by adding attention to pedagogy to any list of censored cultural voices that nonetheless hold absolute power over reproduction. But neither overlooked works nor teachings that introduce to histories of rhetoric its multiple cultural settings and varied metadiscursive tasks will direct historical attention only to leftovers from a main meal. The well-taught emotional force of many situated forms of persuasion accounts for shifted emphases in the systematic theories now included in legitimate rhetoric. The traditional, reversed narrative that begins with legitimacy as a given condition of interest omits cultural history. For instance, systematic handbook treatments of rhetoric since Aristotle and before might not be dismissed or treated only as formalist outlines were they taken up as simultaneously comprising descriptions of practice and prescriptions for placing their users in specific societies of the educated, as many treatments of later conduct books by cultural historians argue. Directions for producing disembodied speeches and other texts, which both genres make available, teach how to behave in language in ways that allow disparate readers to acquire signs of the emotional codes that legible discourse affirms.

These resources—handbooks and other supposedly untheorized guides—are the supplement Jacques Derrida and Georges Bataille call a cultural "excess," "underbelly," "subtext" or "static electricity that holds the system intact."[15] Any textbook fits that definition, but those that manage language have special consequence because their examples embody values—even at the level of the sentence to be diagrammed. They teach appropriate gestures and responses that rarely acknowledge difference.

Consequently, the vaguely realized formality of rhetoric's treatises and their sometimes combative or defensive tenor might also be cast as a background—the primer on which paintings appear—that enables stating new cases about persuasion. The return of a repressed rhetorical center might involve following Brown's lead to focus on the circumstances around discourses whose result has been to regulate emotions, especially by directing their situated displays in conventional discursive interactions like appeals to the Muses and repentance for anger itself. Pedagogy that determines the consequences of these and other appeals to emotion foregrounds the culturally honored dispositions I have sketched. It manages identities, in undiminished but now widely disseminated importance, as what "holds the system intact."

In addition to many educational studies, these propositions allude to Louis Althusser's "Ideology and Ideological State Apparatuses (Notes towards an Investigation)." It names ideological apparatuses, chief among them schooling, as invasions of private realms, especially a classed self, by state-sanctioned institutional practices. But Althusser also defines ideology not as a set of beliefs but a process of assent necessary to form what he terms an "imaginary relation to the real" (164). That move does not entirely uncover the power of teaching that holds a system intact through seemingly only informative lessons that suggest such relations by teaching literature, history, and other cross-cultural narratives. But if we explain his model as rhetorical, a metadiscourse that applies to many ways of reproducing culturally sanctioned identities, its uses become less deterministic. For instance, paideia is neither a state institution nor a centralized system equivalent to a titled ideological apparatus. But its diffusion among a class, not only in one nation-state, expanded its power. Its students draw on trust that can be called into play provisionally, to erase or modify official differences and ultimately to create precisely countercultural associations. If shared elite access to the Muses becomes elite solidarity, it also operates independently of local standing and uneven power relations like those Brown describes in Roman provinces. More important, solidarity endures as a discourse, a relational rhetoric, among others whose powers are not determined by articulated class structures.

This exemplary theoretical limit demonstrates that the trouble with rhetoric *and* emotion is different from and greater than issues I attach to either member of that pair. If we hope to theorize that relationship as correlative, its incapacity to reward straightforward investigations that produce predictable outcomes, however theoretical, becomes visible after only a glance at the messy nature of human interaction. Histories of emotion, their separate definitions, and empirical studies aimed to expose their singular causes and matched results emulate similar treatments in contemporary rhetoric studies. In its treatment of specific emotions, what counts as either an essential or a disciplinary definition of rhetoric tells how to measure the effects of persuasive moves. Rhetoric studies adds to these parallel cases a history that places its vehemence in unseen consciousness that it treats as an always to-be-interpreted phenomenon, not as a result of custom, schooling, and overlayered cultural scripts. Both its theories and its histories also remain distant from the often overlooked subtextual energies that mark interactions with what we do not know and may decide. In this view, modern dispositions are rhetorically layered results of variously nuanced instruction from many sources, including religious and political institutions. They may be imagined within the rhetoric George Kennedy recently defined as a "form of emotional energy" (*Comparative* 3).

To take one instance that clarifies these relations among trust, cultural dispositions, and discourse: As Socrates took trouble to show, knowledge of rhetoric is not knowledge of medicine. But neither is it knowledge of nothing. The metadiscursive processes that medical discourses realize show how mutual trust and authority work in particular cultures and, specifically in this case, how medical discourses persuade us to act in ways that on their face require peculiar leaps of faith. As we know from perhaps the oldest extant medical document, written circa 2100 BCE, the Mesopotamian scientist-*ashipu*, evidently referred to earlier as a sorcerer-doctor, who read signs to determine the sin, heredity, or other extrinsic cause of illness differs from his cooperating peer, the physician-*asu*, who diagnoses on the basis of physical symptoms and precedent cases to prescribe a drug, tonic, or washes, bandages, and plasters for a sore spot. Educated patients trust both and might also visit the Temple of Gula for a diagnosis.

Yet so far as we know, none found a palm reader a safe source of treatment. Given the qualities of our own medical practitioners, this example vividly reminds us that trust is culturally educated to move us to act or not. And from our perspective on discourse, that feeling obviously derives from recognizing hierarchies that the subtexts of various rhetorics create and verify, dispositions based on Hamilton's "routines and pathways . . . the rules of appropriateness and eligibility." A rhetorically encultured patient recognizes the logic and aesthetics of hierarchic eligibility, which are inculcated, never memorized for a test.

These hierarchies also inform trustworthy self-presentations, where the same conditions apply. It does not matter if we go to a seminary to learn pastoral care, or to a university to absorb the terms used in postmodernism, or to medical school to learn how to wield a stethoscope with authority. Our credibility in these cases is not derived from directly taught information, nor from credentials, nor from practice exercises, nor even from personable projected personalities. But those preparatory settings allow us to access systems that require trust, especially in their secret knowledge. That enculturation, not into knowledge but into knowledge *of* knowledge systems, allows us to occupy expectations: we grasp symbolic significations of holding and of being held within various forms of unverifiable knowledge.

Another way to say this is that accounts of persuasion need to consider the emotional effects of charisma. A later doctor in an expensive suit whose educated speech is familiar to us projects a whole range of charismatic signifiers that makes some of us think she will be a trustworthy clinician. But others might infer from these signs that she is a slick upper-class jerk who has ripped off the working class to afford that suit. In either case, choices between faith healers and doctors, and choices by them, will result from comfort within a particular unverifiable code, emotional ways that we trust, or not, different purveyors of knowledge to which we have no access.

These cases suggest consequences for teaching rhetoric. All differently assert that we are not persuaded by argumentative proofs, nor by signs of expertise, knowledge, and fairness in their sources. We trust discourse we perceive to contain unknown, secreted if not secret content, when we feel that there is more to be known, yet that we already know more by virtue of our teachers' access to a metadiscourse whose very existence promises that the unknown is not unknowable. This is to say that many mechanisms around uncertainty function symbolically and charismatically, not logically or analytically.

It follows, logically, that in addition to the demands we impose on theory when we recognize many rhetorics, full accounts of a unified oratorical rhetoric and Aristotelian argumentation cannot be only logical and coherent. Often neatly categorized but inchoate nonetheless, our self-contradictory, overdetermined, and certainly culturally taught feelings recognize more to be said. Emotion has had little systematic attention until recently, as I have said. But despite a great deal of current notice, emotion is still usually treated as a singular creature of rationalism. Only a few articulate an aesthetics of emotion as a way to explain our personal theories of life and choice, our ways of imagining ourselves as occupants of good or bad stories. But in any version of rhetoric, that self-aestheticizing result of modernism—like style, our illusion of control—invites attention. Here, I ground that consideration in only a nonce definition of reality: as Catullus had it, I hate and I love. In that overdetermined multiplicity of feeling, which in Poem 85 includes the poet's tortured curious awareness,[16] we individually join a history like the one I have been suggesting. Its logic is self-contradictory, and its chronologies are obvious projections of our own emerging present. We form and trust these narratives individually, precisely until, as we do and do not use conceptual definitions of rhetoric, we do not.

1 *Decentering Rhetoric*

> If rhetoric is the potent tool by which the passions of men are not only expressed but also fashioned, the forms and figures of rhetoric are themselves fashioned in imitation of the way men naturally give voice to feelings.
>
> —Jacqueline Miller, "The Passions Signified"

> Mediocrity is the series of ideas and discoveries demonstrating that Earth is a relatively common planet orbiting a relatively common star going around a relatively common galaxy that is one of countless others in a giant, perhaps infinite, universe.
>
> —Copernican mediocrity principle

Scientists still disagree about whether Earth is one of many planets like it that orbit many stars like our sun that nurture life much like ours. We may not be the center of the universe. We are in any case much like each other, even if Copernicus's hard-won mediocrity principle is false and we are unique creations inhabiting a unique planet given life by one special sun. So far as we can now tell beneath those stars, however, only small differences in genetic markers write our biological scripts, whether sexual, racial, or emotional. Our explanations of life, arts, and behaviors also now take for granted that it is only small differences among us that are revealing. That is, in keeping with Copernicus, our likenesses are both obvious and in some areas embarrassing to emphasize, as the fearful reaction to his theory in his time demonstrates.

We share not only these cosmic and systemic characteristics but also yet another manifestation of Copernicus's principle: our chosen topics are neither distinct nor all that out of the ordinary. Few would be able to complete specialized schooling without believing that their particular interests are the most consequential of problems of any sort. But immediately after that completion, it becomes clear that any specialty now allows for the mediocrity of interdisciplinarity. That is, we have much in common intellectually because our once discrete objects of study turn out to share generic, historical, and functional purposes that good scholarship requires us to acknowledge. Not only is my work not the center of the universe, but I can no longer expect to imagine that center alone.

Thus too of rhetoric. This chapter's attention to the ancient rhetoric that produces justifiably fine-grained analyses of limited topics also acknowledges a different principle of analysis: rhetoric is neither "Queen of Sciences," a title its proponents conceded to theology some time ago, nor unique among other discourses about discourse. What follows thus attempts to sort through studies of antique writing, of literate practices and education for them that moot the application of oral/literate as a tool of analysis, and of historical interactions that are defined by successes and failures of persuasion. But it goes a step beyond drawing from many disciplines to recharacterize ancient rhetoric. It also suggests that "ancient rhetoric" is many manifestations of guided communication in many sources of instruction.

To make that latter point, this chapter relies heavily on various forms of instruction in the moral character threaded through the identities of seer, prophet, poet, physician, philosopher, hero, and orator. In different ways that link these figures, each mediates between secreted truths that comfort us as assurance that more than we know might become known and the illusion that we know more already insofar as these figures make statements we trust but cannot verify. And paradoxically, what is said of those secrets is trusted in proportion to its ability to be unsettling. Much hangs on that schooled character, as demonstrated by the three treatments of it that are separately attached to reason, feeling, and the stylization of both in Aristotle's *Rhetoric*.

Yet the mediocrity principle invites us to reconsider the elevated place of the centered "rhetoric" I have just cited. Contemporary English studies now attaches authoritative theories of rhetoric to philosophical hermeneutics, great philosophers—Aristotle, Plato, and perhaps Cicero—and one curricular sequence of lessons in their uses. Many have noted that this rhetoric can be glimpsed in poetic, dramatic, musical, medical, and deliberative techniques that obviously precede it. But most who do so take for granted that glimpsed examples are abridged parts of one larger whole that was abbreviated by generic purposes, accidents of composition, and undeveloped knowledge. This chapter instead takes pains to emphasize that the rhetoric we study is but one of many discrete forms of teaching and practice that are variously manifest in liminal spaces of cooperation, discourse that credits what E. R. Dodds calls "an 'occult' self" who participates in exchanged linguistic acts of trust (153). These now othered sites of guidance—many forms of lore, observed examples, handbook sources, specialized legal and ceremonial templates from Greek and other trans-Mediterranean locales—certainly recall mediocrity as Copernicus explains it. Epistolary, handbook, and nonce rhetorics abound and are inhabited by what we must assume were familiar ancient figures. Yet only recently is their parity among theories realized or deemed interesting after it is described. Nonetheless, on that cosmic principle, this different historical view understands ancient rhetoric as many cultural formations of variously guided discursive conventions. They witness a pervasive distribution of linguistic self-consciousness across class ranks, gendered identities, and temporal and geographic settings.

These principles of analysis inform each section of this chapter. It in turn takes up that historical and prehistoric distribution of linguistic self-consciousness ("Reviewing Rhetoric"), links forged by trusted characters among separate classes and interests ("~~Everyone~~ Knows: Antique Characters"), and not entirely discrete precedents that continue to inform moments of provisionally shared beliefs ("Everyone Knew: Rhetoric as Its Precedents"). Each of these sections addresses emotion before its absorption into evaluative paradigms and procedures, yet inside the suspended disbelief that agreement always requires.

Reviewing Rhetoric

Most studies of rhetoric begin with its Greek Athenian appearance, for reasons that need periodic review. That is, given the tenor of its traditional Western histories, this rhetoric is easily thought of as an elevated source-text: both the best system for describing discourse and the best prescriptions for its production in all likely cases. This starting place of course implies an original rhetoric that renders earlier and later systematic expositions of discursive practices as partial and usually unfortunate allusions to one archetype, which itself appears to be only partially represented in rare holistic theories, even Aristotle's *Rhetoric*. The prominence of these master texts has varied. Their losses, recoveries, uses, and attributions trace an uneven, indirect trail. But that unevenness continues to be described as though windows open and close, and open again, in one group home whose inhabitants often repeat themselves and others.

For instance, Aristotle's *Rhetoric* is not an obvious contributor to medieval education, at least not apart from other works that accompanied it. Poggio Bracciolini (1380–1459), in December 1416, found previously unknown manuscripts that included a full text of Quintilian's *Institutes* and commentaries on eight of Cicero's orations.[1] Many of the textbooks of Peter Ramus and Omer

Talon were used extensively in Germany in the early seventeenth century, but at least in Bremen, they disappear from curricula by 1645 (Freedman 141). And as Carol Poster points out about the uses of Aristotle's *Rhetoric* in the nineteenth century, that century's "Aristotle" (or other canonical name and era) is not the available twelfth-century Aristotle, nor the author of twentieth-century Aristotelian principles for writing essays.[2] Knowledge of a canon's existence does not indicate that it is prominent, nor that when it has been known and distributed, its meaning has been other than a product of its uses at a particular time. In addition, the ease with which poetics, philosophy, rhetoric, and ethics were blended and read together in Athenian culture makes it unlikely that conversations among canons that constitute this "rhetorical" as a known way of thinking and talking *about* discourse were conducted from a disciplinary perspective. If one or another work answers, refutes, or confirms another, asserting that relationship does not substantiate it as other than an assumption based on a teleological historiography. And even as modern rhetoricians turn from philological accounts of rhetoric to unfold its philosophical and material subtexts, they often impose this Hegelian historical method and thus de-emphasize the specific materiality of history and the specific politics of discrete cultural contexts.

Difficulties with various elements of these patterns have been addressed by many and ignored by many others who still find the truth of rhetoric's unified yet always uneven expressions in fifth-century and later texts that are taken to be canonical and thus to have always been so. For many whose knowledge of this rhetorical centrism is derived from twentieth-century literary and writing studies, rhetoric is known through a sequence of elusive Sophists whose remains are in fact fragmented: Plato's *Phaedrus* and *Gorgias*, the Aristotle of the *Rhetoric*, Isocrates as the speechwriter of democracy, and a better organized but politically repressed group of Roman writers like Cicero, the Republic's martyr, and Quintilian. That obviously implausible caricature of course suggests that we lack more complicated information that would undo it and other mythological and historical commonplaces. For instance, many already acknowledge that a story of two Sicilian ambassadors to Athens peripherally delivering "rhetoric" on a diplomatic mission is at best difficult to verify. Nonetheless, mythological narrative thinking motivates the almost universal desire to find origins. And that longing easily overrides skepticism about the plausibility of still other stories of rhetoric that round out the eleven centuries (750 BCE to 400 CE) from which such sketchy narratives emerge.

As Trevor Ross points out about pre-eighteenth-century canons, their texts were "something to be produced, not reproduced" (402). This fine point is important for reconstructing an inclusive approach to this history beyond a series of authorial transmissions, partial or copied. That is, opinions of any text's value may circulate independently, outside the conditions for canon formation, which require that it be "possible to insure the reproduction of the work, its continual reintroduction to generations of readers" (402).[3] Thus before reproductive institutions designated their value—in schooling, but also in cultural formations like vernacular usage dictionaries and elocutionary reading—"works from the distant past could be deemed canonical only if they could be clearly shown to contribute in some way to the productivity and stature of the present age, or to the circulation of contemporary values. The classical canon stood as a pedagogical model of rhetorical eloquence, and as an ideological model of poetry-making in the service of empire-building" (402).

Ross's point might be expanded: Rhetoric's status is continually affirmed as a source of eloquence in all genres and as a positive source of poetic forms. It circulates values in every era insofar as linguistic technologies determine textual conventions. However, another source of status and value is often chosen from within rhetoric studies, an assertive logic in which we can solve for x (rhetoric) by addressing its arithmetically cast relations to democracy algebraically, placing it over, and under, literacy. Obviously, any of the terms of this equation can be made its solution by determining relations between the other two. But it might also follow that before this historical rhetoric comes under one roof reaching from democratic Athens to Washington, D.C., it informs and is informed by cultural issues other than democracy and alphabetic literacy.

Nonetheless, views of a continuous and therefore generically unified "rhetoric" are now greatly qualified from the edges of this disciplinary history. Other perspectives might make us more willing to suspend its truisms in favor of undertaking the descriptive research that is now possible in textual archaeology, whose results radically alter the subtexts that commonly support narratives of textual and political origins, democratic results, and consequent universal literacy. Pre-Athenian discourses are not pre-intellectual foils for later abstractions that the alphabet is said to create by making them visual. The Athenian oratorical rhetoric and all that follows from it have precedent versions, earlier laws and speeches, and certainly sophisticated experience in sailing that formed a system of communication across cultures and genres that was far more flexible and extensive than is usually imagined.[4] Greek naval victories resulted from millennia of practice. Thus, a tripartite amalgamation of rhetoric/literacy/democracy need not continue to dominate and cannot rehabilitate the singular conceptual rhetoric whose current histories claim to see its beginnings and endings in Athens and, for instance, courses in written composition.

Each of these underdeveloped propositions suggests that what follows does not review rhetoric so much as preview other ways of imagining it that would expand on its extant root metaphors and their historical narratives by allowing us to distinguish between Athenian oratorical models and many other metadiscursive guides and practices. Other "rhetorics" need not be othered, that is, treated as peripheral fragments or as separate discourses apart from a now highly questionable model.

I realize of course how such an assertion raises the hackles of most of us, for it suggests not only the pleasures of further research but the possibility that representations of rhetoric have lately been partial and in some measure inaccurate. This very limited preview of another sort of rhetoric does, however, already have wide support. Certainly George Kennedy's definition of rhetoric as "emotional energy" in his study of contrastive rhetoric gives permission to rethink these issues. Considering that his 1972 *Art of Rhetoric in the Roman World, 300 B.C.– A.D. 300* begins with "Rhetoric, defined in the strictest sense, is the art of persuasion as practiced by orators and described by theorists and teachers of speech" (3), it is clear that he has now also undertaken this project. Early in the resurgence of rhetoric studies in the twentieth century, Douglas Ehninger certainly implies a need for such a methodological sea change. He not only identifies "the existence of many rhetorics" that provides my conceptual frame ("On Rhetoric" 242) but also says that the "central task of the historian of rhetorical thought" is exploring how communication intersects "intellectual, cultural and socio-political environments" ("Promise" 7). Thus, I note new information about literacy, alternative views of received wisdom about Athenian oratorical practices, and the equation of rhetoric with democracy with encouragement from those who support all such applications to the old version of "rhetoric."

What follows also depends at least partially on research questions that it necessarily revises. To take the more or less universal example, interest in discourse history becomes differently focused in light of significant new evidence about uses of the graphic literacy that has been contrasted with alphabetic writing. That system, said to have come into existence around 750 BCE, is regularly defined as a more sophisticated representation of speech than what are simultaneously cast as crudely drawn writing systems. The alphabet, because it is supposed to imitate speech itself, not provide only a picture of some portions of speech, results in a broader literacy that in this view can be thought of plausibly as a cause and as a result of democracy, or at the least as a technology enabling an innate cultural leaning toward democracy. Nonetheless, recently revealed evidence makes it increasingly difficult to support such a case beyond its innate illogic.

Growing attention to Mesopotamian cultures 6,000 years ago, arguably forgotten in Anglo-American rhetoric studies until relatively recently because a declared East and West have arbitrarily demarcated Islamic from Christian narratives, can still be set aside to make that case. But as François Zabbal makes clear in his foreword to *Ancestor of the West: Writing, Reasoning, and Religion in Mesopotamia, Elam, and Greece*, a "Mesopotamian legacy" from the fourth millennium BCE began a series of modifications of writing, religion, and reasoning whose earliest manifestations, if better valued, might have saved the twenty-first century from grave ignorance on all sides and its results (vii). As Zabbal explains, the Western result of Mesopotamian civilization "is today in a better position to reclaim its past" after two centuries of archaeological discoveries and their analyses, which were preceded in the nineteenth century by research into biblical geography that "was gradually accompanied by inquiries among Arab nomads" believed to reflect the Hebrew culture before Israel (x).

But even if we push writing's past back only to Minoan texts dating from 1900 BCE and after, we encounter a later (circa 1200 BCE) Hittite tablet that compares words across three languages. I take this example specifically to contrast that evidence with typical categorical assumptions like James Murphy's in *A Synoptic History of Classical Rhetoric*. This still-standard source, with only brief qualification that claims its basis in "surviving evidence," assents to the unfortunate commonplace that "the Greeks were the only people of the ancient world who endeavored to analyze the ways in which human beings communicate" ("Origin" 3). As in many assertions about Greek originality, Murphy's extrapolates from Athenian interest in communication a superior "level of development" in the later Greek culture and its individuals, thought here and elsewhere to be "the only people of their kind." Of course Murphy is not alone in this view, nor culpable for ignoring evidence unavailable to him, although the tacit message of his assertion may reveal why that evidence has waited for discovery and interest. But his practice is habitual, as Sylvia Scribner and Michael Cole point out in "Unpacking Literacy."

That is, it is common to blur specifically situated literate acts into a general cultural characterization and then equate this construction of culture from spotty examples with individual psychological progress (Scribner and Cole 57–70). Thus, many single out fourth-century Greek culture as a cradle of development that nurtured all linguistic bases of Western civilizations, ignoring now available archaeological and anthropological findings to preserve a single origin of a superior Western civilization. Much that has been discovered but not yet entirely uncovered about early literacy and its texts awaits full outcomes of translation, dating, and contextualization.

We do, however, have Kevin Robb's *Literacy and Paideia in Ancient Greece*, a reevaluation of propositions that underlie discussions of distinctly named "oral" and "literate" cultures, practices, and individuals. It describes, for instance, a 1974 discovery of a student's exercises written on a potsherd dated circa 1200 BCE: "Four lines are random letters, no doubt practice forms, but the last—and fortunately the clearest—is an abecedary in the standard order of letters, with minor variations, perhaps mistakes" (275). Robb argues that the Greek alphabet was the primary medium for recording that language, noting that the vowel system was invented "as a whole." That is, his prediction that there would be no transitional texts discovered in which one or a few vowels occur has been verified by their absence. But Robb also accounts for other literate practices among those who do use Phoenician script and other systems, to recast claims by Eric Havelock, the respected father of contrasts between oral and literate cultures and cognitive processes. Robb infers that because one recorded vowel sound implies all the others and thus a whole alphabet, the idea of writing was spread "by stimulus diffusion" (275).

That diffusion scattered motives to adopt this writing system in toto in other ways. That is, when adopted, it expanded the *contexts* in which compositions require metadiscursive principles, not only writing as an idea. It is plausible, for instance, to assert that a 1200 BCE peace treaty between the Hittites and Egypt exposes a literate mentality, if that category is at all meaningful, the superior development that is said to occur only later and elsewhere. We can make this divergent inference even without yet knowing how such a treaty was composed, recorded, and preserved, or the schooling of those who undertook these processes, or their probably distinct class status, whether exalted or demeaned.[5] Similarly, other evidence demonstrates legal protections for Hittite women and slaves. We thus learn from the existence of such records that these groups were controlled not only by family patriarchs and slave owners but also in documented law that settled many conflicts around adultery and property rights. But this evidence, like that of peace treaties, cannot evoke much beyond a deduction that schooling in the techniques of producing law-as-text would have taught various rhetorical skills: awareness of precedent authority, knowledge of technical formats, and expertise in addressing specific audiences. Those composing such documents, not always those who inscribed them, demonstrate sensitivities that are learned and taught, if not in settings at all like the classes and strolls of Plato's dialogues on rhetoric. The obvious inference many now draw is that purposeful inscription does precede the imaginary of late Athenian culture.

And other evidence of pre-Greek interest in varieties of communication implies that other inferences drawn in and from Havelock's theories of orality are at the least doubtful and may undermine still other dubious propositions that regularly inform rhetoric's histories. This evidentiary project is undertaken by the compilation *Language and Thought in Early Greek Philosophy*, which simultaneously honors Havelock's seminal work and collects a variety of critiques of his primary arguments. For instance, Arthur Adkins's "Orality and Philosophy" notes Odysseus's tricking the Cyclops by naming himself "No-One" so that neighbors will think that when the Cyclops says, "No-One is killing me," they are not needed. Adkins infers from this and similar evidence that opposes the idea of a discrete literate mentality that "not only the literate may be consciously concerned with words as words" and "language used in everyday contexts . . . can generate major philosophical problems . . . just as readily as the need adequately to express cosmological ideas" (219). In "The Emergence of Philosophy," Joseph Margolis similarly argues that "there is no reason to suppose that the philosophical impulse had to wait until well into the sixth century" (236).[6] He describes a class of scribes in the (generally) pre-alphabetic world that took responsibility for the preservation—"collection, ordering, management, application, and refinement"—of oral texts. Their non-alphabetic notational system evidences more than primitive "abstract" capacities. In any case, Margolis points out, "*The non-literacy of the general populace* would . . . *be irrelevant*" to privileged groups "with scribal-like or at least literate abilities" (236). Like Adkins, Margolis abandons origin stories in favor of uncovering the complexity of discursive practices before the Greek alphabet.

From the perspective of contemporary writing studies, this evidence might remind us that even were we to accede to simple views that orality is "not-literacy" and the reverse, multiplying uses of alphabetic writing would have been disseminated unevenly. That is, as with precedent forms of inscription, if the alphabet could have singularly enabled abstractions realized as philosophical thought and other discourses called "advanced," it would equally have made possible the practices that receive less critical attention and are thus treated as holdovers from supposedly more primitive, commonplace interactions. As Poster suggests in "A Conversation Halved: Ancient Epistolary Theory," such demeaning designations generally are applied to genres that have produced fewer secondary sources, not lesser significance. The rhetorical theory counted as a total "rhetoric," with speeches thought to comment on modern democracy, are thus also obliquely linked to the supposedly accessible medium of writing with vowels, as though its uses to other purposes are negligible (3). The dissemination of handbooks by Polus, Licymnius, and Protagoras that Socrates complains of in the *Gorgias* are a primary instance: historians often demean their uses among non-elite students even though they obviously create abstract, hierarchical outlines identical to the visual arrangements said to enable philosophy in the new mentality many also attribute to alphabetic literacy.[7] In addition, correspondence manuals, letters themselves, declamations and other school exercises, and ad hoc texts like lists, invoices, and public inscriptions—all of which are relatively difficult to locate and contextualize—might uniformly be said to result from the invention of the alphabet. But it is clear that these "functional" modes of writing exist long before the alphabet is invented and supposed to have generated an original philosophy. Thus, the evidence of alphabetic texts themselves undercuts any essential relation between them and their disbursed results.

This reevaluation of evidence that has made many cases about rhetoric's origins does not, however, deter those who date rhetoric as though it and its critics both originate in a democratic alphabet and alphabetic democracy, not from situated refinements of *existing* means of persuasion through discourse. For instance, when scholars disavow the myth of Corax and Tisias delivering a handbook system of rhetoric to Greece and deny that they were the sole source of the four-part oratorical form and the criterion of plausibility for proofs, they usually do so by questioning the existence of Corax or of Tisias. That is, many ignore the implausibility of these contributions, whatever their sources, doing more than expanding, improving, or citing existing practices.[8] On the other hand, Edward Schiappa acknowledges Corax and Tisias as "a convenient myth," to take an evolutionary perspective on rhetoric that sustains its unified development. But more certain than many about rhetoric's having one identifiable origin, he then carefully sorts through various discourses of history, philosophy, education, and oratory to find a first instance of discourse about discourse, in the use of the word *rhetorike* by Plato and Aristotle in early fourth-century Athens, if not by Isocrates (33–34, 39).

It is obvious that supposed origins of rhetoric also persistently blur into a less abstract Athenian democracy, yet itself cast as an origin. An unstated logic celebrates the positive qualities of Athenian democratic assemblies and then their correspondence to oratorical rhetoric. This post hoc reasoning allows those positive qualities to create an exclusive linkage and thus treats schooled oratory and democracy as the best if not the only representations of each other.[9] Especially insofar as this elision is transferred to the canonical American oratorical performances that asserted postrevolutionary democracy, many historians create a teleological subtext in which modern political ideals are equal to ancient motives, not the more relevant Realpolitik of early modern Europe. They imply that oratorical rhetoric's centered origins can now easily fit—because their neoclassical revivals caused—modern models of village, town meeting, and other face-to-face exchanges that guarantee equal participation.

Much evidence perturbs these often-unquestioned assumptions about smoothly connected democracy and rhetoric. When separated, they become theoretically and historically closer to their messy and highly political natures in all eras. For instance, work that revisits the procedures of Greek democracy shows how the uneven Athenian political system was notably professionalized, not distributed equally in an ad hoc way among the propertied males who constituted a citizenry. That democracy, like its oblique reincarnation in an early modern American version, was not based on equal property and human rights, nor on legal systems accessible to all but the sometimes referenced foreigners, poor men, women, and slaves. As Loren J. Samons says in *What's Wrong With Democracy? From Athenian Practice to American Worship*, "Anyone turning to Athens for political lessons must confront the facts that democratic Athens dominated and made war on the states most like itself, suffered two international revolutions, exiled or executed many of its own leaders, squandered vast public resources, and preserved its autonomy for less than two centuries" (6).

Nor did Athens's golden age invite spontaneous participation in public discourse. Obviously, only a few quasi-politicians make up the limited assortment of canonized orators studied now: *rhetores* who stood in for widely argued positions that warranted particular decisions. As Morgens Herman Hansen's extensive analyses of city-states and their institutions show, those who spoke in the *ekklesia* were not elected, did not make decisions but proposals on which people would vote, and worked as highly trained volunteers, given that pay for politics was criminal, at that time publicly so (50). These rhetores were not in the fifth century leaders of the people, the demagogues, nor *strategoi*, the elected magistrates who conducted war but had nonetheless minimal power when not commanding armed forces. And while in the fifth century, rhetores and strategoi might have been one and the same, in the fourth their democratic functions were separated. As Aristotle has it, when the art of rhetoric grew, "men with the gift of speech became demagogues but . . . are not appointed to commands" (*Politics* 1305a7–15).

Hansen infers that separately identifying rhetores and strategoi, despite their earlier shared function, established leadership of deliberation, but not action, by the rhetores. Laws holding them accountable for the constitutionality and results of their proposals applied even after the signatory wreath conventionally worn during their "one day business" was removed (55). Eventually, this cohort of speaker-citizens helped reify assembly speeches as a genre, one parallel to yet not identical with forensic and epideictic speech. For example, only forensic speeches follow a four-part structure, while assembly speeches contain three parts. More important, Hansen demonstrates that those who proposed acts were commonly not required to speak about them. Thus, Athenian deliberation "was dominated by a narrow group of orators while a broader group of citizens might appear as proposers" (60). In sum, he says, "[The name] *rhetor* was almost invariably used about the skilled speaker or proposer, not the *idiotes,* i.e. the ordinary citizen, who occasionally makes a speech or moves a proposal" (62).

Josiah Ober's *Mass and Elite in Democratic Athens: Rhetoric, Ideology, and the Power of the People* further complicates common assumptions about the mutuality of democracy and unified rhetoric. Ober demonstrates that the ten to thirty men who were active rhetores at any time performed the cultural work of assuring communication between classes (104). As members of the leisure class with resources that provided expensive educations, these speakers—about whom we have a few remaining bits of often contradictory biographical information and few textual remnants—spoke in assembly and law courts (114). But among the five hundred jurors were often poor people who needed the fee they received for this duty. Ober argues that this shifting cohort of judges might be "disabled, old, unlucky and unskilled citizens," a group that included rural farmers briefly visiting town (136). Of course, the potential voting of two very different classes representing wealth and its counterpart not only constrains common assumptions that this democracy was at least in its assemblies a political melting pot. As Ober also argues, communication across classes whose speech habits are famously taken as status markers invites expert mediation. But that mediation also involves constant education and reeducation of a changing and thus steadily unprepared group of judges who develop an identifying register of response: the hectoring, verbal abuse, and underclass network of commonplaces that discrepancies in status and schooling regularly invoke. Given those class-marked exchanges of statement and response, complicated by the possibility of rhetorical self-parody and the verbal interventions of judges, it becomes important for Ober and others to take up the effectiveness of the commonplace proof that begins a statement with "everyone knows." That complex yet offhand trope opens ways to analyze this verbal democracy in light of perspectives that as yet are not commonplace.

Everyone Knows: Antique Characters

Ober's *Mass and Elite in Democratic Athens* is influential precisely because its argument that a few politicians professionalized Athenian oratory opposes commonplaces about Athenian democracy, and thereby many applied to its simultaneous Athenian oratory. Both are taken to contextualize ad hoc participation like that described by J. B. Bury in a historical narrative still often taken for granted:

> The Greek democratic city presupposed in the average citizen the faculty of speaking in public, and for anyone who was ambitious for a

political career it was indispensable. If a man was hauled into a law-court by his enemies and did not know how to speak, he was like an unarmed civilian attacked by soldiers. The power of expressing ideas clearly and in such a way as to persuade an audience was an art to be learned and taught. But it was not enough to gain command of a vocabulary; it was necessary to learn how to argue, and to exercise one's self in the discussion of political and ethical questions. There was a demand for higher education. (Bury and Meiggs 241)

This imagined setting's configuration equally recalls educational films about colonial American congresses and the 1939 movie *Mr. Smith Goes to Washington*. Obviously, it differs markedly from the "mass" and "elite" interactions that Ober demonstrates. That is, traditional views individualize speech—both as a performance and as content—as a mode of action. Beyond their commitments to separate critical priorities, Bury and Ober differ insofar as the cultural subtext of Bury's narrative portrays such individuals as potentially singular outsiders, standing alone against "enemies" unless they "exercise one's self" in skilled verbal exchanges. Ober's very different understanding is expressed in his title, where two differently educated, socially demarcated groups occupy the characters of "socially learned narratives" like those of Aristotle's "sixteen paradigm scenarios" of emotion in Book II of the *Rhetoric*.[10] There, Aristotle argues for the identity between emotional response and generalized characters sorted by age in a theory of the emotions that persuade youth, the middle-aged, and older men but that also express feelings whose description there scripts the emotions of these groups for centuries.

It is less frequently noticed that types of characters are also linked to these feelings in Book III of the *Rhetoric*. There, character types, moral states, and appropriate language are joined, but briefly and in association with verbal signs that bring to presence what "everyone knows." Even on its surface, that commonplace overlaps a trope with socially learned scenarios. It sets aside the idea of interiorized feeling that post-Cartesian eighteenth-century and later rhetorical treatises describe, instead implicating those to be persuaded in well-circulated stories like those of the school exercise *personification*, to which judges of any sort are attuned. Ober assumes that this assertion that "everyone knows" a proposition's context "created the fiction that the entire polis was the sort of face-to-face community that in reality existed only at the level of the *demes*" (150). Since in fact this "everyone" is obviously illusory—a term always under erasure—Ober infers that projecting shame on those who do not already know an Athenian speaker's supposedly commonplace assumptions "may have its roots in village-level judicial decision making" (150).

Certainly his speculation takes energy from Hansen's description of the sizes of a quorum needed at the assembly and of the maximum seating capacity of the last-built replication of its meeting place. That is, a city that required 6,000 to constitute a quorum after 368 BCE, and that could seat 13,800 people at its assemblies from 340 to 200 BCE, was large enough to belie views of Athenian democratic interactions modeled on nuclear families, townships, committees, congregations, and other sites of face-to-face exchange that are characterized by opportunities for regulated equal participation (Hansen 17). But the habit of overlaying one on another set of provisions for judgment—here, intimate village relationships imposed on interactions among many Athenian strangers—reopens the question Ober tacitly asks by emphasizing cross-class mediation by only a few elite rhetores. That is, that situation requires rethinking the characters of speakers and judges as they are realized in descriptions of their interactions.

The *Rhetoric* is the source text for simultaneously addressing speakers and judges, especially in its treatment of arousing emotions within the narrated emotional scenarios it relies on in Book II. But this topic comes up in each book of the *Rhetoric*, and specifically in regard to what "everyone knows." In Book III, what "everyone knows" is used to control an audience who will be "ashamed at their ignorance of what was common knowledge (1408a32–36). On that ground, they will accept a speaker's selection of favorable and unfavorable measures of judgment, for rejecting them "would indicate how little they know of cultural fables and lore" (Kennedy, *Aristotle* 235–36). This analysis also applies to Book I's statement that a speech itself must be both the source and the realization of a speaker's ethos, "not by any preconceived idea of the speaker's character" (1356a7). That is, where it is likely that a speaker has no preconceived reputation for individual character in the populated city's sizable meeting place, face-to-face mutuality with the judges of a proposal is perhaps less likely to carry an argument than a textual representation of the speaker as an already scripted, well-known person. The composed speech itself alludes to conventional life narratives that, again, "everyone knows."

It is thus the value of established measures of propriety, not of glimpsed individuality, that assures familiar and, if not necessarily collective, certainly socially legible character. For instance, Jakob Wisse's *Ethos and Pathos from Aristotle to Cicero* refers to Aristotle's "strict separation of technical and non-technical *pisteis*" (246). Aristotle thereby describes a separation of a persuasive communal ethos from the alternative individual consciousness: a practical, "non-technical" mutuality derived from experiences that remain unframed as conventions, but not necessarily "unconventional." But space and time determine the more relevant generic conventions the *Rhetoric* prescribes, as we witness in the letter Lollianus sends in the late empire, pleading for back pay not on the ground of what we think of as "personal" friendship with the emperor but on the assumed friendly trust among those with shared education (see introduction). In intimate settings, the map is in fact as big as the territory on which proof from character rests. As Rui Zhu says of our current view that motives always arise from discrete interior selves, "There was no distinction between private life and public life, as there is today. There was no such concept as the 'invasion of privacy,' perhaps because *no Athenian felt that he had a private life that was to be kept distinct from his public life*" (232, emphasis added). Thus, a "non-technical" proof of character is one unframed by cultural scripts, whatever its content.

Of course, the word "felt" in Zhu's comment projects onto individual Athenians a model of universal individualism that long postdates their cultural norms. Early modern cultural secularization, which implants in individuals a spiritual relation to God and the Christian "body of Christ" composed of human members, begins the progress of consciousness that mooted Athenian "public" and "private" categories cannot imitate. However, we habitually deduce from cultural remnants the traits of conscious individuals, as we deduce a mentality from available, not specifically used, literacy. On the evidence of the texts we have, representations and receptions of character are clearly cultural productions—even including the personal opinions Athenian rhetores were expected to express to avoid charges of coterie thinking (Ober 123). And as Ober suggests in noting this requirement, the orator stood alone only insofar as he must be perceived as untied from special interest groups and reified causes, not as a socially unmoored, erratically opinionated individual. At least partially in concert with Zhu, he says that political and social roles were less differentiated from each other than in modern societies: "The stress on the necessity of good character for good political action led quite naturally to the politician's life as a whole being open to public scrutiny. . . . His every action was public property and would be judged against the standard of popular morality" (127). Once again, shared conventions set criteria that assess an orator's credible character. Judges who make decisions based on how skillfully speakers recirculate commonplaces affirm their participation in the common *doxa* those commonplaces create, in their "always reciprocal" (Ober 104) commutation with a rhetor.

What "everyone knows" hereby regulates both parties, "mass" and "elite," both by laying down limits and acknowledging the creative stances within them that regulations make visible. In this exchange, morality is an agreed-upon responsiveness to familiar propositions, not to a personal choice of action. Aristotle explains this cooperative perceptual field as an alignment of character with probity. The trope comes up as an example of "Appropriateness, Propriety" in Book III of the *Rhetoric* (7.7) as the last element of an expanded outline of means toward stylistic *copia*. The first three points list the qualities of appropriate *lexis*: It first "expresses emotion and character" in proportion to a subject. It second provides the gravitas fitting "weighty matters," not casual discussion, nor an extreme formality. Finally, "emotion is expressed" if style fits the *character of the speaker* to the topic at hand. This last point of course demonstrates a perceived identity between character and its publicity, the exposure of performed utterances that is fully exploited in much later print publication (chapter 3). For instance, the anger that Peter Brown describes as a political act in the late Christian Empire here appropriately attaches to other interactions: insolence (*hybris*), reluctance to speak to "impious and shameful things," respect to admirable things, submission to pitiable topics. These repetitions of the classification scheme for emotions as separate states in Book III again equate them to reputed credibility:

> 4. The proper *lexis* also makes the matter credible: the mind [of the listener] draws a false inference of the truth of what a speaker says because they [in the audience] *feel the same about such things, so they think the facts to be so,* even if they are not as the speaker represents them; 5. and the hearer suffers along with the pathetic speaker, even if what he says amounts to nothing. As a result, many overwhelm their hearers by making noise. (III.7.4–5, emphasis added)

This analysis of audience responses links them to the fit of style to topic, with no mention of personal, "style is the man" guidelines that describe expression but not trust. In the view of the *Rhetoric*, speaker and audience are engaged in a persuasive dynamic when they "feel the same things" (see below). The "noise" that Aristotle says may accomplish this false affective connection warrants Max Weber's claim that Athenian leadership was "charismatic," thus based on emotional appeals (qtd. in Ober 123–24). But as points one through five are themselves expanded in this treatment of style, Aristotle appears not to limit appeals to emotion to only the sobs and sighs, growls or whispers of "noise." The emotional register appropriate to a topic instead expresses character "because there is an appropriate style for each genus and moral state" (III.7.6). *Genus*, or type, includes "things like age—boy, man, old man—or woman and man or Spartan and Thessalian" and *moral state* (*hexis*) includes the principles by which someone is "the kind of person he is in life." Here, "moral states" are not fixed principles applied in speculation about what one might do or should do in hypothetical situations. What is at stake is instead appropriate language that "creates a sense of character" (III.7.7). Listeners will react to the fit between "rustic" and "educated" language applied to generic types as they will to "expressions speechwriters use to excess: 'Who does not know?' 'Everybody knows . . .'" (III.7.7).

In Kennedy's translation of the *Rhetoric*, "embarrassment" replaces Ober's "shame" as this trope's coercion to agree, a discomfiture that in Kennedy occurs "in order to share in the [alleged] feelings of all others" (Sherman 183). Kennedy notes that for similar effect, Quintilian (8.3.37) advised anticipation ("You may not want to believe what I am going to say, but . . ."). That amplification adds to the list of too frequently used, but entirely effective, ways of framing attention around event and context.

The *Rhetoric* appears to take this treatment of proof by potential exclusion relatively lightly, easily connecting "everybody knows" to embarrassment. Contrary to Ober's paraphrase, "ashamed at their ignorance of what was common knowledge," Kennedy's alternative translation suggests that what is at stake is knowledge of appropriate responses to specific data shared by all. Thus, the trope might be paraphrased as "what everyone feels when confronted with X." This emphasis on character by Kennedy's Aristotle equates "moral states" with "shar[ing] in the [alleged] feelings of" *all* others. In this relatively casual way, the *Rhetoric* reiterates the positive educational program in the moral states that is appropriate in educated elites. As the *Politics* has it:

> [N]othing [is] more important [than] to "become habituated in . . . judging rightly and delighting in good characters and fine actions. Rhythm and melody provide keen likenesses of anger and gentleness, and also courage and temperance and of all the opposites of these and of all the other states of character. . . . Becoming habituated to feeling pain and delight in likenesses is close to feeling the same way towards the things that are their models. (1340a15–28)

It is again taken for granted that "delight in likenesses" will be inculcated, and practiced, by anyone whose moral state joins other persuasive "characters that prevail" (*Rhetoric* I). Trust among the assembled judges and an orator is based on shared responses, those that emerge from "all" accustomed to encountering events, proofs, and scenarios in the courts and assembly.[11] Those feelings, that is, determine how to argue cases and verify their claims against common feelings. As Nancy Sherman's citation of the *Politics* in *The Fabric of Character: Aristotle's Theory of Virtue* puts it, "Virtue is concerned with proper enjoyment and loving and hating rightly" (1340a15–28, qtd. in Sherman 183). Stylistic appropriateness thus has predictable results. It represents an orator's virtue, a "proper" pleasure in having the right feelings.

Michael V. Fox is determined to contrast earlier Egyptian prescriptive views of ethos with Aristotle's in his "Ancient Egyptian Rhetoric." But the ethos portrayed here and elsewhere in the *Rhetoric* makes character more than what Fox calls "an adjunct to proof" (15). Each of its books addresses proof through character—first to explain its importance in judicial oratory (I.2), later as an element of deliberation (II.1), and finally in relation to sign theory, including the signification of what everyone knows (III.7.1–7) as an element of style. In the first instance, Book I glosses that particular appeal as it lists types of proofs: "Some [proofs] are in the character of the speaker, and some in disposing the listener in some way, and some in the argument itself" (I.2.3). Kennedy explains that "ethos" here means character, especially "'moral character,' and . . . is regarded as an attribute of a person, not of a speech" (*Aristotle* n. 40). That personal character imbricates dispositions of the listener insofar as it evokes feelings. But it is not discussed in relation to logical analyses (n. 40). This explanation in the first section continues:

> 4. [There is persuasion] through character whenever the speech is spoken in such a way as to make the speaker worthy of belief. For we believe fair-minded people to a greater extent and more quickly [than we do others], on all subjects in general and completely so in cases where there is not exact knowledge but room for doubt. And this should result from the speech, not from a previous opinion that the speaker is a certain kind of person; for it is not the case as some of the technical writers propose in their treatment of the art, that fair-mindedness on the part of the speaker makes no contribution to persuasiveness; rather, character is almost, so to speak, the controlling factor in persuasion. (I.2.4)

Again, it is not the absolute quality of private dispositions that names character as this "controlling factor." What "everyone knows" is taught, specifically as the appropriate feelings of the elite that are systematically exposed and enforced in the literary education of paideia. But characters that prevail among the schooled class are also defined by their responsive recognition of that appropriateness, sensitivity to what is also "fair-minded" for the judges. Thus, the *Rhetoric* moots fervent discussions of distinctions between intrinsic and enacted character—"nature" and "role." Public and private lives, core and display, are not at issue in events that perform community service specifically by embodying shared values.

Book II's second exposition of persuasion through character also implies that proposition. It makes clear that formalist assignments of ready-made characters to specific types of argumentation is not the primary issue at stake in deliberation:

> 2. But since rhetoric is concerned with making a judgment . . . it is necessary not only to look to the argument, that it may be demonstrative

and persuasive but also [for the speaker] to construct a view of himself as a certain kind of person and to prepare the judge; 3. for it makes much difference in regard to persuasion (especially in deliberations but also in trials) that the speaker seem to be *a certain kind of person* and that his hearers suppose him to be disposed toward them *in a certain way* and in addition if they, too, happen to be disposed in a certain way [favorably or unfavorably to him]. (II.1.2–3, emphasis added)

The *Politics* again elaborates this view of character, as Wisse points out. It names three measures for a person's fit to high office, including being "friendly toward the established political arrangement" (1309a33–39, qtd. in Wisse 159). The other two necessary qualities are "capacity for the work of the office" and "virtue and justice: in each political arrangement the [kind of virtue and justice proper] to the political arrangement. For if what is just is not the same in all political arrangements, then there must also be different kinds of justice" (qtd. in Wisse 159). This point revisits friendliness, not as an insider's pose or willingness to repeat a corporate position but as a politician/orator's moral stance, a character without ambivalence toward the combined public/private persuasive identity of the rhetor of the courts and the deliberative assembly. The application of that socially determined character in fitting styles further characterizes this ethical proof. Book III's explanation of sign theory suggests that orators are judged by their access to extralogical proofs. The Muses Lollianus takes so much to heart are, after all, capable of, if not invested in, artifice and thus deception. In addition, signs and styles require interpretation, as the *Rhetoric*'s acknowledgment of a variable fit of linguistic register to more and less sophisticated characters attests. Thus, oratorical character is fundamentally deceptive and prescribed as such, at least insofar as unstable signs compose its credible argumentation.

Everyone Knew: Rhetoric as Its Precedents

Obvious as it is, few who theorize rhetoric focus on the ancient assumption that trusted persuasion joins a socially legible moral disposition to commonplace proofs whose tenor "everyone knows." Shifting groups of judges share occasional like-mindedness, an artifact of temporary employment and the power of office to embed its holders in traditions they may not consciously know. But that cultural spin on the interactive phenomenology around persuasive speech deserves attention. For one thing, this grounding of persuasion in shared assumptions and shared access to them reveals the relevance to rhetoric of many circulating views of prevailing moral states that constitute persuasive moments among many versions of rhetor and judge. An immediate example is in Plato's later treatise *Laws*, which modifies his negative treatment of emotion in the *Republic*. That is, the Athenian Stranger there allows that education can inculcate a habituation ("ethos") to the correct measure and object of pleasure and pain. He thus defines virtue as a "general concord of reason and emotion" (7.653b). This definition places personal quests for "the good" in a cultural context, as the Stranger's elaboration shows: "But there is one element you could isolate in any account you give, and this is *the correct formation of our feelings of pleasure and pain*, which makes us hate what we ought to hate from first to last, and love what we ought to love" (653b–c, emphasis added). This power of education to create judgmental responses that "we" share again not only focuses on educated feelings that are acceptably "right" but also determines those deployed in the service of persuasion that will be recognizable among "everyone."

These workings of oratorical proof reappear in the immediately following statement that God, not man, is the measure of all things: "[I]f you want to recommend yourself to someone of this [God-like] character, you must do your level best to make your own character reflect his [character], and on this principle the moderate man is God's friend, being like him, whereas the immoderate and unjust man is not like him and is his enemy" (Plato, *Laws* 716c–d). As Dorothea Frede says, Plato here evidences "faith . . . that right habituation through the right kind of education, most of all in the arts, will provide the right inner equilibrium for the good citizen" (sec. 5.2, par. 4). The Stranger also specifies this cultural curriculum. That is, the gods ordain festivals as occasions of rest that are the sites of the first education by "Apollo and the Muses." Festivals teach the divine harmonies and rhythms of dance, music, and poetry, and their attendees see tragedies and equestrian and gymnastic contests and hear rhapsodes like Homer. There, the Stranger argues, people learn to judge by seeing the best performances as twofold lessons: those that inculcate godlike assessments of a fit between goodness and pleasure in performance and those that demonstrate the bad and displeasure in trivial or ill-chosen representations:

> In either case, the best-educated men judge correctly:
> [T]he pleasure must not be that of chance persons; the fairest music is that which delights the best and best educated, and especially that which delights the one man who is pre-eminent in virtue and education. And therefore the judges must be men of character, for they will require both wisdom and courage; the true judge must not draw his inspiration from the theatre. . . . He is sitting not as the disciple of the theatre, but, in his proper place, as their instructor, and he ought to be the enemy of all pandering to the pleasure of the spectators. . . . But this custom

has been the destruction of the poets; for they are now in the habit of composing with a view to please the bad taste of their judges, and the result is that the spectators instruct themselves. (*Laws* 7.659)

Were connections obvious among the discourses Plato cites—poetry, drama, tragedy, rhapsody, and epic—and the formulation of systematic rhetoric, the enduring philosophy/rhetoric dichotomy that continually repairs rhetoric's secondary status or reinforces it might be set aside in favor of articulating the ad hoc, class-based, experiential, and especially educational bonds that enable persuasion. That is, in neither its early critiques or positive representations—not in Plato, Aristotle, or Isocrates—is rhetoric yet discretely theorized. Nothing equivalent to literary theory, for example, explains its operations as a cultural formation, a "rhetorical" equal to an eighteenth- and nineteenth-century "aesthetic."

That missing equivalence might apply as well to the tenor of shared experiences of value that underlie persuasion. That is, insofar as rhetoric describes a cooperative space of performance, participation in decision-making of any sort requires suspension of disbelief in an inspired, *mantic* realm. That state, later theorized as aesthetic appreciation, was deemed readily accessible not only to its seers, poets, and other cultural mediators but to their audiences—those who must already be persuaded of the powers of art if its discursive forms are to result in action. Before categories of logic and emotion were definitively opposed or emotion was in modern philosophy defined as a cognitive assessment of more and less immanent experience, the spaces of mixed connections among poetry, divinity, prophecy, and philosophical speculation in Plato's *Ion, Republic, Phaedrus*, and *Gorgias* at least invite the inference that examples in Aristotle's *Rhetoric* derive from a commonplace circulation of those discourses among their sister arts, especially the metacraft of rhetorical composition.[12]

That fit among these discourses and positively systematized rhetoric is obvious to many. Adele C. Scafuro's *The Forensic Stage: Settling Disputes in Graeco-Roman New Comedy* is but one treatment, with Simon Goldhill and Robin Osborne's collection *Performance Culture and Athenian Democracy*, James F. McGlew's *Citizens on Stage: Comedy and Political Culture in Athenian Democracy*, and especially Jeffrey Walker's *Rhetoric and Poetics in Antiquity*.[13] Translator Benjamin Jowett points out that Aristotle, living in Athens when Plato's *Laws* was written, refers to that treatise more than twenty times (1). But despite the usually identified oppositions of their positions, Plato links performance to its judges in ways reflected in the *Rhetoric* and *Politics* (see Aristotle, *Politics* 1309a33–39). Both emphasize that stable standards should instill moral states. That is, both appear to address those markers of character from within already well-circulated philosophical positions, themselves derived from settings like the contests and performances Plato defines as educational. Unlike Aristotle, however, he proposes divine origins whose powers were articulated long before alphabetic writing.

Such notice of divinity of course touches not only the arts of poetry, music, and others assigned to the Muses but all of antiquity's rituals, which are both practical and performative educational settings. In fourth-century Athens, the persuasive force of various precedent practices gathers in formal treatments of rhetoric, both as partial theories like Aristotle's and Isocrates', and in a very different handbook tradition. Aristotle prepared a compendium for his students, a *Sunagôgê Tekhnôn*, summarizing the work of predecessors reputed to include Corax, Tisias, Gorgias, Protagoras, and, according to Quintilian, Isocrates himself.[14] Harvey Yunis points out that Plato's outline of a positive rhetoric in the *Phaedrus* might count as "the first systematic theory of rhetoric," not because Plato has originally used the word *rhetorike* but because this outline represents the gathering of traditions that enable this para-theory and Aristotle's (223). In this light, the overdetermined composition of the legible character of a rhetor draws on many forms of shared emotional assent to a character-in-performance.

That mode of proof is shared across the work of orators and, at least in Socratic dialogues, in philosophy. That is, despite competition as modes of access to Truth, rhetoric and philosophy more directly than oratory uncover the linguistic basis of agreement—not trust in either discourse's celebration of human communication but as the Socratic method of *elenchus* that becomes dialectics: the question-and-answer method that performs attention to ways in which language mesmerizes. As Jacqueline de Romilly's *The Great Sophists in Periclean Athens* stresses, the Sophists—including Socrates—repeatedly demonstrate, present themselves, and are represented by others as teachers of a specific subject: persuasive uses of language that mesmerize audiences precisely in the mode of poets (68–70). She cites, for instance, Hippias's technical treatments of grammar and prosody to demonstrate sophistic attention to language as the tool of philosophical persuasion (74). Shared moral states constitute persuasion from speaker to many forms of judgment in a variety of registers in which that sharing occurs, not in the acceptance of philosophical abstractions. Thus the language-truth relationship is much less revelatory than the directly persuasive language-trust relationship that informs the *Rhetoric*, numerous handbooks, sophistic and Platonic theories of discourse, and the few classical orators we know from speeches.

This observation is not singular. For instance, Edward P. J. Corbett's 1971 *Classical Rhetoric for the Modern Student* acknowledges the multitude of rhetorical practices in pre-fifth-century Homeric, philosophical, and historical discourses.[15] But that conglomerate is usually treated not as spaces that define persuasive interactions but as a source for one description. That is, poetry, drama, history, or philosophy is treated as a singular link to its imitations, or to its supposed sources, in rhetoric. Yet Plato, if unexpectedly in light of Socrates' famous views, also alludes to enactments of persuasive processes across medicine, religion and its history in antique divination, and, of course, education (7). From a perspective that looks for persuasion within established means of assuring trusting acceptance, any history of rhetoric has many plausible beginnings, or many rhetorics to account for.

Thus, it makes yet another sort of sense to imagine the rhetoric its historians have cast as a central metadiscourse as instead codifying long-extant and widely dispersed sites of persuasion that comprise cultural infrastructures even beyond and before their evocation in ancient city-states. Of course, each of those practices has had extensive treatment already. But these expositions rarely take up how some extratextual practices are framed as traditions that always hinge on persuasive force. Nonetheless, oratory realizes other sites of linguistic regularities, other narratives of characters whose predictable emotions conjure expected behaviors and outcomes, and other appeals to the strength of cooperating numbers demonstrated by many forms of family, tribal, community, and eventually national citizenship. The abstraction of these experiential texts now gathers them in a textual ontology that differs, essentially, from the immediate interactions and commonplace situations that create their persuasiveness by virtue of repetition. But all make it plausible to identify their devices—for example, imitation, allusion, and certainly "what everyone knows"—as metadiscursive precepts and technical procedures, not as their results.

So many references affirm that ancient persuasive discourses of many sorts are realized in oratorical rhetoric that it is impossible here to identify them all, much less pretend to do the topic justice. In addition to de Romilly's work on rhetoric and magic, which designates poets, seers (practitioners of divination), and Sophists as united in the project of cultural education, many sources like those I have cited from Aristotle and Plato explicitly include ancient poetry, drama, festivals, and medicine in the ways of thinking and talking that inform cultural education through discourse. These sites not only precede rhetoric's canons but also vividly demonstrate how shared emotional states and commonplace memories are their core bases in trust.

Poetry

Literary compositions are perhaps the most obvious proofs of these propositions. Of course, it is also commonplace to connect epic, lyric, and drama to rhetorical devices, if usually without noting that interactions among these separate forms and their techniques were inevitably recursive, with one modifying another while responding to it. Thus, "influence," if not mutuality, is moot in all but the broadest terms. A relevant illustration is Jakob Wisse's notice that handbooks before Aristotle's *Rhetoric* differ from his in their lack of organization and especially in failing to treat ethos and pathos. He infers from this evidence that historians of rhetorical theory should focus on the enthymeme as Aristotle's primary contribution. But Wisse's evidence is at best very indirect: the omission of character and emotion from handbooks may be an artifact of the discrete purposes and uses to which rhetorical devices are put, not certain evidence that their compilers were in fact omitting topics they designated as irrelevant to the practices that were their sources. We can thus only be sure that these manuals, like the poetry, epic, and drama circulated in the antique world, compile *other* particular persuasive devices that, taken from their contexts, become abstract outlines that produce further variations on the practices they compile (Wisse 13). And as suggested by the diversity of these and other persuasive discourses that precede Aristotle's and other systematic rhetorics, the arousal and potential enchantment of emotion are old news of another sort well before the incomplete collection of guides and examples that we have. Thus, when Wisse strongly rejects the argument that pathos is central to Aristotle's conception of rhetoric, he is assuming a unified circulating theoretical statement of rhetoric from directly inherited sources, an assumption that undermines his case. Yet he obliquely supports this criticism himself by noting that the ethos of Aristotelian rhetoric is taken from directions to actors to represent "oneself as a certain sort of person" and put the judge in a "certain frame of mind" (II.1.3.77b24). It thus is reasonable to infer that the designed pathos of actors—in Denis Diderot's term, the actor's paradox (*"Paradoxe sur le comédion"*)—occasions ongoing discussion in rhetoric of whether an orator must really feel, or can effectively only seem to really feel, the emotion portrayed in a speech. Wisse himself asserts that Aristotle's *Poetics* and the later Horace also promote acting emotional to buttress an audience's identification with the poet (*Poetics* 17.4.1455a32–3). The *Ars Poetica*, he says, is concerned with *signs* of emotion, so it describes the style that makes displayed feeling convincing while "the problem of 'poetic sincerity' is not even mentioned" (265).[16]

It has been so important to equate poetic excellence with a sensitive individual consciousness rather than with skillful uses of lyric conventions that this relationship between poetry and persuasion is only recently revived. Thus, in his preface to *Poet, Public, and Performance in Ancient Greece: From Homer to the Fifth Century*, Maurizio Bettini takes pains to contrast modern with ancient poetry. The latter, he says, links poetry "to the realities of social and political life, and to the actual behavior of individuals *within a community*" (vii, emphasis added). Paul Allen Miller also stresses this difference in *Lyric Texts and Lyric Consciousness: The Birth of a Genre from Archaic Greece to Augustan Rome*. He argues that only a multi-referential, multi-temporal world of writing can enable modern consciousness, which he describes as a nonlinear, recursively interrelated series of temporal loops that connect a person to the world from a space of interiority (2). The conscious self, "compulsively analyzing and reinterpreting the same multivalent experiences," is not the poised ancient lyric poet who, like the orator in a space of composition, is "not simply . . . a 'strong personality,' but . . . *a particular mode of being a subject*, in which the self exists . . . as part of a continuum with the community and its ideological commitments" (4, emphasis added).

Miller's extension of this argument additionally suggests that modern assumptions can equally deform the oratorical ethos at stake in Aristotle's and Plato's assumptions about decidedly typified characters. In this specific poetic case, histories often portray a speaker as a heroic voice of an interesting individual who has control of both language and audience response. Miller explains it differently:

> The *ego* [in these poems], especially in the archaic period, is not that of the author or the author's persona, but that of the object actually bearing the inscription. Moreover, this object-ego is only given life by the reader, who lends his . . . voice to the inscription, making it come to life for his largely illiterate bystanders. The *ego* then is in no sense private or idiosyncratic, but very precisely paradigmatic, in that it is assumable by anyone capable of making it sound forth. (7)

Charles H. Kahn further associates texts that themselves have symbolic functions with early literacy, which he dates in the eighth century BCE and before, saying that some form of writing was by his guess "indispensable for the composition of both [Homeric] epics" (110). However, "for a long time the written text would probably be the privileged possession of professional singers—perhaps the guild property of the *Homeridae*" (110). Miller stresses the relational values such property represents, much like those associated with the holographic illuminated Christian Bibles in scattered medieval churches: "What we understand as a psychological *affective* and moral terminology in reality denotes relations between the individual and members of his group" (18). By this reasoning, that affective moral terminology applies equally to the circulating texts of oratory, as our many analyses of the few speeches we have suggest. They are not simply the works of Gorgias or Isocrates, but Foucauldian "statements," cultural representations.

Drama

These circulated linguistic powers more obviously attach to ancient drama, for its festival productions and prizes already connote its cultural work. For instance, tragedy repeatedly portrays choices that simultaneously derive from interpretations of group values and assert the dangers of individual choices based on singular motives. Thus, many studies of drama echo the problematics of character and consequential choice that can be said to underlie declamations, handbook examples, and staged poetic voices. Contemporary critics easily recognize this connection, as for instance in Maria Grazia Bonanno's "All the (Greek) World's a Stage: Notes on (Not Just Dramatic) Greek Staging." It notes the "psychosomatic pleasures" that join epic and lyric to dramatic performance principles. Bonanno further argues that the frequent uses in literary performances of "metaphors, images, and similes[,] . . . an esoteric coterie language," indicate that the paradigmatic authorial voice and the equally typified attention it receives both display its entirely conventional stances toward a community (113).

Of course, many treatments of ancient Greek texts additionally categorize them as "not-oral." That view of literature as advanced beyond a spoken world easily elides individual uniqueness and literacy, without reference to the ancient assumptions about poet, poem, and texts to which Miller and Kahn draw attention. But categorical assessments of literacy's progressive results are not simple. Bruno Gentili's translator, A. Thomas Cole, points out in his introduction to *Poetry and Its Public in Ancient Greece: From Homer to the Fifth Century* that Milman Parry treated formulaic language in oral composition as a way to project "the hearer at once into a world of shared values and assumptions—to be accepted or rejected as known quantities—without interference from what we could now call the self-referential or intertextual overcodings that come with the literate artist's search for individual expression" (xvii). In addition, of course, we should note that without noting textuality, Parry's work on ethnic orality cannot take into account the impossibility of the ancient poet who is not a personage preexisting a poetic utterance. That is, antique ritual recitals that are accepted as broadly literary attend to performing the social paradigms they also produce. Scafuro connects this performativity to rhetorical theories in *The Forensic Stage*, where she notes that "our readings of orations suffer from one of the same deficiencies we have begun to correct in our readings of ancient drama: we forget that the (original) orations were, in a very real sense, performance texts" (57). That definition is omitted from current rhetorical theories, perhaps to assure that these texts' relation to later elocutionary rhetoric remains silenced (see chapter 3).

George Kennedy's *New History of Classical Rhetoric* echoes that reminder that oratory, not all rhetorically guided texts, is performed. Kennedy treats drama as evidence of developing rhetorical traditions. He says that "although Greek literature from the earliest times was 'rhetorical' and illustrates techniques that were eventually defined and described, the fifth century was . . . crucial . . . in the emergence of a consciousness of rhetoric on the part of speakers and audiences" (25). But Kennedy does not take up how tacitly suspended reality and inherited myth create dramatic persuasion in ways that oratorical rhetoric adapts. With others, he instead reverses that order, saying that dramatic speeches "share many of the features of invention and style of contemporary Greek oratory." That is, he takes these homologies to be evidence for multiple applications of emergent rhetoric (17), not as evidence of common techniques of persuasion across discourses that accrue trust literally on their own, situated ground. Kennedy does point out, however, that by the late fifth century, rhetorical handbooks clearly incorporate the devices of Homeric epics (25). John Poulakos's treatment of the Sophists further complicates that connection, for he notes other recursive interactions of dramatic and other traditions within codified rhetoric, as for instance in theatrical spectacles that are imitated in courtroom theatrics (*Sophistical Rhetoric* 3).

It would be useful to elaborate these and other plausible but rather piecemeal connections among literature, its ritualistic cultural content, and systematic guides for oratorical performances. To do so would not only enact a less linear, more credible picture of rhetoric as multiple, differently intended pedagogies that are never rendered as a reified theory-of-everything-discursive, neither then nor now. That project beyond this brief survey would expand already recognized connections between the Platonic dialogues and the formal structures of tragedy and comedy. As James A. Arieti says in *Interpreting Plato: The Dialogues as Drama*, Plato clearly adapted dramatic forms to prose in ways easily traced to the exchange patterns of even earlier dance rituals and the binary exchanges of the *Dissoi Logoi* (404?–397).[17] Taking up less noted connections might also shed light, for instance, on shared infrastructures of writing processes, acting and voice lessons, trans-historical religious speech acts, and the specific geographic locations of recovered texts. Arieti's lead also suggests we might notice how traditional agonistic drama creates a narrative structure that audiences finally take to be a template for otherwise disordered lives. These forms lead to and follow from a later systematic rhetoric's five-part structure of argumentation, as "the argument of the play" suggests. They may have been templates for the four-part oratory supposedly delivered by Corax and Tisias. But they certainly insert into modern consciousness the expectation of a life with development, crises, high points, and denouements—the good death, the heroic sacrifice.

Of course, the plots of drama and much fiction are well described, for instance by T. W. Baldwin's *Shakespeare's Five-Act Structure*, which demonstrates the endurance of Senecan five-part theater. Baldwin describes that sequence moving from a point of entrance (scene, setting, context) to a defining event that presents a protagonist. The protagonist, a person or force, encounters an opposing human or natural or conceptual counterforce, as is modeled earlier by the strophe/antistrophe statements of Greek choruses. After these forces meet in a *crisis* (the "crossings" of encounter), a *climax* (the realization or highpoint of the conflict) follows, seemingly inevitably leading to a "final event": a *denouement* or stabilized outcome easily projected into a future state. In argumentation, the disposition of materials also eventually follows this pattern of exchange-as-progress, moving through *exordium* (contextualizing introduction), *narratio* (facts, situation), *confirmatio* (positive evidence, support), *refutatio* (engagement with opposition), and *peroratio* (concluding summary, statement of implications). Obviously, both drama and five-part argument formally trace sequences of daily, if notable, acts and the conventional turn-taking of conversation.

This comparison demonstrates mutuality among performative sites that create their credibility by reiterating familiar patterns of language and action. Expositions of past action and wished-for events produce such paradigmatic positive and negative forces (for example, stock characters, conceptual dilemmas, political choices for good and ill) and effectively invest both a teller and those who can be drawn to identify with a tale in its plausible alternative outcomes. Poulakos describes this formal realization of persuasion, saying that "if the orator's display succeeds in firing the imagination of the listeners, and if their hopes triumph over their experience of the world as it is, the possibilities before them are well on their way to becoming actuality" (*Sophistical Rhetoric* 69). Those possibilities are at least tacitly excited in Plato's dialogues, which imitate comedic dramas, a genre Arieti explores in this context beyond others who only acknowledge dialogic exchanges without classifying them as theatrical (3–4).[18] But when their conversational turn-taking is read closely, it becomes clear that various forms of interaction are the primary topics of *Gorgias* and *Phaedrus*. Both dialogues exemplify Socrates' frequently failed argumentation—his apparent inability to convince his interlocutors of his point of view. Thus, we might usefully set aside the well-worried prosaic sense of these comic dialogues in favor of noting that they express not always reassuring "Truth" as the nature of interactions. *Gorgias*, for instance, persistently opposes its own cases against rhetoric, especially by demonstrating question/answer *elenchus* that Socrates insists must preempt oratorical speeches. In this sense, the dialogue is actually *not* a way toward a shared Realist critique of rhetoric but toward picky quarrels among its characters. *Phaedrus* also has less to say about the nature of love than about the powerlessness of the phallus against textuality, the "already said" traditions that swallow that dialogue's literary myths and examples along with its failed seduction.[19]

Of course, these dialogues do seemingly replace rhetoric with philosophical Realities, at least by casting out stylistic excesses and trivial proofs. But their examples suggest normal antique associations among practical arts and their functional counterparts, if such categories are meaningful in this early emergence of prose. The most obvious examples are Plato's famous analogies with rhetoric as like cookery rather than medicine (*Gorgias* 465; *Phaedrus* 270), like cosmetics rather than "training" or "gymnastic strength and beauty" (*Gorgias* 463; *Phaedrus* 270), and like pandering to desires rather than wisely leading the soul to Truth (*Gorgias* 463; *Phaedrus* 260ff.).

In Aristotle's *Rhetoric*, these exemplary arts become illustrations, appealing examples of strategies. "The virtues of the body" (such as health, beauty, strength, physical stature, athletic prowess; I.5.4) contribute to happiness, so appealing to them is persuasive. Medicine is here portrayed as rhetoric's twin, not its superior, insofar as both require generalizing from specific instances: "The art of medicine does not specify what is healthful for Socrates or for Calias but for persons of a certain sort" (I.2.11). But medicine is also a proof by sign, in which we infer from a fever that someone is ill, or from a woman's milk that she is a recent mother (I.2.18).

Cures

This positive later association of rhetoric with authoritative generalizations and signs suggests that its ancient theories draw on examples from established ordinary discourses whose achievements require assent, approval, or at the least a measure of cooperation. That is, beyond the literary arts, rhetoric is also much like otherwise commonplace but equally scripted activities usually ignored in its histories by those who privilege not only drama and poetry but systematic handbooks and sophistic thought. Yet unregulated deceptive practices have more complicated implications for rhetoric than simple oppositions of it to more civilized Truths. The *Satyricon* and enormous current attention to gourmet and culture-specific "cookery," what we know of both ancient and contemporary Olympic training, and recent theoretical attention to fashion and cosmetic improvement of (equally theoretical) "natural" appearances all argue that metadiscourse subsumes its everyday culture to a purpose.

For instance, in the case of medicine, the problem of its purchase on accurate diagnoses and effective treatments has long legs. Mesopotamian medicine was reportedly successful in many ways but was based on beliefs that disease is a sign of sin, perhaps the sin of a family member or ancestor finally come to punishment in the current patient. Here the issue becomes whether any period's science—for example, a germ theory of disease—is at all relevant to emotional investments in other forms of conviction—for instance, trust in the truth and efficacy of the following Mesopotamian prayer:

> Loosen my disgrace, the guilt of my wickedness; remove my disease; drive away my sickness; a sin I know or know not I have committed; on account of a sin of my father or my grandfather, or a sin of my mother or my grandmother, on the account of a sin of my elder brother or an elder sister, on account of a sin of my family, of my kinsfolk or of my clan . . . the wrath of gods and goddesses have [*sic*] pressed upon me.[20]

Considering how we still easily liken illness to punishment, that prayer is not so odd as first appears. And given the actual opacity of the ancient body and its fictionalized integrity in early modern views of individual consciousness, there is a consequential history of cures that mystify doctor, patient, or both.

Nancy Struever's "The Discourse of Cure: Rhetoric and Medicine in the Late Renaissance" also argues that both medicine and rhetoric can be described as "shaky empirical science[s]" that necessitate interventionist tactics (277). The inductive credibility of both forms of persuasion is based on accumulated guesses. Both realize this apprehension in "a self-questioning that invests both disciplines in their self-evaluation and, in particular, in their peculiar ambivalence about their commanding discourses" (280). Struever cites Aristotle in the *Ethics*, which compares the two arts on the basis of "things that occur as a result of our efforts, 'though not always the same way'" (280). Struever's comparisons with early modern medicine also resonate pan-historically. For instance, she describes both clinical and oratorical discourses as combinations of "upsetting power claims" and "a tendency to weak or confusing arguments" (280). She also links oratorical uses of the passions to their definitions in antique medicine. Before emotion becomes psychologized as a cognitive process, it is frequently treated as a disease to be excised from specific parts of the body where feelings reside. In this scheme, its moderate forms result from the balance of the four humors. These beliefs have held sway from the earliest reading of entrails by seers to the modern hysteric's heart palpitations and vocalized joy (285–86).

Struever's account might be expanded. For instance, it does not take up the paradigmatic secrecy associated with both arts, nor the tense deliberation and resulting revelation that turn exchanges between an authority and an auditor into scripted scenes. The outcomes of those scenes also depend on trust on both sides of that pair. Thus, her essay only suggests the congruence of the two arts' persuasive tropes, despite its notice of their shared self-doubts. But like the credibility of the orator's performed character, medical standing involves reputation and credentials as well as an appearance of empathy, charismatic bedside and assembly-side manners that are legible to their audiences. The triumphs accomplished by chefs, physical trainers, fashion designers, poets, actors, playwrights, and philosophers equally take place in rhetorical/aesthetic spaces of suspended disbelief. They all depend on whether a client, patient, audience, or reader will act in some way on the diagnoses, inferences, and plans these social managers prescribe.

Sophisticated Rhetoric

These connections among what Struever calls "low sciences," rhetoric's history, and highly regarded literary and philosophical discourses were already noted among the Sophists, who are usually treated as direct forebears of theoretical rhetoric and its combats with philosophy. Yet both G. B. Kerford's and de Romilly's important studies place sophistic precedents to Athenian rhetoric among other circulating discourses that do not rely on heroic speakers. For instance, Kerford's description of the work of Antiphon of Rhamnus makes this point in its survey of genres, topics, and precepts relevant to evidence and argument:

> [Antiphon is] credited with manuals of rhetoric, perhaps in three books, with an Invective against Alcibiades, with composing tragedies, and an intriguing *Art of Avoiding Distress* (*Techne Alupias*). Paralleling the treatment given by physicians to those who are ill, he was said to have set up a kind of citizens' advice bureau or modern-style Samaritan service in a room near the market place at Corinth, claiming to be able to treat those who were in distress by asking questions and finding out the causes and so by his words encouraging those in trouble. We do not know what words were used. But . . . anxiety is recognised as a pathological state. . . . Euripides in a fragment . . . makes a character say that he has learnt from a wise man to contemplate disasters such as unseasonable deaths in advance so that they will not come unexpectedly when they do come. . . . [Antiphon's interest in psychological problems also appears] in his work on the interpretation of dreams. He says they are not direct perceptual origins as "held by the atomists, or a direct and natural predictive value" but "followed the path later labeled that of *divinatio artificiosa*." . . . On this view dreams were signs which required the opposite of what they appeared to say. (51)

Kerford thus makes explicit the relativity of truth to discourse, to emotional states, and to its persuasive literary versions of the self that are realized in life-as-a-narrative self-fashioning. That latter connection is realized, for instance, in sophistic beginnings of language theory, which acknowledge that philosophical considerations of human experience are prefigured in linguistic creations of the subject in grammatical forms such as pronouns and verbs of location like "here," "now," "then," and other markers of place in self-narration.[21] But Kerford also notes the medicine–rhetoric connection. His work points out that a "full account of the sophistic movement in the fifth century B.C. would require a consideration of . . . the collection of medical writings attributed to Hippocrates" (57). It also cites as examples the para-medical treatises *On the Art* and *On Breath*, by still unknown authors, which are less examples of antique science than "epideixeis or exhibitions of sophistical argumentation" (57). Thus, in its defense of the art of medicine against those who vilify it, *On the Art* appeals "to sophistic doctrines about the relation between names and classes of things" (58). Of course, the sophisticated taxonomies that create boundaries around specific technologies—medicine, astronomy, and a host of practical crafts—not only indicate the importance of linguistic forms in the creation of identity. They as well trouble philosophy's equally strict but Idealized definitions by implying the possibility of unstable referents, the difference between a word's common and technical uses. And that problem for the purity of philosophical reasoning returns it to confronting the unintended implication of hanging Socrates' arguments on the nominalism of *elenchus*: that "Reality" can be (only) a concept in language.

De Romilly attaches that conflict between language and abstract Truth to Protagoras and his measurement of "all things" against man, not the gods. She calls this standard "total revisionism" that ruled out "all theories of transcendence or certainty" (*Great Sophists* 85). As I have said, Protagoras's view moots discussions of autonomous reality that stabilize it by reference to its plausible fit to language. Citing Socrates as the voice of philosophy's complaint in *Cratylus* (386A), de Romilly summarizes: "Everything now depends upon man's feelings and opinions, feelings and opinions that can be neither challenged nor confirmed and vary from one person to another and according to circumstances." These feelings are "the only yardsticks: things are to me such as they seem to me" (98). That precept obviously renders rhetorical persuasion a matter of emotional trust, as precisely a "delight in likenesses" (*Politics* 1340a15–28). De Romilly also notes Plato's perception of this difficulty in his citation of Protagoras in the *Theaetetus*, asserting that Sophists and doctors treat their audiences in precisely identical manners in regard to Truth (166b, qtd. in de Romilly 100).

It is plausible to connect this conflicted measure of truth to the ways that poststructuralists describe language, and to liberatory pedagogies, to establish theoretical analogues that link rhetorical history to current composition studies.[22] But the historical pull of Ludwig Wittgenstein's "rope of many strands and family images" (qtd. in Berchman 2) does not necessarily tie either poststructuralist critiques of reference or socialist collectives to ancient conditions for trust in linguistic meanings. That is, both of these twentieth-century philosophical contributions stay well within post-Cartesian rationalism. Sophism's language philosophy did not. It instead emerges from extra-rational practices whose means of persuasion represent a still largely unsorted collection of belief systems.

This is to say that despite usually accepted histories of one rhetoric, meta-discourses theorize persuasion and engage linguistic performances in light of precedent religious, mythic, and prophetic systems. The effects of these discourses remain invisible in rhetoric studies, not only because its assumptions about supposedly unified Athenian theory and practice use them only as allusions and examples. In addition, these ways of thinking cannot help defend oratorical rhetoric as a philosophical or interpretative theory acceptable in studies that tacitly rely on binary pairs: body/soul, brain/emotion, logic/intuition. Nonetheless, the force of extra-rational discourses continues. Fifth-century and later obsessions with credibility, with the power of education to overcome a "natural" weakness in character, and especially with the status of probability in a corporate field of consensus all emerge from pre-sophistic practices now regularly divorced from these ancient themes.

Of course, I make these points in full awareness of their uncertain history. We have almost no surviving evidence of sophistic rhetoric and therefore know it primarily through fourth-century reports. Yet my points are supported by connections between that future and the sophistic movement's past, as Yunis's "The Constraints of Democracy and the Rise of the Art of Rhetoric" points out:

> Rhetoric turns the natural talent for or poetic uses of linguistic manipulation into a systematic consciously deployed discipline aiming specifically at persuasion, so that, for example, a complex message . . . an unendurable message . . . or one that nonbelievers might find improbable . . . has a good chance of being accepted precisely when it matters that it be accepted. Rhetoric . . . by systematic, rational means . . . therefore puts in our power that eloquence which the gods supply according to their whim. (226)

Those rational practices of course include sixth-century quasi-scientific writing, however fragmentary: for instance, a geography attributed to Hesiod, the Nautical Astronomy attributed to Tales, and evidence of a *Kataploi* (a versified description of harbors). It is notable as well that these texts were composed in hexameter verse. Thus, as Charles Kahn points out, it is plausible to accept Heraclitus's tacit claim that in the sixth century, there was a "body of technical literature, primarily Ionian in origin, which by the end of that century would have been almost entirely in prose" (114). Meager evidence of such writing may result from the technical, easily outdated nature of such practical works. But however common, their evidence of movement from poetry to prose is more complicated than belief in an oral-to-literate shift in memory, as any such formal change is. Like sixth-century prose storytelling, this work follows from the extra-rational yet applied means of persuasion that precedes it.

Divine Rhetoric

The whims of the gods are less available to us than other evidence of sophism's conceptual precedents, although entirely relevant to them. They are, for instance, visibly threaded through the antique sign theory adopted in the description of common topics in Book I of the *Rhetoric*. It categorizes signs in terms of their completeness or infallibility, categories appropriate to protocols for logical analysis. Thus, taking up the favorite physical symptom of lactation, this passage from the *Rhetoric* connects signs to symptoms and other visible processes:

> Now the materials of enthymemes [include] Signs, which we can see must correspond respectively with the propositions that are generally and those that are necessarily true. . . . Of Signs, one kind bears the same relation to the statement it supports as the particular bears to the universal, the other the same as the universal bears to the particular. The infallible kind is a "complete proof" (*tekmerhiou*); the fallible kind has no specific name. By infallible signs I mean those on which syllogisms proper may be based: and this shows us why this kind of Sign is called "complete proof": when people think that what they have said cannot be refuted, they then think that they are bringing forward a "complete proof," meaning that the matter has now been demonstrated and completed (*peperhasmeuou*). . . . Now the one kind of Sign (that which bears to the proposition it supports the relation of particular to universal) may be illustrated thus. Suppose it were said, "The fact that Socrates was wise and just is a sign that the wise are just." Here we certainly have a Sign; but even though the proposition be true, the argument is refutable, since it does not form a syllogism. Suppose, on the other hand, it were said, "The fact that he has a fever is a sign that he is ill," or, "The fact that she is giving milk is a sign that she has lately borne a child." Here we have the infallible kind of Sign, the only kind that constitutes a complete proof, since it is the only kind that, if the particular statement is true, is irrefutable. (I.2.9)

This passage retells the conditions of credibility for a particular kind of ethos. That is, it emphasizes a represented character's logic, reasoning from authority to oppose charges that an always-deceptive oratory relies on pandering proofs (Wisse 19). But as I have stressed, this is not the *Rhetoric*'s last word about bonding with audiences by deploying what everyone knows, here about signs of illness and motherhood. Book III connects locally held beliefs to issues of character by explaining signs as the familiar experiences of bonded groups. *Copia*, prescribed here as stylized examples that resonate broadly, transfers the credibility of a speaker from processing verifiable knowledge to creating appropriate, commonly understood linguistic signs of accepted insights. Thus, this last treatment of ethos in overlooked *Rhetoric* III might be said to be its most "rhetorical." That is, its basis in sign theory suspends the defensive logic of Book I, instead treating character as a stylized manifestation of the cultural temperament around it. As it says in identifying a sense of what is appropriate as the trustworthy propriety of an interlocutor, "6. Proof from signs is expressive of character, because there is an appropriate style for each genus and moral state" (III.7.6).

This separate acknowledgment of style as credibility demonstrates Aristotle's moderate realism. That is, he accepts that the minds of men share perceptual habits that produce conventional meanings and tacit agreements about their implications.[23] These agreements depend on shared associations: "they feel the same about such things." But the signs of this comforting emotional space of "getting it" also include a notably stylized male code. As Maud Gleason says in "The Semiotics of Gender: Physiognomy and Self-Fashioning in the Second Century B.C.," "Men enacted their manhood through body language—the firm walk and glance, controlled body, athletic dancing" (qtd. in Stehle 12). She connects this culturally fashioned identity to the overriding importance of reputation, which the *Rhetoric* acknowledges earlier in its contrary wish that precedent reputation remain separate from a text's trustworthiness. But Gleason also points out that the rustic language that emanates from the rustic "type" is delivered in a reinforcing system of performed gender (qtd. in Stehle 12). As Eva Stehle also says about the persuasive sign as a legible demeanor, "Self-presentation must be in and through the discourse that is meant to influence the audience's conception of life, state, or world" (19). In light of Aristotle's statement that spoken words are signs of things and written words are signs of spoken words, we additionally note that language is its own sort of proof.[24] It blurs moral types that accomplish trust in one speaker's ability to appropriate "everyone" directly.

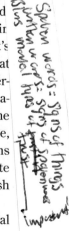

This linguistic view of credible character suggests that the actual appeal of the enthymeme derives from shared values—from *pathé*, as Jeffrey Walker argues in "*Pathos* and *Katharsis* in 'Aristotelian' Rhetoric: Some Implications."

That is, the missing term that has traditionally defined the enthymeme does not operate as a truncated syllogism, a failure of deductive rigor. And even if this proof were logical shorthand, its uses despite that lacuna imply that all know what can be omitted without harming an argument. Thus, both incomplete signs and enthymemes may be effective if mutual experiences supply their punch lines.[25] Of course, the reverse is also true: Neither clichéd symptoms nor quasi-logical inferences have force apart from what everyone in a particular rhetor's (or poet's or dramatist's) audience already knows. That knowledge may derive from propinquity, class status, or, ironically, from exclusion from particular forms of access. But without it, signs *and* enthymemes are opaque and thus can entirely destroy always unstable illusions of rhetorical control.

As cited, some signs are deemed "complete," or infallible. Giovanni Manetti stresses in *Theories of the Sign in Classical Antiquity* that physical signs like mother's milk in the *Rhetoric* and elsewhere warranted sure inferences about motherhood in any time. With others, Manetti also points out that before Aristotle, the semiotic vocabulary had been entirely in the realm of the sacred. He says it continued there until its adaptation to "strictly secular use" (xv). Thus, the "semiotic paradigm" visible in the last treatment of ethos in the *Rhetoric* emanates from a sophistic and tacitly Aristotelian measure of all things. Manetti also argues that its longest roots—and equally those of framed persuasion across many cultures—grow from "divination and magical medicine" (xv). Lollianus implies that source in his letter requesting back pay in the name of "the Divine Muses." That reminder contains shared contact with nonmaterial forces beyond them. Thus, while stylistic devices—metaphor, metonymy, symbol, allusion, or onomatopoeia—do not reenact the set theory of the syllogism, they establish sets: groups who share enduring textualities beyond citation.

There are, of course, many powerful, persistently renewed attempts to efface "the irrational and the unconfirmable" (Manetti xv) from Western history. Logic, dialectic, monotheism, rationalism, various forms of science, and other sobering doses of designated realities trace that story of supposed progress toward control, another Hegelian narrative. But divination and its corollaries are ubiquitous in antique Mediterranean and many other early cultures and, while no longer official in modern cultures, are retained still. A curative/predictive/directive collection of extra-rational discourses testifies to human curiosity and to a hope that other forces know the vexing mysteries of a present circumstance. Across Mediterranean history and later, Manetti traces such extra-rational practices well after the occult's pre-alphabetic modes, certainly in post-Athenian rhetoric and philosophy that build on the diverse Greek precedents I have outlined here, which are insightful but not purged of the irrational.

To take one example, divination notably characterizes Stoic theory of the truth-conditions of conditional (if/then) propositions. The antecedents and consequents of these propositions are joined much as they are in signs that Cicero calls "verisimiles," the *Ad Herennium*'s "Presumptive Proof," both forms of evidence that things usually happen in a certain way. In Stoic logic, such preconceived connections, like enthymemes sensible only to those already within their cultural commonplaces, are proposals, not definite predictions, as in fact were the predictions and readings of the earliest diviners. They—like rhetores—were often held responsible for their forecasts and thus emphasized the provisional nature of this proof.[26] Divination and its sister arts also come up in Plutarch's early second-century Delphic dialogue, which blends discussion of divination by signs with logic (Manetti xv). Yet Cicero's discussions of signs and the two types that appear in Aristotle, in which he pairs certain proof of physical signs with verisimiles (*De partitione oratoria* 34), turn out to be misleading. In *On Divination* he calls all divination, and thus this proof, absurd superstition. He tells Quintus, his brother and interlocutor, that he is publicly quiet because divination is a foundation of the state's religion. But privately, he can say how ridiculous it is. He dismisses the philosophical schools that argue for it, as most did then, especially the Stoic belief that signs confirm the divine, not the reverse convention that the gods send signs (xii.28–xvii.41; li.116–lv.125). Despite his certainty, however, the meanings and relationships that divination seeks are corollaries to biblical "things unseen" (Hebrews 11:1), which motivate belief and faithful action. Divination accesses not only hope but also the play of conjecture, imagination, and other inferential processes that require trust, even of the most sober text.

Of course, the most well-worn sober model of communication in ancient attention to things unknown is the written text. It is obviously so in the many types of divination that operate through marks and objects: divination by flour (in which a note is balled up and placed in flour to emerge as a version of our modern enigmatic fortune cookie), by skywriting observed and read by Babylonian diviners, by the marks on the folds of the liver, by the direction of the flying birds that Nestor reads to guide the *Iliad*'s ships (I.69–72), by reading configurations of tossed sticks and clouds, and by many other accidents and projections of chance. Such techniques persuasively extend ordinary reasoning about recurring symptoms and appetites: fevers, flushes of many sorts, and a host of inexplicable but eventually telling markers that permit still iffy weather forecasts, crop predictions, and guesses about the sex of a child. All of these physical manifestations are easily made prophetic about hidden parts of the body like the liver and lungs. In this sense, reading—interpretation, divination, prophecy, and oracular prediction—precedes writing.[27]

But writing does follow. Its phenomenology imitates the exchange of Plato's "mantic individual" who receives a vision and the prophet who is its interpreter (Manetti 16). Like writing, the work of what Plato calls "Natural" divination and its "intuitive" or "inspired" pronouncements results from responses to questions. Perhaps the most famous is the Delphic prophecy in answer to Croesus's question about whether to attack Persia in 550 BCE, roughly, "If you cross a river, a great empire will fall." This familiar if/then logic omitted to tell Croesus that it was his empire that would be lost, an example of a linguistic politics of exclusion that writing makes inevitable. In this instance, the oracle may have been more mantic than needed, too under the influence of the ritual psychoactive smoke that accompanied these inspired gnomic texts. But Plato refers to these Delphic pronouncements as "true and inspired divination," which does require being out of one's rational mind, which the smoke assured. Its counterpart form is the artificial "*mantike technike*" that results from engaging inductive *or* deductive processes like those claimed by Romantic poets recollecting experience. Plato distinguishes the two in *Timaeus*: "No one achieves true and inspired divination when in their rational mind, but only when the power of their intelligence is fettered in sleep or when it is overcome by disease or by reason of some divine inspiration" (71e–72a). He restates Socrates' claim, typical of writers, that anything to do with divination is garbage except his own divine sign that sets him aside to apply critical reason—insight—to its fullest. In the *Ion*, that vocation is detailed as a three-part transmission from a divine spark, not from knowledge or reason. It is given to a poet by God, then transmitted in the special text of the early poet's writing to a rhapsode, who finally enacts its light for an audience (534b7–d1, 535e7–b4).[28]

Obviously, both the nature of occult persuasion and the offices of the priest/prophet/seer point to the universal ability to suspend disbelief and its result: participatory attention that endorses epic, lyric narratives of history, projected creation myths, philosophical Reality, and, of course, oratory. But that oratorical space is not the center of oracular forms disseminated across other genres—epistolary, philosophical, or educational writing. Like the textuality it joins, oratory projects fragments of experience in narrative forms, where they become the narratives-as-lives that smooth over differences, precisely differences from experience.

That accomplishment is, of course, the access to ancient definitions of acts of writing and written texts as opposed to their decipherment as "readings." Like divination and organized religions, inscription simultaneously reveals secrets and keeps them, inscribes novelty and repeats it.[29] Thus writing, especially in cultures whose elites and craft-servants read consequential texts, is also entirely revealing and authoritative. It is a disembodied but reliable voice, yet a graphically materialized sign of potential misinterpretations. Whether pictographic cuneiform or alphabetic script, it is always literally a system of signs intended to designate what they depict, to bring it *to mind*, not necessarily as a translation of what would be or has been spoken. For example, amplification could inflate a pictographic sign, such as when an enlarged sketch of an ox becomes a once-removed sign for a cow. Thus, while the alphabet has been celebrated for its recording direct speech, the larger progress of inscription—from pictorial cuneiform to increasingly abstract signs that represent things to later connections of signs to words—attenuates the directness and reliability of texts. By accumulating allusions attached to signs of words rather than things, alphabetic writing thereby stacks accepted, conventional "meanings" of signs, tacitly re-forming them as stories of intentions. This ability to repeat associations among fixed words, like a sign's ability to combine a picture of the ox and signification of it and the cow, rehearses the hold of writing on persuasion insofar as everyone's ox and cow join their representation. Yet that process of assimilation also effaces writing's authority, no matter how direct its records of spoken words appear to be.[30]

These examples demonstrate at the least that like powerful human characters, signs that constitute magic, prophecy, divination, dream interpretation, mystery cults, and oracular proof continue to prevail well beyond the *Rhetoric*. Their power clearly appears now in explanations of events as "meant to be." In all of these practices, as in Neoplatonic Christianity, Truth is an essence visible in instances yet outside any particular material circumstance. But prophetic practices also recall how persuasion depends on trusted relationships. That is, signs can only signify shared experiences and their stylization. Their enduring uses in divinatory and religious persuasion represent a strand of rhetoric's history only briefly knotted as the status of oratory is made an artifact of the alphabet and democracy.

But as de Romilly suggests in *Magic and Rhetoric in Ancient Greece*, poetry more readily than democracy represents this congruity among magic, religion, and mesmerizing words and styles. To contradict Isocrates in *Against the Sophists*, the poet's persuasive power enforces the words uttered by orators. De Romilly notes that "poetry was more and more treated as a kind of proto-rhetoric" (7).[31] Of course, this prototypical poetry is also informed by curative medical and prophetic spaces of persuasion, all included in the orator's many presumed characteristics. But those offices cannot be fully explained as collecting in so simple an additive equation. Refreshing as it is,

Christopher Johnstone's assessment that "classical rhetoric may have been an invention of the fourth century, but it was invented using tools and materials that had been crafted during the preceding two hundred and fifty years" (16) again turns rhetoric studies inward, to retell a story of one discourse replacing another in a sequential march toward rationalism and democracy. It does not take up the more obvious coincidence of persuasive genres and extant texts that suggest how emotional interactions have been approved and sustained across many other pointedly rule-governed situations. Discrete forms of trust characterize the many genres that Stanley E. Porter's *Handbook of Classical Rhetoric in the Hellenistic Period, 330 B.C.–A.D. 400* identifies as "Rhetoric in Practice." These forms remind us that favored genres are constituted by and constitute specific interactions realized in discursive practices. The epistle, poetry, biography, oratory and declamation, homily and panegyric sermon, romance, drama, and others all obviously teach linguistic behaviors by gathering and circulating their conventional forms. Those conventions in turn mirror and determine their participants' accepted dispositions, and transgressive versions of them. They readily gather unframed temperaments into textual types. And, as many note about philosophical dialogues, more or less intimate modes of statement attach to still other genres—the love letter and the encomium, for instance—to characterize discursive purposes and their equally conventional modes of performance.

Thus, to consider rhetorical instruction as lessons in the emotional ties that bind our convictions, historians might also consider how emerging genres create anxieties. Uncertainty about specific functions of discourse surround not only the processes of definition I have singled out for their problematic relation to certainty. That concern is also obvious in any case where being wrong—not just "out of touch with reality"—is imaginable. The spaces I hope to have opened to consider these topics thus contain that accumulation of audiences and the auras around them, common places where trust, inclusion, exclusion, and the emotional persuasiveness attached to them take many forms.

2 Trusting Texts

> Everything is now becoming public property from which scholars hitherto
> had been able to secure the admiration of the common people.
>
> —*Collected Works of Erasmus*

Certainly Renaissance/early modern histories of rhetoric recognize discrete forms of metadiscourse. Examples include attention to a revived poetics, rediscovered oratorical pedagogies, and a long epistolary tradition held over from church and other administrative chanceries, which is enlarged and complicated by the retrieval of Cicero's familiar letters. Histories of these separate generic lessons address discourses across the European Renaissance, the seventeenth-century English Revolution and Restoration, and the earlier half of the "long eighteenth century" (1660–1745). That period, defined in English literary studies as the "early eighteenth century" or as an "Augustan Age" of imitations of classical texts, blends these eras into the subsequent multiplication of vernacular political, philosophical, and literary texts that is treated as a later "Eighteenth Century." Thus, the early modern period, the term used here, ends after the deaths of Alexander Pope (1744) and Jonathan Swift (1745) and the concurrent birth of social activist Hannah More (1745–1833), whose books about the rhetoric of conversation and female schooling indicate discursive sea changes that will characterize modernism.[1]

The wide range of early modernism's cultural changes across Europe is in large measure overseen by Michel de Montaigne's skepticism. Traced through numerous settings, it might be said to characterize reorganization of the political and property rights of one catholic Christianity through reformation and rebellions, the consequent redistribution of wealth among merchant explorers and those who benefit from their introduction to Europe of new foods and commodities, the expansion of Ottoman Turks into southeastern

Europe, and, among still other vectors of change, both Christian and Muslim justifications for articulations of racism and a gradual gendering of males and females into new social typologies that continue to constitute discoursed domestic identities for men and women. The anxieties attending all of these economically, philosophically, and religiously driven shifts, schisms, and signs of mobility characterize the era for good and ill. Ambivalent worries are visible in new political systems and political events, coloring absolutism, emerging nationalism, and varieties of their enforcement in constitutionalism, widespread uses of gunpowder, workers' and peasants' revolts, and, for instance, the execution of 1,000 witches in England and around 5,400 in the Swiss Confederation. Obviously, any sort of history of the time must be built from revisions of discrete historical narratives.

Nonetheless, almost any source of information about early modernism addresses the new Western, secularized trust in God, which shifts bureaucracies from church to state institutions and their offices, and consequently rearticulates individual character—commonalities so general as to flatten most of their explanations into elementary generalizations. To avoid that result here insofar as possible, we might think of early modern discourses as differently fitting the eras within their scope. The metadiscourses that guide the cultural practices I have noted and others persistently layer one set of social tropes onto another across an indeterminate period in which an unstable flow of information and interpretation carves more than one trail. Thus, this chapter presents necessarily uneven cases about this movement, all of which note increased reliance on print and its results, a phenomenon rhetoric studies rarely addresses except as ancillary to a literate/oral divide.

In "Thumbing Our Nose at the Public Sphere: Satire, the Market, and the Invention of Literature," Christian Thorne provides a context for these considerations as they apply to "ourselves and our modernity," a pointed summary that I further abbreviate here:

> My first story: Europe was once full of imbeciles; then came the printing press, and there were imbeciles no more; for with print came mass literacy, and with literacy came learning . . . [and] new democratic self-fulfillment in some guise or another. . . .
> This story is out of favor, although . . . readers who have long since parted with any belief in the essential value of great literature are likely to harbor some residual attachment to the value of the printed word . . . [that] indulges in a crudely progressive technological determinism. . . . [P]rint is not necessarily or inherently liberating. . . . [It] may have played something like a democratizing role, but it has done so only insofar as it was enmeshed in other phenomena. . . . [The] limits of its

democratizing project have been the limits of . . . other institutions. . . . The technology does not exist apart from the politics that assigns it its meanings or functions; print is not prior to culture. (531–32)

Thorne's narrative suggests that were the word "oratory" substituted for his "literature" and "alphabet" for "print," we might recognize it in histories of rhetoric that do not bring either pair—literature and print, or oratory and the alphabet—to this period's more prominent manuscript/print juncture. Recent rhetoric studies has not translated all of its "residual attachment" to the privileges of speech into investigations of written discourse except as "the texts of X author," an object of study that creates the field's authority to judge a written record as an event's reality rather than its performance or its transmission. Recent studies of media also regularly ignore modern alphabetic literacy, which is absorbed into the supposed cognitive cultural impact of media and thus rarely noted as a material intervention in discourse production (see chapter 3).

Perhaps ironically, the absence of these discussions in part results from versions of "technological determinism" that Thorne omits. For instance, historians may celebrate the invention of print at the expense of equally interesting developments of legible scripts. As one of many examples of this scribal energy, a 1567 printed French writing tutorial names seventeen discrete varieties of handwriting and says that there are "others you can invent at will and name as you please" (Craig-McFeely 10). Julia Craig-McFeely thus notes that "during the period 1550–1650, although printing was becoming more widely used, hand-written books and documents were still the norm, and so handwriting had a far more fundamental position in terms of both social status and the power structures surrounding local and national government than it did by 1750" (10).

Obviously, ignoring manuscript technologies like handwriting and the forms of manuscript books sets aside the impact on discourse production of cultural circumstances, here those that had made print their foregone conclusion well before Gutenberg's press opened. Thorne also notes that both versions of his narrative cast alphabetic literacy as equivalent to print and that both the alphabet and print have iffy links to democracy. He is thus more open to the claim that rhetorics are multiply formed and enacted. Neither Augustine's uses of oratorical systems to characterize Christian sermons nor the historically rich era of post-Roman Christian oligarchy is lost, in his view, to an alphabet or a democratizing oratory. Instead, powerful cultural formations realign various metadiscourses.

Nonetheless, Story One, long accepted as common sense rather than as a spin on social history, only recently gives way to the complex cultural fortunes of trusted discursive sources and credible texts. While technological determinism clearly has not implied that just after the alphabet is invented, speech-making voters suddenly appear among tribal illiterates, the exclusionary focus on the alphabet's power to change cognitive processes, and thus political institutions, has turned attention from parallel, non-oratorical metadiscourses. As I have noted, rhetoric's historians regularly separate its seemingly dominant oratory from a lesser epistolary rhetoric, which is nonetheless powerful pre- and postclassical guidance for producing discourse, and both rhetoric's historians and literary scholars have disallowed the alphabet's possible equalizing of various classed emotions. For instance, the lower-class anger now recognized to have motivated not only an otherwise seemingly mindless medieval peasant revolt against Richard II is also admitted as having resulted in at least six complaining petitions at the time. That is, unexpected writing outside privileged educated classes has been systematically misread, as though original accusations against peasants correctly named them as representatives of the Antichrist come to earth. Their anger is not acknowledged to have been a plausible peasant emotion, at least partially because it is enacted officially only as a ruler's prerogative. Lower-class writers of these petitions are thus described as expressing "animal rage," not an appropriate politicized resentment. And their six separate texts have only recently been cast as other than variants of one writer's work or transcriptions of prior speeches. Medieval history, like rhetorical history derived from Story One, prefers to explicate texts as examples of the literary paideia distributed among the entitled. Neither has a historical category that recognizes that peasants wrote at all.[2]

This is not to suggest that histories ignore new evidence about early modern rhetorics nor other arguments that complicate this data. Lawrence Green's "Aristotle's *Rhetoric* and Renaissance Views of the Emotions" takes Renaissance recoveries of Greek and Latin texts as a theme, specifically to identify not only the textual tradition of the *Rhetoric* but its "principal contexts" at this later time. He identifies Renaissance Greek editions of the *Rhetoric*, Greek editions with Latin translations, Latin editions, and vernacular translations. These textual variations constitute three educational projects: The *Rhetoric* is used as a *Latin* scholastic treatise allied with dialectics to prescribe ethics. It is also *Greek* intellectual work whose retrieval and applications contribute to a Renaissance "literary present." And it is *cited* as a source text that informs emerging interest in Cicero's and Quintilian's rhetorical texts. These sorted textual types and separate ethical, intellectual, and especially literary contexts for interest in the *Rhetoric* also identify discrete versions of Renaissance trust in ancient languages and discursive purposes.

Green's is one of many ways of framing an analysis of the intervention of classical texts in early modern cultural regroupings of religious, political, and social institutions. That reorganization is commonly described as a contest between scholasticism and humanism, two sequential pedagogies whose conflicts are regularly exaggerated. That is, after the addition of legal and ethical instruction and rhetorical lessons by humanists, scholasticism's introductory logic and semantic theories do slowly fall from favor in curricular change, which combines them to serve composition needing both the equipment of logic and the elegant prose of new trans-European communication.[3] However, the differing methods of scholasticism and humanism do not attach to the uniformly testy personalities of their prominent supporters. Competitive emotional dispositions create personalized critiques on both sides. In addition, nationalism complicates actual curricular differences, as itself an artifact of successful and of failed religious imperialism.

Pan-European Latin scholastic traditions hereby meet humanist educational counterparts over recovered classical texts like Aristotle's *Rhetoric* and *Poetics*. The result is a new-identity identity politics that marks humanist critiques of scholasticism across national borders. That is, humanists are not anti-religious nor opposed to hermetic schooling so much as they are unhappy with multiple interpretations of texts, which scholasticism encourages through the pedagogical exercises of dialectics. But that use of dialectical exchange tacitly contradicts scholasticism's multiperceptual hermeneutic promises to exclude human elements from the logical-authoritarian imaginary. Diverse humanist energies merge, to include human, or rhetorically situated, elements. They join the reform rebellions of Martin Luther and Henry VIII with international excitement about retrieved classical texts and the promotion of vernacular Bibles and thus of widespread reading, for instance, by Henry VIII. In this mix, characterization rather than rational debate becomes the norm. As John Colet, the early sixteenth-century Catholic humanist who founded St. Paul's School, says of scholasticism, it is a "sign of a poor and barren intellect to be quibbling about the words and opinions of others, carping first at one thing and then at another, and analyzing everything so minutely" (qtd. in Perreiah 4). In this and other criticisms, an *ad pedagogum* tone is the issue, not the relative value of scholastic traditions or novel humanist curricula that nonetheless is used as grounds for vilifying competitors for pride of place.

The dissemination of these methods relies on migrations of individual humanists who remain in conversations like those among Desiderius Erasmus, Peter Ramus, and Rudolph Agricola. Most prominent in English rhetoric are portable scholars Erasmus (1466–1536) and Juan Louis Vives (1492–1540), both of whom import different versions of classical rhetoric to England in the sixteenth century: Erasmus authors *De Copia* (1512), which the German

Philip Melanchthon refers to in his own sixty-page rhetorical handbook, *Institutiones Rhetorices* (1523), which is published the same year as Vives's *Education of a Christian Woman*. Erasmus taught Greek at Cambridge, if briefly, and Spanish; Vives was a son of a forcibly converted Jewish family, invited by Henry VIII to tutor his Catholic daughter, Mary. Royalty is here, as in the education of Elizabeth by her tutor Roger Ascham, well equipped to address the issues raised by increased secularization by study of the classics and by a cosmopolitanism that in Elizabeth's case will preserve new European nationalist interests from disaster.

In Italy and France, revived classicism was well established earlier as a literary rather than grammatical tradition. As Dante's pleas for vernacular writing suggest, a different Italian humanism after 1550 is detached from the grammatical tradition and focuses on Aristotle's rediscovered *Poetics*. In France, reformers known as "La Pléiade" (comprising Thomas Sebillet [1512–89], Jacques Peletier [1517–82], and poet Pierre de Ronsard [1524–85]) apply classical learning to theories and practices in vernacular poetry. Sebillet wrote *The French Art of Poetics* (*L'Art poétique Français* [1548]); Peletier translated Horace in 1545 and published *French Poetic Art* (*Art poétique française* [1555]). Ronsard's *Sonnets for Helene* (*Sonnets pour Hélène* [1578]) enacts the vernacular momentum of all three theorists of a new poetics in which invention, disposition, and elocution explain literary plot, order, and style.

But the slight difference in national emphases on the grammatical part of the trivium may mirror an already culturally constitutive ambivalence toward rhetoric. Changed early modern political and social conditions around new canons that are only partially derived from one classical tradition still cohere around shared elite education. But competing religious dicta enormously complicate these conditions in equally new international and national politics, especially insofar as its Machiavellian base encourages turning words on themselves and on those who use them. As those already transmitted lessons in strategy are newly perceived in revivals of classicism and rediscoveries of classical texts from Aristotle and Horace, they also move with vernacular language to less credible and then more authoritative print documents,[4] which are more regularly commodified throughout these processes. If early modern trust is an "event," its drama results from discursive technologies, these textual revivals, and contiguous moments of competition between the registers represented by Latin and the vernacular.

Wayne A. Rebhorn's helpful anthology of excerpts from traditional Renaissance rhetoric extends these conditions to characterize its collected pieces—from the Italian Francesco Petrarch's "Letter to Tommaso da Messina" (circa 1240) to Jean-François Le Grande's *Discourse on French Rhetoric* (1658)—as "deeply conflicted." Rebhorn says these texts demonstrate how uses of the same technical vocabularies, citations of the same anecdotes, and appeals to the same authorities nonetheless result in one contention over the "nature, goals, and value of rhetoric" (3). Of course, assuming that goals and values should be consistent in all rhetorical cases implicitly honors the tradition of repeated analyses of an ancient oratorical canon to find its essence. But Rebhorn also acknowledges that an extra-oratorical context for this contention includes threats of rebellion and insurrection; a concern about any writer-speaker's potentially unregulated social mobility outside categories of degree, rank, and access; and another version of that fear in renewed complaints that rhetoric seeks contingent conclusions, not Truth. He says that putting into question religion, monarchy, and the doctrine of degree results from rhetorical exemplars that are "special sites where some sort of important cultural work is going on" (10).

That cultural work is, however, more comprehensible if we not only imagine rhetoric as many varying metadiscourses but also account for material conditions that produce and circulate texts. In early modernity, two crucial concerns call for that different approach. First, new monarchic patriotism demands the creation of a literary vernacular whose authority cannot entirely rest on fixed style or vocabulary. That is, once divorced from the ranked identities that speech projects, the vernacular is never so stable as classical Latin and Neo-Latin are in its different projections of one nation's reliability among others. But inevitable attempts to create that stability raise the stakes in precisely that attempt to regulate the style of English prose and of French poetry guided by the *Poetics*. As a corollary, the social conditions that enable print's invention also allow print to become the up-and-coming technology of consequential statements. Possibilities for social and political affiliations are obviously increased by a newly favored and widely available print vernacular. But that medium's distance from its sources can also disable earlier signs that had prevented character forgery. Shared rank, religion, education, genealogy, and even propinquity may be mooted by a print text. If trust in written statements had been an issue that called for elaborate seals, signs, even household thresholds to accompany titles, bills of sale, and other correspondence to verify their credibility, both the distance created by print and its likely errors could create even greater anxiety. For instance, according to the *Oxford English Dictionary* (1979 edition), our word "syllabus" derives from the *printed* word "syllabus," which was perhaps a compositor's mistaken typesetting of Cicero's intended *syllobos*, in his also unintended as such yet highly influential model for epistolary textbooks, *Letters to Atticus*. In its first setting, the word meant something like a label on a book; in its first recorded English use, however, it represents a title or index that locates where individual matters are *in* a book (D. Hamilton 1). Of course, scribes identically skew meanings. But the enormously increased possibility for distribution beyond even multiple transcriptions has far greater potential to repeat the error in typesetting, one accepted and widely distributed as Cicero's intention.

These multiple disturbances are not single troubles for the unified rhetoric that might have been resurrected after scholasticism diminishes and a humanist curriculum expands its use of classical canons and new textbooks that incorporate them. Despite Thomas Elyot's influential *Booke of the Governour* (1531), a manual for developing a humane humanist pedagogy, we still retain dialectic divisions in René Descartes' *On Method* and in Sir Francis Bacon's *New Method*. Both have lasting beneficial influence on logic, if not from their insistence that "method" divides knowledge to conquer it. But that dialectic proposition is also well established in other pedagogies: the practicable and easily visualized categories of Ramus's enormously if briefly popular prototypical textbook[5] and illustrations of how to teach John Comenius's *Orbis Pictus* (1658), which includes a picture of God.

This is to say that pedagogic energy is everywhere in this period, a sign of concern to stabilize the vernacular both linguistically and as a new discursive sphere serving national politics, local religions, authoritative science, and learned discourse. That energy is consequently expressed in guides to language and style: Sir John Cheke, a Cambridge humanist and tutor to Edward VI, devises both a controversial method of Greek pronunciation and Anglo-Saxon compounds like "endsay" for "conclusion," "forsayer" for "prophet," and less obvious "wespeakinges" and "overstraight." Roger Ascham's *The Englishe Scholemaster* (1570) calls pretentious foreign words dragged into English from Latin "inkhorn terms." But one person's neologism, like "endsay," might be another's remedy for an inkhorn term from earlier English, as was the resurrected "inwit" for "conscience." Translation is also energetically pursued, not only to create vernacular Bibles but international treatises. For instance, Thomas Hoby translates Baldassare Castiglione's *The Book of the Courtier* (1561) to produce an archetypal English conduct book.

However, metadiscourse is more relevant to the fortunes of oratorical rhetoric. George Gascoigne and George Puttenham respectively publish *Certain Notes of Instruction Concerning the Making of Verse in English* (1575) and *The Art of English Poesy* (1589), after Sebillet's *The French Art of Poetics* and Peletier's *French Poetic Art*. With Samuel Daniel's *A Defense of Rime* (1603), these texts praise writing in English and complain of scholasticism's rules and fixed precepts. Thomas Wilson also says rules should be used flexibly, in the service of the writer, not to prove the writer can apply them (16). Puttenham agrees, again to object to scholasticism as "studious persons fashioned and reduced into a method of rules and precepts" (qtd. in Smith 2:5).

Other sources differently regulate vernacular writing. Thomas Nashe's 1589 preface to Robert Greene's *Menaphon*, written "To the Gentlemen of the University," attacks the practice of plagiarizing from classical authors, praising the Englishness of Edmund Spenser and Robert Greene. Nashe's *Anatomie of Absurditie* (also 1589) satirizes contemporary but foreign-born romances. And the lesser-known John Hart (known as the "Chester Herald") writes *An Orthographie Conteyning the Due Order and Reason Howe to Write or Paint the Image of a Mannes Voice* (1569) and *A Methode or Comfortable Begining for All Unlearned, Whereby They may bee Taught to Read English* (1570). These templates for Thomas Sheridan's elocutionary textbooks and pronouncing dictionary of the later eighteenth century make it clear that vernacular delivery will from nationalism on be at issue in any discourse instruction that shares with these authors the purpose of securing one or another form of patronage. That is, mobility is always at issue among these works, which in addressing language describe and create movement toward national identity while assuring attention to their authors' trustworthy guidance.

In toto, this work points to the mistake in oratorical rhetoric's trivialization of figures, an attitude that drastically oversimplifies the semiotics of figural terminology. As Carol Poster's "Being, Time, and Definition: Toward a Semiotics of Figural Rhetoric" puts it:

> Late antiquity and the middle ages, the periods of "decline" so deplored by [historians] Baldwin, Vickers, Kennedy, and others, were those in which figural rhetoric flourished, and both the sheer volume of extant figural treatises and the continuity of figural rhetoric from the Hellenistic period through . . . contemporary semi-popular books . . . demand attention from the historical scholar. (116)

Of course, early modern handbooks that highlight figuration also increase attention to the status and possible malleability of the vernacular, a project that never completes itself but has moments of increased energy from early modernity on. In the late eighteenth century, figuration will be equally important in exchanges that determine the status of oratorical vehemence and the emotional persuasion that its figurative language accomplishes for new consciousness. Thus language and its new print medium become rhetorical domains themselves, neither elementary nor after-the-fact concerns. Of course, official New Latin endures well into established North American university requirements, like the seventeenth-century insistence at Harvard that Latin be spoken within the college grounds. But the symbolic cohesion of humanist scholarship will be lost to situated extra-curricular rhetorics that fit another, emerging world.[6]

Trusting Printing

It is precisely the failure of print to revolutionize the mind, or any sort of rhetoric, that draws attention to this technology's more interesting relation to extant discursive practices just after its invention. Still completely embedded in a phenomenology of holographic texts, not in the orality some claim that it finally cured, print is taken in by metadiscourses whose lessons appear to ignore it until long after it is common, when elocutionary rhetoric attempts to overcome issues it imposes on individualistic models of direct communication (see chapter 3). The space between oral delivery of a composition and its many print deliveries is infrequently discussed, if perhaps alluded to in discussions of how ancient sites of persuasion and instruction in its techniques might be transposed to contemporary teaching. Histories give substantial attention to sorting out the interlaced emphases of scholasticism and humanism, perhaps because both curricula stay in touch equally with oratory and transmitted Ciceronian precepts. But few place these attitudes toward pedagogy in material circumstances—for instance, to point out that the drill and memorization associated with scholasticism had important purposes in a world of scarce texts and no access to Google. In addition, assumptions about rhetorical stances and signs of authenticity were for centuries attached to both new and copied holographic texts. But how do texts that are not thought of as records of oratory, as oral compositions, or as surrogate interpersonal spoken exchanges earn their credibility or suffer from its absence among those who base trust on a shared paideia and an outsider's deference to it?

The most accessible treatment of this historical difference is Walter Ong's regret for a loss of intimacy in a number of books that address dialogue through the oral/literate dichotomy, especially his *Ramus, Method, and the Decay of Dialogue.* Reversing Socrates' priorities, Ong equates close interactions with oral communication, yet eventually restates his point, arguing that print communication attenuates relationships. Harold Love's *Scribal Publication in Seventeenth-Century England* complicates Ong's view. It takes up the period of transition in which print displaces manuscript circulation. At the time, it was not the number of copies of a work that determined its status as a publication but its circulation among "communities of the like-minded" who shared sophisticated means of circulating a text, not only education that determined its meanings (32–33). However, as Love's study and Peter Beals's *In Praise of Scribes: Manuscripts and Their Makers in Seventeenth-Century England* demonstrate, the category of "intimacy" does not apply either to speech or to seemingly hand-to-hand manuscript transmission within those like-minded communities. As long after print is invented as 1631, for a pricey twenty pounds a year, a country family could subscribe to John Pory's weekly manuscript newsletter, which circulated parliamentary speeches and other political news (Beals 10). Lawrence Stone reports that Pory had been sending such inscriptions to the Earls of Shewsbury, Derby, Pembroke, and Hertford in the 1590s (338). Love points out that much more could be said in a handwritten letter than in print and cites Ben Jonson's "Newes from the new world, discover'd in the Moone" (1620): "I would have no newes printed; for when they are printed they leave to be newes" (vii).

Obviously, manuscripts were not primarily single poems like those written for patrons or fellow members of the Sidney circle. In these and their other forms of practical distribution, manuscript texts suggested how print might work and later still competed with its duplicated texts. Beals also describes the implications of common scribal and authorial anonymity in an era that often satirized professional scribes while socially elevating individual exemplars among them.[7] That is, it is unlikely that either scribes or those who read manuscripts automatically treated them as direct communications in a continuing social authorship. Issues of attachment to a text's material sources, or detachment from them, come up among various cohorts of readers, but they are imagined apart from a text's physical form.

Thus, no matter how stable a universal rhetoric is made to seem, it is also unlikely that one system, or even the two prominent oratorical and epistolary rhetorics transmitted from the ancients through the early church and scholasticism, were untouched by the forms of texts and their patterns of circulation. As David Hamilton notes in his study of early modern schooling, "Since the 1950s, the history of moveable-type printing has moved from studies of 'communication' to the analysis of the mutually-constitutive practices of writers, printers, book-sellers, translators and proof-readers who, collectively, are implicated in the organisation [sic] and use of communication technologies" ("From Dialectic" 3).

A primary example of such literary production is the 1623 folio edition of Shakespeare's first collected plays. Charlton Hinman's *The Printing and Proof-Reading of the First Folio of Shakespeare* and W. W. Greg's *The Shakespeare First Folio: Its Bibliographical and Textual History* describe how the plays' composing, regulations controlling publishing, members of acting companies, and compositors play out the gathering into one text of their available multiple parts. In that instance, these classic, extensive, and often contested treatments of the folio include how variant sources affect the published texts and how participants in that process modify it as the play is read and printed. Specifically, the folio's sources include separate "partes" read by actors, the foul papers of the playwright's draft, sometimes actors' own transcripts of the spoken play, or a (sometimes unwritten or missing) prompt copy that gathers these individual scripts. Censors might later alter the text to exclude statements and allusions directed at particular critical audiences at court and elsewhere. The folio may also vary drastically from separate quarto editions in details that appear crucial to its credibility, again upending the conceptual authorship of the 1623 volume. As with the Plato and Aristotle evoked in various times, the 1623 plays are neither precisely those that were produced earlier, nor later.

The process described in this work precedes possible errors and other changes that may be introduced in a publication process. Compositors create errors and even in a supposedly stabilized print version may inconsistently manipulate texts, for instance in deletions to fit the space available on the bottom of a page for transitions from one to another scene of a play. Proofreading occurs as printing proceeds; already-printed sheets are not discarded, so error is retained in some pages but also appears later in new errors. As Paul Werstine summarizes, "single agents" are neither accountable for nor credited with Shakespeare's plays. "These texts were open to penetration and alteration not only by Shakespeare himself and by his fellow actors but also by multiple theatrical and extra-theatrical scriveners, by theatrical annotators, adapters and revisers (who might cut or add), by censors, and by compositors and proofreaders" (86).

Obviously, ambivalent trust in the origin of a print document results at least partially from its differences from manuscripts. For instance, Michael D. Bristol and Arthur F. Marotti further note "the mobility of the [printed] book and its general indifference to the social status of its readers" (8). But conditions that enable a potentially class-blind distribution of printed texts, which had also encouraged print's invention, accelerate other social changes that may be complicated by this unanchored circulation (Bristol and Marotti 8). In this instance, the distribution of political speeches across much larger populations than their manuscript circulation would allow suggests that print can capture immediate purposes of speech, just as later reading of transcribed ancient oratory may appear to do. But differences in material form are not only phenomenological. A primary example is that while it is clear that the preserved speeches of Elizabeth I lose power, they do not lose it to lifeless print. As Leah S. Marcus argues in "From Oral Delivery to Print in the Speeches of Elizabeth I," records of these speeches multiply complicate the "almost mystical integrity" attributed to spoken words. As she describes, Elizabeth first composes thoughtfully, "using the classical arts of composition and of memory." Her speeches may then be delivered as seemingly extemporaneous monologues, as are other rhetorically crafted political exhortations like the St. Crispin's Day speech to gathered troops in Shakespeare's *Henry V.* The speeches also become edited transcripts that do not exactly duplicate their situated oral delivery and are revised still further for print distribution in a form that takes into account currently sensitive issues and the advice of counselors (343–48). As in the composition of Shakespeare's folio, this progress includes interventions of script in printing and the reverse. And that interaction suggests that a widely circulated print version of one of Elizabeth's speeches might be further from her words than other unstable renderings.

Despite his more aggressively cultivated literary/dramatic persona and a continuing construction of competition between him and Shakespeare for authorial status, Ben Jonson's notable expressions of a "bibliographic ego" only redraw a still choppy line between early printed compositions and much later assumptions that individuals author a separate "literature."[8] These problematics of print authorship include Jonson's assertion that a playwright might also be the publisher of his or her printed work, even if not its owner, printer, or official licensing agency. For instance, Jonson indirectly inserts himself among the ancillary figures of the induction and epilogue in *Bartholomew Fair* (1614). This dramatized metacommentary represents the character of "Author" as what the acting company calls "our poet," a common term that in this context might suggest the proprietary rights of others. Characters also include a Scrivener who appears onstage holding a contract allowing "*Spectators* or *Hearers*" in the most expensive seats to have rights of censure proportionate to their payments. A Prompter who adds a separate prologue accompanies them all, to form a crowd of embodied metadiscourses, later supposed to be gathered in one person's authorial control. Prologues like this one might be printed with the text of a play but performed only at an opening performance.[9]

Jonson thus successfully displaces the acting company to "reshape literary market relations" (Lowenstein 103). His displayed authorial situation is not unique in form but in its references to the contemporary economics of drama and to representatives of wealth who rearrange relations among language, culture, early modern textual production, and the circulation of texts. As Lowenstein says, "Jonson's permanent contributions to English literary convention . . . [are] at the social level, the construction of a literary coterie (the nearest model, the Sidney 'circle,' being merely a slight elaboration on the aristocratic household) [and] the development of literary marketing, the publication of the 1616 folio *Workes of Benjamin Jonson*" (101). Even without reference to dramaturgy, the circumstances that produce early modern texts and privileges of judgment around them create a theoretical perspective that was difficult to formulate before print. For Jonson, neither one person's intentions in composition nor readers' expectations for a text that approximates those intentions can control decisions that later writers will take for granted as their prerogatives, however infrequently they may realize them: choosing recognizable sources of a work's plots and heroes; constructing the stylistic figures and commonplace arguments of actors' speeches; overseeing the textual changes created by omissions, additions, and emendations; and accepting or rejecting changes that these editions will inevitably incorporate. This view erases the force of a literate "mentality" associated with stable, "best," or "correct" texts. It sets aside minds changed by their invention of the instruments of that supposed change—an alphabet or a press—in favor of attending to how patterns of manuscript circulation and emerging print genres necessarily rework the ground on which their precedents were trusted.

Trusting Rhetoric

This different view relieves at least some of the anxiety within rhetoric studies that may be expressed as disapproval of an early modern fragmentation of a classical unity. As I have pointed out, when early modern discursive pedagogies are at issue, competition between scholasticism and humanism immediately appears the more important topic. Yet the two traditions share a pre-Renaissance history in which they operate as parallel, usually mixed curricula suitable to particular social and institutional contexts.

The more interesting issue here is thus the accusation against scholasticism by its pupils and by humanists that in addition to extraordinary pickiness, it promoted specialized uses of language. Vives says its practices create what he calls "pointless, irrational, strange and unusual meanings and word order, wondrous suppositions, wondrous amplifications, restrictions, appellations" (Vives qtd. in Perreiah 4). Katherine Elliot van Liere adds to this and other well-known self-promotions of humanists' good sense the example of five student orations from the prominent University of Salamanca. In "Humanism and Scholasticism in Sixteenth-Century Academe," she argues that these student exercises enacted an opposition to humanist celebrations of "arms and letters" as the best education for a versatile courtier in state service. The exercises combine traditional scholastic forms of argumentation with humanist themes, but they emphasize that the legal profession that scholasticism continued to inform rightfully deserves the honor and privileges accorded to ancient soldiers. Nonetheless, humanists had many ways of making their good cases appear even better in staged self-promotions. In *Erasmus, Man of Letters: The Construction of Charisma in Print*, Lisa Jardine illustrates manipulations of his and other reputations. She shows that the long-delayed publication of Agricola's treatise on dialectic was part of a campaign to present Erasmus as a founding father of a northern European humanist genealogy. In addition, a servant may have transcribed Agricola's 1479 *De inventione dialectica* "creatively," to make it appear a source for Erasmus's 1512 *De Copia*.

Intellectual anxieties occasioned by such maneuvering among pedagogues readily add to new doubts about oratorical rhetoric's claims to be more than one of many cooperating central metadiscourses. Scholasticism's contributions to language theory include an explanation of suppositions unknown in Aristotle and elsewhere, and examples of how meanings of words change in the context of sentences (Perreiah 14). And humanism includes literary texts in its metadiscursive interests, reinforcing the international community of letters represented by Thomas More, Erasmus, Vives, and others who taught a European royalty in need of shared allusions and other elements of a monarchic paideia. And as I have stressed, humanist poetics focuses on stylistic devices deployed to create vernacular vocabularies and syntax worthy of nationalist patriotism. Thus, both of these curricula, competitors only in highly qualified ways, re-form templates for composition that absorb some precedents in oratorical rhetoric in the additionally disruptive context of increased reliance on print.

Those who equate print with a vaguely named "writing" often also treat oratory as equivalent to orality. But in this case, as Neil Rhodes demonstrates in *The Power of Eloquence and English Renaissance Literature*, it is easy to mistake functionally separate metadiscourses for extensions of each other. That is, oratory remains the political weapon of choice, while *copia* in written composition is taught as a method of invention, as in Erasmus's textbook. But Rhodes pits the masculine courage promoted in Niccolò Machiavelli's 1520 *The Art of War* and its association between military success and oratorical power against the study of figures of speech. He says that Tudor schooling's punishing exercises enact a male focus in emphases like Henry Peacham's on the "physical power of language" (45). In Rhodes's view, Peacham nonetheless turns that manly characteristic of rhetoric on itself in his name for what he calls a compendium of the "military function of tropes and figures" (Peacham 46–47). Rhodes's point is that "during this period [we witness] a transition from a culture which was in some respects oral to a predominantly written culture, and hence from rhetoric as powerful speaking to rhetoric as fine writing" (45). By implication, fine writing is less physical, warlike, and forceful, a view that also extends Ong's claim that writing is less intimate than speech.

The logical problems with this and any such historical characterization are obvious. For instance, the association of poetry with rhythm, and of both poetry and rhythm with witchcraft, may allude to the orator's place among other antique figures whose mesmerizing language conveys special access to secret knowledge, what William Webb calls "'inchuntment, as it were to perswade them anie thing whether they would or no'" (qtd. in Rhodes 7). But in Rhodes's scheme, these oral models are not sources of vernacular poetry, which instead is an artifact of a transition to written language. In addition, both Rhodes's numerous examples and Peter Mack's detailed analysis in *Renaissance Rhetoric: Theory and Practice* demonstrate that the many vernacular manuals included in rhetorical education in England, as elsewhere, took Latin texts like the *Rhetorica ad Herennium*, Book IV, and Quintilian, Books VIII and IX, into another milieu, the humanist schooling that at least glimpses social mobility (Mack 77).

These manuals are in some measure vernacular tools that help students decipher Latin texts. But they also help their users cope with linguistic issues brought up by increasing numbers of authoritative uses of English, which make visible difficulties that arise when word order in the vernacular changes to replace inflected Latin. Mack embeds handbooks' vernacular lessons in their Latin precedents and continuities, in keeping with his general argument that Elizabethan schooling in Latin and in vernacular rhetoric demarcates an elite. That is, rhetoric wields power in all uses of language, written and oral. But those who master both Latin and vernacular rhetoric also extend the bonding achieved by ancient paideia to a differently schooled group who begin to need Latin a bit less, but vernacular skills more, in an emerging secular, politically contested culture. The "flowers" of figurative writing guided by vernacular handbooks like Peacham's *Garden* juxtapose fine writing and combative oratory yet also point to how the power of Latin language is at issue in this transition to vernacular print authority. Added to this mix, of course, is the rule of England by a childless female, a woman warrior whose duality warrants, if indirectly, the imitative importance given to male dress and costume—to personal style—at the time.

Yet the more common assumption is that one transmitted rhetoric remains stable as a system that unfortunately falls into unevenly rescued fragments, a tacit accusation against history that assumes that detached parts of a system do not already contain and reflect its other domains in a recursive mixture that Aristotle's treatments of character in each of the *Rhetoric*'s three books indicate (see chapter 1). In addition, it is telling that vernacular rhetoric manuals that teach formal systems of invention or arrangement do not accompany surviving vernacular handbooks. They instead highlight linguistic infrastructures of discourse in ways that require attention from rising social ranks. As I have noted, early modernity's poetic metadiscourses, like those of the French Pléiade, are imbricated in oratory. As in Aristotle, rhetoric and poetics obviously share treatments of style, vocabulary, and figuration. Thus, newly overlapped, multiple social spheres result in a spate of new instruction in the vernacular, in handbooks, in the composition of emergent literary genres, and in the occasions for public persuasiveness that are later worked out to support empirical political epistemologies.

Of course, shifts in the relative powers of inherited privilege as against civic entitlements undermine social systems precisely through the offices of crafted language and available lessons in its construction. If we find few vernacular compositions that detail formal rhetorical domains, many formal and informal modes of secular persuasion are presented in the self-help tradition continued in printed, portable vernacular conduct books and writing manuals. The most famous of these guides, Angel Day's *English Secretorie* (1586), follows Erasmus in classifying correspondence in the familiar categories of classical rhetoric. He says letters may be deliberative, demonstrative, judicial, or ceremonial. But Day additionally advertises that he has written the crucial sample letters himself, a practice that earlier translated manuals do not undertake, for instance, in often-used books by William Fullwood (*The Enimie of Idlenesse* [1568]) and Abraham Fleming (*A Panoplie of Epistles* [1576]). Day thus suggests that his letters have immediate currency because they contain current practices.[10]

Yet extending practical vernacular guidelines is not an entirely classed phenomenon. Day's popular manual, dedicated to powerful parliamentary secretary Sir Francis Walsingham, emphasizes preparation for a secretarial position, not how to write private letters. His work appears just as sons of the squirearchy increase university enrollments to prepare for employment as official clerks of state.[11] Richard Rambuss points out that Day's second edition was also expanded to address another sense of "letters," literary composition, which added to it adapted instruction in rhetoric. Rambuss notes that Day portrays a secretary not only as a keeper of a master's secrets but in a secret relation to a master and at times a living human "secret" who stands in for the state, the prince, or the equivalent, much like ancient Egyptian scribes and their counterparts in Mesopotamia. All of these overlapped identities suggest what he calls a "formative relation between writing, secrecy and subjectivity: in the secretary's closet (among other places in early modern culture) an interior private subjectivity begins to be scripted and secured" (321). The secrecy associated with the secret/ary is also picked up in Spenser's poetry. A secretary for bishop John Wilton, a messenger for the Earl of Leicester, and a secretary to the Lord Deputy of Ireland, Spenser published his *Shepheards Calender* anonymously as annotated by someone who is named only "E. K." Sir Philip Sidney's *Astrophel and Stella* also indifferently hides its author. Both of these works follow Gascoigne's *Hundreth Sundrie Flowres*. Its masculinity evidently intact, it relieves E. K. from punishments by portraying him as a supposed anonymous editor. Following this self-conscious self-concealment,

Spenser introduces more than a dozen personae whose acts and comments bring into question connections between writing and the representations inside its texts as it covertly states that texts easily hide what is outside them. These writers hereby set an agenda for ambivalently anonymous literary writing that, with Jonson's, includes its own interpreter, apologist, and confidant in its author. As I have noted, Jonson's plays enact this figure's functions through more than one character. These writers first undertake that project in English poetry, establishing a template for a "secretary" who in Spenser's case has already lived the part. In "The Early Modern Closet Discovered," Alan Stewart adds that the complex relation of secretary to a male or female master involves sexual anxieties created by the secretary's access to the study/closet added by Elizabethan architects, a room where men interact in suggestive ways alluded to in a number of secretarial guides, including Day's. Stewart finds that space to be an inevitable influence on the actual writing the secretary performs (82–84).

Despite the novelty of Day's homemade model letters, the new credibility of traditional handbooks for life and language traces many precedents. As John Gillingham points out in "From *Civilitas* to Civility: Codes and Manners in Medieval and Early Modern England," the ideal early modern gentleman had already been described in Daniel of Beccles's twelfth-century comprehensive courtesy book, *Liber Urbani* (Urban Life or The Book of the City), which itself follows the third-century *Distichs of Cato*. This even earlier source takes up rules of conversation, how to deal with friends and enemies, how to choose a patron or a wife, and other topics that the *Liber Urbani* replicates, which will also appear in Renaissance and later conduct books, as in current codes of etiquette and self-help advice. The genre is thus already well known, credible in itself as an imitation of such precedents and their presumed connections to spoken advice.

But there are severe limits on taking a *plus ça change* approach to aligning histories of genres with social commonplaces. Many metadiscourses that reemerge in shifted economic and political circumstances encourage mobility among classes acting on novel epistemological assumptions. In the first instance, some early modern texts called "histories" traverse the generic spaces of Anglo-Saxon chronicles, Shakespearean and earlier history plays, and reports of explorations. They entertain both profit-oriented sponsors of exploration and audiences seeking sensational narratives. The genre also includes the "true fiction" adventures of picaresque Renaissance heroes, tales that continue through Jonathan Swift, Daniel Defoe, Miguel de Cervantes, Tobias George Smollett, and Henry Fielding. Apparitions, marvelous coincidences, and various *dei ex machinis* endow these true-life fictions with spiritual qualities, useful as new secular verification that God's plan is realized in human happy endings.[12] New ways of knowing are also realized in formats that "prove" the truth of the historical account—for instance, by the composition of lists, maps, eyewitness journalistic accounts, dated diary entries, exemplary case studies, and letters that will also constitute epistolary fiction. All of these visual and other guides complicate the separation of classical rhetoric's artistic proofs from its inartistic data. They add to them and to topics of invention many forms of genre knowledge. And that knowledge is further complicated by the impossibility of decisively marking ironic verisimilitude in a print text whose author and purpose are unknown.[13]

However, we do recognize the irony involved when the emerging modern scientific report appears to connect an actual writer to truth by openly redefining the credibility of "experience," which in early modern English means "experiment," not individual living. Paired with the essayistic writing of natural philosophers, the two scrupulously distinguished discourses accumulate credibility from the reputation of their human sources yet equally from displaying results based on new instruments and standard measurements. But insofar as either genre verifies hypotheses or disproves prior assumptions by deploying the credibility of its writer's new "experience," both also diminish the force of authoritative sources, especially Aristotle, which had found truth in conventional oratorical arrangements of arguments. As Peter Dear argues in *"Totius in verba*: Rhetoric and Authority in the Early Royal Society," new scientists and natural philosophers replace Aristotle's definition of experience as evidence for a case that is always true—for example, Aristotle's famous "bees reproduce parthenogenetically." One might then reason, "I saw the sun come up in the east, so I know what they say about that is true." In this new reassurance, direct observation has its own currency of credibility. Using this "experience" and experimentation as well, evidentiary claims of the Society's research reports are not tested against authority, what "they say" about a phenomenon, but by the specificity of their details and, notably, the presence of other observers. "The ideal research resulted from an 'association of individuals' with common interests who were engaged in work that was commonly perceived to be of value; cooperation in the work itself was not part of this ideal" (Dear 158). In these discrete, object- or goal-oriented sites, different evidence of shared paideia establishes trust, but in relation to objects that its circle of students observes within community affiliations.

Apart from the observations and experiments of new science, by the seventeenth century multiple sources of credibility support other, often unreasonable hypotheses of a separate natural philosophy. With no agreed-upon definition of this discourse except as "not science," its credibility is at issue. As Adrian Johns explains in "Identity, Practice, and Trust in Early Modern Natural Philosophy," this "not science" raises epistemological questions about why some claims are accepted or rejected without obvious cause in this time of multiple, fanciful attempts at science (1133–34). His answer suggests a new rhetorical intervention in epistemology:

> A new *persuasive strategy* deployed in the mid- to late seventeenth century [attempted] to provide common ground for an intellectual, not social, community who share common-sense attributions of credibility. This was the practice known as "experiment." Experiments were staged practical demonstrations, designed to manifest "matters of fact" before witnesses whom contemporaries would *just know* to be reliable. (1133, emphasis added)

It is clear that Johns is renaming the appeal to what "everyone knows" to show that the sense of things that communities hold in common becomes a new, increasingly individualized "common sense." To do so, the early modern natural philosopher claims membership in a group of *virtuosi* who are skilled in various discourses whose dispersed rules will be seen to undermine stable rhetoric. Bacon and Galileo are obvious examples of this membership. But Bacon died from a cold caught trying to freeze ducks in the snow, as one of the *virtuosi*'s credited "improvers" of society.[14] Other designs include Robert Boyle's imagined (and ultimately workable) air pump, proposals to evacuate fleas from a room by placing warm horse piss under a bed, and visions of creating cranes that would fit in one's pocket yet be able to lift buildings (1137).

This multiplication of genres and of the primarily rhetorical rules applied to their evidence is also visible in early modern rehabilitations of various passions, to use them as rhetorical devices. For instance, *acquisitiveness* (avarice) can be treated as a newly valued context for contract agreements,[15] just as Adam Smith's *The Theory of the Moral Sentiments* (1759) later makes feelings of *sympathy* a matter of assessing the value of another person. Lori Branch points out how shifted perceptions of emotion fulfill Scottish colonials' self-interest in sharing *The Wealth of Nations*. As she puts it, "Once social mobility or interchangeability is posited, the ultimate terms of value naturally become one's esteem in the eyes of the crowd or of the moral market economy, as it were" (22). That is, if people no longer inherit the standing and education that create credible public speeches, their community "worth" is precisely, and only, equal to opinions of it.

Thomas Miller objects to such interpretations, especially to Smith's "not rhetoric." He says they undermine the oratorical rhetoric that he equates with democratic action, but not with varieties of invested persuasion:

> Several aspects of [Smith's] stance were very deleterious for rhetoric: the shift from purposeful action to *appropriate motivations*, the disloca-

tion from the perspective of the political agent to that of *the disinterested observer*, the devaluation of public discourse to *merely persuading other individuals to do business,* and the consequent displacement of rhetoric from its *civic relationship to politics, with rhetoric moving to emphasize belletristic criticism on responsive sentiments.* ("Is Rhetoric American?," emphasis added)

This view does not connect Smith's "disinterested observers" to his teaching of rhetoric nor to the scientific experiments and "just knowing" proofs of Smith's immediate predecessors. But until recently, many whose work joins Miller's[16] do not recognize emerging discourses and the material conditions of their production and distribution, nor attend to the ordinary writing and literary texts that the precepts and separate purposes of many rhetorics form. Nonetheless, as Ronald Walter Green comments on anxieties akin to Miller's in "Rhetoric and Capitalisms: Rhetorical Agency as Communicative Labor," this anxiety appears to be firmly entrenched:

[C]lassical models that hoped to harness rhetorical agency to the making of the "orator-statesman" must re-imagine political participation in terms of publics and counterpublics, social movements, electoral campaigns, communication media and technologies, as well as supra- and sub-national institutional settings. As the classical norms of citizenship rub against (post) modern realities, a permanent anxiety over the meaning and potential of rhetorical agency seems destined to be lodged in the critical imagination of rhetorical studies. (188)

In this light, it is unfortunate that the emerging novel is a primary instance of work that Miller's position also excludes from early modern rhetoric, for it often treats individual motives precisely as a character's self-interest. That new emphasis effectively disconnects modern motives from a classical rhetor's focus on the primacy of cultural preservation, thus offering a historic place-marker unavailable within oratorical records. The genre thus works through cultural changes that impinge on individuals, in the cultural contexts of the moral lessons of ancient fables and other myths, but not as their defender. But as Nancy Armstrong's *Desire and Domestic Fiction: A Political History of the Novel* comments about the novel and gender formation, to separate fiction from rhetoric and to divorce persuasion from a not yet articulated aesthetic perspective on internalized assent hide the genre's pedagogic management of feeling across Western cultures. Instructive novels and picaresque stories, some of which favor not only classed conventional morals but individual awareness of them, are thus only obliquely recognized as continuing classical creations of certain kinds of trustworthy characters that will remain cultural models, for good or ill. *Don Quixote, Clarissa,* and *Tom Jones* share that purpose with other genres: Greek dramatic satires, judicial speeches that expose the character of prosecutors and witnesses, and Isocrates' claim to be writing the first prose biography/encomium of Evagoras, King of Salamis.[17] That is, drama, oratory, biography, and fiction carry forward various textualities that had instructed Western character from its earliest theorizations.

In this case, a novel's authorial rhetor also purveys political precepts. They are visible in the motives of the characters of Pamela, Evelina, Amelia, and Jane Eyre, as they are in the misfortunes of unentitled men like Fielding's Tom Jones, Smollett's Humphry Clinker, and Thomas Hardy's Jude. Information about rank and power becomes character-ized as truths about relationships and misfortunes. Strategies for negotiating both are displayed in a persuasion that does not overtly argue to groups for due process.

The emerging novel also continues to elaborate rhetorical purposes that mark other genres, for instance, history, edict, and scripture. A fictionalized individual character-in-action soon occupies science and economics, redirecting popular absorption of the emotional motives appropriate to persuasion. Nonetheless, with significant exceptions, rhetoric's history does not normally address representations of minorities, marginalized women, or non-elite men, who are taken to be more relevant to "literacy," despite many copious vernacular archives that would belie that assumption.[18] But such exclusions from heroism of all but male Universal Individuals and their potential mates do not only serve the maintenance of disciplinary boundaries. They also gradually move trust outside both rhetoric and literary interpretation, oratory and sensitive individual readings, which rarely account for prescribed inferiority among democratized individuals.

"Sincerely, and Prudently, Yours"

These partial arguments about early modern investments of trust in generic discourses precisely *as* genres obviously omit the "deleterious"—toxic and deadly—issue that Miller raises to criticize sociocultural approaches to rhetoric: "the shift from purposeful action to *appropriate motivations*" (emphasis added). Certainly "consciousness" becomes a vexed issue that eighteenth-century rhetorics will incorporate in moral philosophical approaches to universal human nature and its individual taste. But before John Locke's *Human Understanding* (1690) constructs a unique yet simultaneously universal (male, Anglo-Saxon, propertied) individual, still earlier versions of a self defined by actions through discourse set terms that will encourage this later creation. Religious, political, and precisely rhetorical contexts address this problematic new self and the emergent fortunes of ancient rhetoric's characters. As John Martin's "Inventing Sincerity, Refreshing Prudence: The Discovery of the Individual in Renaissance Europe" shows, one rhetoric cannot account for the gradually realized, always overdetermined cultural identities that layer one on another concept *and* on actions that enact credibility across early modern Europe (1321).

Classical and later discussions of oratorical displays of emotions address sincerity as a condition of trust, treating both feelings as congruence within a person that was recognized probably well before Solon's antique instruction to trust character more than promises. But the nature and test of that character after it is unmoored from visible entitlement, rank, and power or from their absence is complicated in ways that become visibly highlighted in early modern constructions of a self. The fortunes of the terms "prudence" and "sincerity" expose theoretical difficulties for rhetoric that will be fully realized in eighteenth-century moral philosophy. But immediately prior meta-discourses, especially epistolary rhetoric, outline a European historical space for a fashioned individuality that is elsewhere less easily seen.

Of course nineteenth- and twentieth-century master narratives appear to easily imagine the complexity of that early modern self. Jacob Burckhardt's *The Civilization of the Renaissance in Italy* argues that the Renaissance created individuals and individualism and thus the possibility of testing one person's authenticity; Stephen Greenblatt's *Renaissance Self-Fashioning: From More to Shakespeare* demonstrates that cultures and institutions inscribe that same individual in ways that by definition will moot such tests. The first view relies on a Hegelian model of progressive Western history that, as Martin's "Inventing Sincerity" argues, depicts increasing *revelation* of the individual in terms of increasing freedom. In the second narrative, derived from Greenblatt's work and other New Historicism, that same individual is not a portable nor emerging core identity but realizations of a self in specific situations at particular times. This view is now the common interdisciplinary explanation of identity in almost all studies of early modernity (Martin 1320).

Martin takes these separate influential models to ground competing narratives that differently address identity as both moral and social self-presentations, which early modernism comes to value on the basis of opinions of them. In that relationship of society to morality, people obviously experience a difference between some feelings and some immediate responses to events and conventional, appropriate, and socially cautious displays of those feelings (1321). Petrarch, Sir Thomas More, Luther, John Calvin, and Montaigne all write of such crannies and fault lines in the emblematic "human heart." But among these writers are theologically educated martyrs who must choose between physical and spiritual death (Martin 1321). As Judith Rice Henderson further notes in "Humanist Letter Writing: Private Conversations or Public Forum?," "The individual conscience faced hard choices among competing theologies and political allegiances that threatened exile, death, or eternal damnation to their enemies" (35). We therefore cannot simplify early modern choices about whether to survive or to be "honest," or imagine a "true self" based only on a psychologized view of decisions that could be neither private nor individualistic. Such choices result from identification with a community and a community's changing view of *its* identity (35). The language that expresses them is neither Aristotle's signs of being a character that prevails or an argument solely within a self.

Martin extends this distinction by treating self-definition in relation to self-presentation. He specifically takes up how rhetoric and religion conceptualize the changing implications of the concepts of "prudence" and "sincerity." Thomas Aquinas and Luther thus can demonstrate differences within an emergent, conceptual self. That is, prudence, the Aristotelian *phronesis*, is also one of four cardinal Christian virtues through Aquinas's time. It is the focal point of the medieval portrayal of the soul's relation to God and to other Christians. Of course, a later early modern prudence is reinformed by secular wariness about communicating one's thoughts. But this virtue is not entirely suspended in a situated, theatrical self-fashioning of a mysterious aura around a self. It involves self-protection: the earlier secrecy required of Machiavelli's Prince and Castiglione's courtiers becomes in the politics of early modern revolutions and religious reformation a more general counsel to mind our own affairs and, to be socially and politically attractive and powerful, to remain tacitly mysterious about our thoughts (Martin 1. 324–25). In this Renaissance view, the authors portrayed in Spenser, Sidney, and Gascoigne write a prudent reticence, as would secretaries closeted with their masters.

This shifted understanding of prudent self-protection frees the human will for decisive control, or the appearance of it. Prudence hereby becomes more involved in human feelings as it is less attached to organized instruments of salvation, informing the expressions and self-protective deliberations of an emergent inwardness (Martin 1. 326). Yet in tandem with this surfacing self-construction of a social identity, the earliest implications of "sincerity" as "purity" are taken to associate a person with the Creator. Thus, individual identity is still seen to participate in a model community of flawed imitations of God who engage in self-purification rituals of many sorts in the name of individual self-correction. Sincerity hereby connotes well-intentioned concord among *and* within people who want to feel in harmony with their community of believers.

However, that communal identity begins to fragment in the face of a forceful Protestant assertion that man is fallen and unlike God, the ground of both its justification by faith, rather than impossible standards for living, and its very different logic of predestination. In either narrative, the fallen are unable to constitute the community Body of Christ, so sincerity becomes only individual interior harmony. It is visible in an agreement of thought with language, a felt sense of "telling the truth" that is more likely to remain institutionalized in Catholicism. Luther, for example, praises the Psalms for their earnest expression of the writer's deepest thoughts, treating the psalmist as an individual with access to spirituality, not as a poetic voice of corporate godliness (Martin 1. 330).

This Protestant acceptance of fallen humanity paradoxically isolates the early modern self's expressions by removing a church authority's intercessions on the self's behalf. In that isolation, people are more or less sincere (pure), not representations of a human essence communicating among its selves, as it were, to build up communities that are flawed imitations of a Body of Christ incarnate. In a later Enlightenment, prudence and sincerity will be further discoursed as identical to isolated, individual expressions of supposedly universally shared truths and then absorbed into the insight of the singular Romantic poetic voice. But the place of this early modern subject's language is between a fundamentally relational act of prudent participation and individual isolation in sin, not in a personality or from contact with a more general Nature that can only account for sincerity from within the individual. This grounding of a novel self in both individual credibility and community discourses helps explain our ready acceptance of both Burckhardt's and Greenblatt's views of the Renaissance. The early modern invitation to form and hold to dual narrati̶ ̶ ̶ ̶ ̶nd contextualized sel̶ ̶ ̶ ̶ ̶ ̶d within and at odds w̶

But th̶ ̶ ̶ ̶ ̶ ̶ ̶ ̶ ̶ ̶ ̶ ̶ ̶y ̶ ̶rhetorical abstraction. That is, realized sincerity results from fitting our speech to feeling, not the more common ancient outcome of adapting feelings to conventional human and linguistic styles. This context of course makes it easy to misrecognize the Hellenistic debate about the orator's expression of genuine or feigned feelings as a modern problem. But the emotional issues of classical orators are not identical to our self-consciousness. Martin's summary tacitly makes this distinction: "The primary cultural factors in the making of Renaissance individualism were the emergence of Humanism and the development of Protestantism, both of which deeply problematized the relation of what contemporaries viewed as one's inner self to one's words and actions" (1. 341). That duality cannot be resolved by resolutely direct classical action. Over time, it will inevitably support philosophical concepts of "being," which ultimately make credible an ethos sincere in proportion to its revelations of self-doubt (see chapter 3). For instance, some now admire Montaigne's essays for their encouragement to readers to share self-revelations that enact the "discursive fortitude" in which "the word replaces the deed" (Posner 56).

Of course, shifting implications of two words cannot contain the total early modern experience of the self. But these fluid terms do provide access to how trust of conventional discourses intersects nationalist faith in language and in its social stratifications, a faith that creates a much more knotty meeting of connotations than any single explanation or analysis of concepts can untie. Thus, the implications of "prudence" and "sincerity" raise further questions, for instance, about how human acts may fit the rhetorical systems available to represent them. That is, the new, precisely moral imperative to express oneself with prudent sincerity is, at this point, a question of representation, but not yet representations of the containers for isolated individualism. As this evidence also argues, emerging attitudes toward discourses and the material-ized institutions, practices, and economies that connect them trace discrete earlier formations, metadiscourses that they modify but do not erase.

Yet trusted orators are hard to come by in urgent revolutionary and reli-gious politics. Its designated speakers are by definition advocates of conflict-ed positions about enemies who are also family and friends. And obviously, as rank and reputation may be at least partially irrelevant to the emerging secular bureaucratic and relative economic independence of those who ac-quire them, locales of trust become increasingly immanent in documents themselves. Thus, the letter and epistolary rhetoric, always more prominent than oratorical histories acknowledge, take on a different urgency. In un-avoidably material early modern realizations of credibility, it makes sense to highlight not a diminution of oratory, even in the American pamphlet politics to follow, but how the oxymoronic prudent sincerity of early modern selves replaces Aristotle's and classical rhetoric's certain kind of person as the letter becomes its illustrative medium.

Although many sites of persuasion are treated as "minor" because little secondary work exposes them,[19] early modern epistolary rhetoric, its prec-edents, and its later manifestations as guidance for surrogate polite conversa-tion all demonstrate how cultural pedagogies shift in exigent circumstances, specifically in this case to construct plausible secular credibility. Of course, this rhetoric is easily enough mapped on classical origins. For instance, José María Gutiérrez Arranz and Ricardo J. Sola Buil locate the familiarity and individuality of the modern letter in the rhetoric of disputation of Corax and Tisias. In an extensive review of "The Late Medieval Epistle," they identify the formal judicial relation between accuser and accused as an obvious pre-cursor to discourse that contains "individual attitudes and ways of acting" that "emphasised the primacy of spoken expression, where the presence/absence of a subject became more remarkable" (par. 1). However, that insight—the crucial point of credibility in an epistolary text—need not be attributed to a "precursor" as likely to have followed as preceded it.

But the issue of presence/absence that focuses many recent expositions of epistolary rhetoric is precisely the infrastructural point of prudent sincerity, if not in regard to the physical presence of interlocutors that the letter displaces. Arranz and Buil explain it in terms of the "problems outlined when we want to establish, from a pragmatic point of view, where is the subject who writes and which is the *real message* behind what he/she says" (par. 3, emphasis added). They also point out that epistolary traditions arise not only from formal rhetoric—Aristotle and the *Ad Herennium*—but are subject to "the implicit controversy between form and subjectivity" (par. 4) that is realized in the rise of a "literary" subjectivity immediately after the early modern "economic subject" is formed. They focus on the shift around 1400 from a market to a monetary economy, when a literary (textual) subject's identity is literally its exchange value, an identity that only appears in its textual context, on a rough analogy with a closed monetary system whose cash is valuable only when it is exchanged. The literary identity they describe is not attached to specific words, nor is it the direct source of records of a person's speech (par. 4). It is much more phenomenal than an "authorship" assigned to a name or to a copyright, the later, culturally recognized author whom Foucault imagines and Martha Woodmansee separately sees as an artifact of the changing legal status of texts.[20]

Of course, the exchange value of authorship is played out and complicated later, as we have seen in Spenser, Sidney, and Gascoigne. Their secretarial personae gloss the historical gendering of the epistle in which the intellectually trained noblewoman chooses this marginal form to reveal personal experiences. In "Female Explorations of Literacy: Epistolary Challenges to the Literary Canon in the Late Middle Ages," Albrecht Classen notes how the characteristics of the genre—its prescribed greetings, salutations, closing statements, rigid conventions for arranging its parts, and seals and signatures that verify authorship and privacy—permit female writers a safe deception. In yet another sort of secret knowledge, they can at least hide feelings in narrative conventions (95). Arranz and Buil infer that "all the difficulties enclosed in the recognition of a [letter-writing] subjectivity are increased when the remittent is a woman." Omitting difficulties inherent in the situations of literate members of lower classes of either sex and of other unentitled or fearful writers, they conclude that "it seems now clear that it was precisely women who with greater strength broke free from the rhetorical formalisms and used all the emotional possibilities that the letter provided to them" (par. 13). Nonetheless, letters by upper-class women with secretaries are dictated and read aloud by recipients in many settings, well after public postal services replace messengers. And they are often instruments of home teaching, checked for correctness not only by recipients recruited for that purpose but also before they are sent, overcoming their privacy in more than one way.

Perhaps again imposing unneeded causal and influential relations on parallel metadiscourses, Arranz and Buil add that a postmodern proposition was realized in the medieval epistolary tradition. They point to *Artes Dictaminis* of both Guido Faba (*Summa dictaminis*, 1228–29) and of Conrad de Mure (*Summa de arte prosandi*, 1275–76) to identify three formal elements that evoke recent critical attention: "the authenticity, the confidentiality and the fact of making present the absent to whom the letter is sent" (par. 5). Recent epistolary history and criticism take up each of these elements of this discrete metadiscourse, assuming the broad availability of the genre to all readers and writers, as female correspondents evidence, tacitly theorizing how letters are trusted.

However, that theory is colored by a more prominent debate in rhetoric studies about an early modern falling off of medieval epistolary traditions. The Spring 2001 volume of *Rhetorica* addresses the fortunes of medieval *dictaminan*, with less concern about the credible subjectivity of correspondents than about a recurring disciplinary interest in epistolary rhetoric's "decline." This falling-off is described variously: as absolute change dated from the late fifteenth century, as a temporary result of repressive politics, as a (more likely) move from one to another genre—for example, from official, exclusively transmitted medieval prescriptivism to the ingratiating, commodified modern conduct manual. The volume includes Martin Camargo's introduction ("The Waning of Medieval *Ars Dictaminis*"), John O. Ward's "Rhetorical Theory and the Rise and Decline of *Dictamen* in the Middle Ages and Early Renaissance," Malcolm Richardson's "The Fading Influence of the Medieval *Ars Dictaminis* in England after 1400," and Judith Rice Henderson's "Valla's Elegantiae and the Humanist Attack on the *Ars dictaminis*." These essays do not emphasize how letters assure trust among those who read and write them or the obviously changing fortunes of rhetorics designed to produce that credibility. But their attention to noncanonical instruction nonetheless assumes that letters create or bring to mind and heart ad hoc emotional bonds. Those situated attachments help account for shifting methods of discourse education and practice and for cultural norms that education entitles in specific times.

But other scholarship makes clear that the early modern letter participates in an explosion of preprint discursive practices with much earlier beginnings in Cicero's *Epistulae ad Atticum*,[21] the letters to Atticus noted earlier as having enormous influence on epistolary rhetoric and on letter writing as surrogate conversation by providing models in informal, conversational Latin. These letters inform all early modern arts of conversation whose sociolinguistic categories parallel those prescribed by epistolary rhetoric to determine variations that depend on who is speaking to whom on particular occasions about specific topics.[22] In the *Rhetorica* volume, John Ward's "Rise and Decline" calls the earlier, eleventh-century highpoint of burgeoning interest in epistolary rhetoric a "veritable communications maelstrom," which on many fronts furthered responses by "various learned vested-interest groups . . . [who required] effective and comprehensive modes of communication" (177). Obviously, that energy is sorted out over the next four centuries: differences among multiplied epistolary purposes and audiences—for instance, the new audience for a political "open letter" that may become a printed tract—require and socialize systems of correspondence, as they also regulate uses of print technologies.

But Ward also emphasizes "why and how a society codifies into theory and transmits as such . . . its communication practice" (176). That is, the letter is an example within a larger outline of various abstracted and well-circulated metadiscourses. He applies to that comprehensive project the fortunes of classical rhetorical theories, showing the relevance of skillfully written Latin compositions of both poetry and prose to "the elegant, polite, humanist, intimate letter." Again, rules applied to epistolography "according to medieval treatises and manuals on the subject" (176) may easily borrow across metadiscursive precepts that make up an elite paideia yet do not demand the authority of one unified precedent. Thus, these discussions of epistolary rhetoric and practice after Cicero identify multiple traditions in which, for instance, Italy and the Papacy assert an official epistolary identity distinct from French and English uses of rhetorical precepts in epistolography. Some note recursive interactions between classical rhetoric and the letter, especially the Ciceronian *Ad Herennium*'s transmission of figures through the Middle Ages, in treatises that finally separate situated groupings of practices to form a larger dedicated epistolary tradition. Some identify that tradition as unique, citing how rarely it is included in volumes of rhetorical theory.[23] But as we have seen, others emphasize epistolary rhetoric's derivative uses of parallels they present as its precedents.

In addition, organized epistolary instruction that is based on classical rhetoric distinguishes the three elements of uncertainty about identity, content, and trustworthiness that I noted earlier. Such instruction takes up the didactic uses of many kinds of letters, which are often overlooked even when the letters themselves request correction and advice, especially in women's correspondence.[24] As Richard McNabb says of Juan Gil de Zamora's exemplary *Dictaminis Epithalamium* (*The Marriage Song of Letter-Writing*, circa

1277), in addition to standardized derivative treatments of salutation, narration, petition, and conclusion, the book "supplies an exhaustive list of words and phrases one may use in letters to praise a person's virtues or to censure his vices" (229). A broad outline of the progression of this separate tradition is therefore differently traced among its generally agreeing but particular scholarly histories.

A few inferences from this work are especially relevant to rethinking early modern rhetoric. First, English epistolary practice dates from Anglo-Saxon administrative uses of the letter through the eighteenth century. That practice consequently endows the English letter with a distinct content related to the organization and the infrastructures of administration, apart from the later influence of papal chanceries. The English administrative influence is visible at least through early modernity in time and work schedules and in instructions for accomplishing the social tasks that many familiar letters regularly assigned and monitored. Second, the rise of this epistolary theory need not be taken to be a humanist creation or a "break" with classical rhetorical traditions, despite the popularity of Cicero's rediscovered *Familiar Letters*. Rhetoric as a theory gives way to the many more frequent uses of these letters as models. John Ward hedges about this result from Cicero, in the main concurring with Paul Grendler's *Schooling in Renaissance Italy*: "In renaissance classrooms Cicero's letters seem to have largely replaced theoretical rhetorical treatises as generalised guides for epistolography, but within a classicising rhetorical context" (218). In "Humanist Letter Writing," Henderson agrees that epistolary rhetoric is a separate building on the same grounds (31). Third, the outcomes of specific sources for letters differ. As I have noted, letters written to meet the necessities of royal administration are credited differently than papal writing, which in some measure extends the voice of the Pauline epistle. The administrative letter follows much earlier sources represented by ancient bills of lading and other niche professional and merchant literacies (Hoskin 35). The Pauline epistle follows the classical *topos* through Augustine: letters are "windows of the soul" (Cicero, *De Oratore* iii.221).

But epistolary categories also follow material circumstances that will determine a text's content. For instance, letters intended only for manuscript circulation among a limited group employ a private tone and content that will nonetheless generate publicity. Warren Boucher also names a corollary category that may have no purpose but to establish the writer's reputation for a good Neo-Latin style. Others, like Erasmus's famous intellectual missives, promote a philosophical, educational, scientific, or other intellectual/social program. And some letters routinely acknowledge courtesy, disseminate news, fulfill the exchange obligations of friendship, or contain narratives contrived to support broader policy decisions among correspondents without becoming printed newsletters, tracts, or contracts (Boucher 138). Even among less fine-grained categories of "private" or "intimate" letters as opposed to "public," "official," or "business" correspondence, none commonly accomplish decisions or actions between two people or even members of one and another household. That is, as Boucher notes, "You had to be of a certain standing and importance before you could make yourself an issue in a letter of civil business" (138).

That standing is dispersed as Cicero's familiar letters substitute for direct epistolary instruction and as dedicated epistolary rhetorics become popularized (Camargo 139).[25] Malcolm Richardson, attempting to complicate this relocation of the *ars dictaminis*, notes that middle-class literate people could not have accessed the many official models in extant manuals that date at least from 650 CE. But these models nonetheless shadow new occasions, where they trace hierarchies and institutional assumptions, not a Ciceronian imitation of intimacy (231).[26] Thus, the increasing number of homemade letters after about 1420 is met by a concurrent gap in the production of letter-writing manuals over the next 125 years. Instead, at least until circa 1545, imitation, copying, and allusions to legal forms preserve the content of earlier precepts in a widening and re-regulated literate sociability. These modes of preservation allow conduct of official interpersonal matters we now treat as personal, like courtships, marriage proposals, and the ritualized emotions of dueling. In the last case, correspondence written according to strict social protocols manages that early modern phenomenon with precisely nuanced challenges and apologies that prevent most quarrels of honor from ending in a death, the result that safe epistolary distance discouraged.[27] Letters also negotiate complicated matrimonial contracts between literate propertied families that became written records of financial and domestic promises. Of course, their imitations of official documents can completely displace a model's successes, as in the Renaissance example of a response to an accusation that "is forced unnaturally into a structure filled with 'whereases,' 'wherefores,' and 'whereupons,'" in which "the [rhetorically prescribed] 'narrative' turns into a grotesquely drawn out 'whereas' clause of the normal royal missive, except that no 'therefore' clause resolves it" (Richardson 228).

But letters may also maintain inappropriate distances insofar as the models applied to accomplish early modern official business and distribute community news cause frequent unease about writing them at all. As the later sixteenth century produces manuals and conduct books that restate the chanceries' epistolary precepts, they transmit to ordinary exchanges the force of institutional agendas and the model letters' never exactly applicable differences in rank. In these new publications, the letter and instructions to write it are encrusted with conventions that re-impose uncomfortable social relations that had often been meant to be precisely that. That is, distinct yet accumulating relationships among writers and texts, writers and readers, and readers and texts eventually demand that the varieties of epistolary instruction I have surveyed here enter a new, at times distorted, register. Early modern interlocutors evidently mistrust expression, or print, or formal rhetoric alone, but nonetheless rely on the joined, well-executed controls on distance that well-formed letters always entail.

This is also to say that rather than indicating a fragmentation of rhetoric, early modern epistolary practices and the handbooks, conduct books, model letters, and self-instruction traditions that inform them might demonstrate the anxiety attached to original and copy. In this case, that anxiety will be extended to the distribution of imitative yet novel instruction whose acceptance will depend on the production of print copies of already imitative originals. Their wide uses and acceptance thus again reveal the unnecessary limit placed on metadiscursive history by ignoring the intercession of print in its narratives, despite the ease with which we may note that it is impossible to maintain oratorical rhetoric's staged control of thought and action in a letter. But many comments on early modern literary discourse extend this view of the period's focus on the relation of original and copy that the prudent sincerity of represented feelings also necessarily involves. Harold Love notes that inconsistencies in John Dryden's seventeenth-century poetry demonstrate that he valued ideas for their usefulness, not their conceptual stability ("Dryden's Rationale" 298); Jennifer Richards says that the period's experimentation with dialogue allows self-interest to be expressed in light of other, competing interests that the voices of interlocutors contain (3). Kristine Haugen sees early modern discomfort with commonplace originality in the battle between the ancients and moderns, begun with William Temple's seventeenth-century assertion that the first instance of any creation is always its best occurrence (3).

Such urgency about trusting an absent source whose charisma is nonetheless "to hand" in either manuscripts or compositors' early print technologies is also played out in the vast multiplication of variously pre-indexed printed commonplace books whose blank categories are filled with citations for the sake of their owners' originality. Some are indexed according to relevant concepts, some according to biblical references, and some only alphabetically. Thus, both before and after Locke's *A New Method of Making Common-Place Books*, accusations of being a mere copyist are literally meant, not allusions to plagiarism. But such charges also oversimplify how these printed compendia allow us to read and "work up" what Locke calls "material," here the textual resources that universal individualism invests in and thereby owns.

Just as imitating model letters allows their writers and readers to assimilate still another, differently trusted charisma, commonplace copying creates property that its owners may use at will. This differently trusted character can only imitate the privileged membership in power that Aristotle assumes to be the source of persuasion or the specific prudent sincerity that will gradually occupy the persona that the letter's conventional greetings and salutations convey and teach.

In this different historical narrative, reproduced formal structures of discourse have created trust in antique oracular speakers and their language, which was in turn valued in proportion to its display of conventions that accessed a community's actual experiences and esoteric knowledge. But as separate oratorical, epistolary, and bureaucratic rhetorics redefine the social place of religion and inform burgeoning democratic, monarchic, and republican political arrangements, those rhetorics also respond to disseminated print, which creates ad hoc, often unexpected relationships. These processes thus create a *textual* imaginary. It is made of persuasive conventions and mesmerizing language but is then separated from personal, localized, even national experiences. In this early modern matrix of emblematic relationships, handwritten letters to strangers for whatever purposes rely for acceptance on prescribed formalities—graphic markers of status and of feeling that stand in for ancient participation in what everyone knows. But disconnected from the energy of a shared past, markers of status and feeling in letters are finally (only) identical to this social energy—as Socrates threatened about all writing, are perhaps without memories at all.

3   *The Mobility of Trust*

It is reasonable to think that, in general, the recurrent use of a concept in communication would favour the introduction and stabilization of a corresponding word in the public language.

—Dan Sperber and Deirdre Wilson, "The Mapping
between the Mental and the Public Lexicon"

We must be permitted to say, that we do not hold the art of oral delivery in so low an estimation as the learned sometimes affect to do. . . . It is not altogether so superficial and insignificant as is imagined.

—Review of *An Introduction to the Art of Reading*

Style has an absolute value, like the product of any other exquisite art, quite distinct from the value of the subject about which it is employed, and irrelatively to the subject.

—Thomas DeQuincey, "Language"

The rhetorical tradition is a fiction that has just about outlasted its usefulness.

—Thomas P. Miller, "Reinventing Rhetorical Traditions"

So far I have attempted to disrupt the default historiography that regularly narrates rhetorical theory and practices through one oratorical root metaphor. This traditional approach prevents accounting for the historic multiplicity of metadiscursive pedagogies that constitute cultures, seeing them as separate theories and practices. This current-historical tradition in rhetoric studies also implies that homologous features among separate practices indicate that we might find an ancient Rosetta Stone inscribed only with Athenian oratory and only in the Greek alphabet. But it is possible that Aristotle's definition of rhetoric as the "art of discovering all the available means of persuasion in a given situation" (*Rhetoric* I.14.1355a) captures a transcultural commonplace: discourses have much in common, yet distinct situations, purposes, and conventions of composition require their teachings to call attention to their material circumstances—differing occasions that create nonce communities in various settings. We consequently must look everywhere, not only at formal systems within us. This is to claim that framed language is trusted in proportion to a perceptible fit between its conventions and the locally intelligible charisma of its sources. Those sources share metadiscursive teachings—practice for oratorical delivery emulates acting lessons. But such lessons also differ historically in accommodations to available resources and altered ends that characterize their temporal, always material settings.

Of course Aristotle puts it better. I emphasize that only from a formalist, feature-driven view of texts can we accept a touchstone approach to rhetoric's history. That approach disallows the now obvious, post-Cartesian predisposition to trust crafted language insofar as it acknowledges its mediation of specific immediate circumstances and what they do not reveal. Trusted persuasion, which any framed statement necessarily attempts, requires diverse versions of *kairos* insofar as opportune moments are by definition constituted by a sense of something missing.

This chapter attempts to support these views again. It examines the overdetermined Anglo-European imaginary that is built by eighteenth-century elaborations of Cartesian rationalism, especially its result in the Lockean naming of a "human nature" that these principles about trust imply. It discusses the guidance of the century's moral philosophy in reforming metadiscourses in the first extensive explanations of linguistic psychology. These treatises by David Hume, Hugh Blair, George Campbell, and Richard Whately—whom John Schilb calls "the usual suspects" of eighteenth-century rhetoric (343)—embed consciousness in discursive practices. In addition, the chapter takes up renewed attention to refining and standardizing spoken and written vernacular language, realized by widely published dictionaries and elocutionary lessons. Perhaps most important, it argues that the self-reflexive nature of consciousness provides ways to re-imagine the phenomenology of texts as a material realm parallel to that of consciousness: a differently materialized *published* textuality that locates trust in media, not as conveyors of messages but for their own sake. That is, while holographic and print texts obviously still carry individual and official presence, disseminated publication regularly compromises that conception of presence itself. Thus, the discrete, published text stands in for immediate interactions; it does not contain them; and with increasing frequency, it does not attempt to.

For example, the always ambivalent status of the letter (see chapter 2) constitutes the self-reflexive aesthetic of epistolary novels. Yet these narratives also rework the genre's constitutive possibility for mis/trust insofar as they display the letter, without comment, as a framed fictional nonfiction. The invention of the genre is universally attributed to printer Samuel Richardson, who became master of the book trade's guild, the Stationers' Company, and published a book of model letters (*Familiar Letters . . . on Important Occasions* [1741]) the same year that his *Pamela: or, Virtue Rewarded* appeared. Thus, this hybrid genre based on self-reflexive consciousness is an eighteenth-century intervention in discursive practice—a novel that imitates interiority, not a Swiftian "history." But it is also entirely embedded in the fact of published privacy, which verifies that the (published) genre, if not its letters, may be trusted fiction.

These formations exemplify a literary/affective shift that simultaneously establishes and erodes Enlightenment confidence in the Universal Individual's control of linguistic meanings. For instance, conventional persuasive characters here embody a distinct subjectivity, a republican citizen whose ethos is an emblem of a self-governed nation constituted by self-governed individuals.[1] This necessarily published character results from new values assigned to cultural keywords, but it also reassigns value to an older vocabulary. Formerly religious and monarchic structures become the secular "heart," "spirit," and "salvation" of patriotism and commerce.[2] In addition, legislation authorizing a postcopyright, reproduced canon realizes new independence from church and monarchy by making published texts available across class, gender, race, and other categories of exclusion from centrist education based on vocation and region. Yet for this often-noted new readership, expensive or esoteric print texts become "rare books," a special category that no longer enacts social exclusion on the basis of coterie politics yet preserves it in limited mass access to collected archives.

To support these generalizations' difference from casually repeated historical stories, this chapter also revisits both dismissive opinions of elocutionary rhetoric and their occasional rehabilitation. It speculates that this cold spot in rhetoric's histories is an unrecognized yet definitive theoretical place-marker. It indicates a disruption in the force of a unified oratorical model of rhetoric, which is easily overlooked without attention to the importance of language reform at the time. But this unhappy topic includes that refinement of vernacular language in newly complicated workings of any modern metadiscourse. That is, the energy around elocutionary rhetoric in the eighteenth century demonstrates a splintering from *within* oratorical rhetoric, not one imposed from outside, nor, apart from acting lessons, a parallel metadiscourse. It not only responds to postrevolutionary political agendas that would prevent crowds from gathering to hear fiery oratory but would also create a new hegemony of published textuality. Elocutionary lessons require re-theorizing the credibility of texts apart from traditional paths of authority in a process that indirectly results in fully detaching already well-established print from the ranked texts of manuscript cultures, which nonetheless continue to circulate Latin and other esoteric texts. The elocuted publication of a text further impinges on a historiography that relies on progressive canons, despite its contrary illusion of stable reproduction. That is, elocution contributes to a reconception of texts as "media" to be used. It (literally) punctuates the shifts from a seventeenth-century "conduit" to a twentieth-century "economical" way to get a story "over" in the least time. Publication ultimately dissolves trusted ancient character into material signs of its diffusion.[3]

In *Rethinking the Rhetorical Tradition: From Plato to Postmodernism,* James L. Kastley notes that before this theoretical turn, rhetoric is already under the pressure of modernism's revision of Enlightenment precepts. That is, theories grounded in uncertainty and simultaneity set aside earlier positivist objectivity because they recognize that "the perspective of the subject cannot be eliminated" (137). Social sciences also displace the centered subject as the conceptual nation diminishes under an international and global politics of late capitalism. The most significant of these modernist developments is that the decentered subject recognizes that "thought cannot transcend the language in which it is embodied," which is to say that "language is not merely a medium that is employed by thought but . . . is inescapably *constitutive for thought*" (137, emphasis added). In this view, the political oratorical project becomes complicated "by the clear evidence that political debate is not a rational exchange but a stylized contest" (137).

Of course, these listed changes have undermined the rhetorical tradition, but not in one blow. Kastley sees evidence of that erosion in lost faith in human abilities to fulfill the modernist dream of rational persuasion. But this erosion also cooperates with two forces emphasized here. The first is the formerly improbable but now habitual assignment of interpretative literary reading to students who are to be empowered by mass literacy, yet who nonetheless are not already positioned to produce culturally consequential discourse nor are likely to become so. The second is the absorption of oratorical ethos, pathos, and logos into an internalized universal psychology that eighteenth-century moral philosophy ascribes to the split consciousness of a soon-to-be Freudian model. This latter adjustment of self-identities also transfers John Locke's sensational access to knowledge from individuals to the "insides" of unsettled cultural programs. There, language systems and a superstructure of social procedures recast conventional ancient character as (deeply) hidden, not merely prudent, psychologized "personalities."

As these two redistributions of character take hold, a modern human subject whose nature exceeds rational argument does not require for either sociability or responsible citizenship a rhetoric of democratic principles and precepts. That is, in and after the Anglo-European eighteenth century, citizens constitute political systems that do not depend on naming their parts— neither "free speech" nor "rights." They form a "world as task rather than as object of knowledge" (Kastley 137). The centrism of oratorical rhetoric is hereby visibly dissipated into multiple, ad hoc discursive exigencies. A world in process around its broken formal categories places any second incidence of such personal or social exigency in quotation marks, marking it precisely as "event" by virtue of its recurrence. In this world-as-task, traditional infra-structures also appear only in and as performed media, not in their statements nor in those about them.

That is, without culturally predictable yet suddenly opportune moments of *kairos*, the success of an oration's attempt to fit direct speech to local circumstance becomes iffy; professional concern for continuity in the "rhetorical tradition" of that circumstance fades. As Chaim Perelman and Lucie Olbrechts-Tyteca recognize, the audiences judging arguments can no longer be cast as cooperative resident participants in civil democratic exchanges (16). Nor are they abstractions but self-contained, ad hoc subjects of representations who normally access cultural events through the trope of irony, as is evident, for instance, in their apparent ability to suddenly stage an unexpected street interview with only momentary glances toward a camera. Diffuse, self-contradictory global economic politics, implausible objective/rational decision-making processes, and suspicions about even our own "direct" communications and righteous motives supplant ordinary access to cultural identity.

Of course, the simple view that a text that is often reproduced in precisely the same widely accessible form can re-initial the speaking body of oratory is also incomplete. It remains partial even when complicated by Derridean readings of Plato's *Phaedrus* or very different Bakhtinian privileges for interactive, embodied dialogic processes.[4] Trust in direct human interaction through language does not easily slide to the space of publication I am describing, which takes only an ambivalent interest in the authority of unseen voices that emanate from material sites. Nor does adding charisma to the authority of publication explain how trust endures, if it does, as more than a flat inference from recognizing a publishing house, a name, the possibilities implied by a title, or high production values.

Thus, it is easy to identify with the anxiety that marks prominent eighteenth-century projects as they replace indifference to Shakespeare's erratic spelling with a moral determination to get published texts exactly right. We know that consciousness is an unreliable source of trust in discourse even as we become persuaded that it is the essence of evidence. Its multiple perspectives precisely equal its ability to take another side altogether, in a trice. So it is also clear that gradually accumulated complications of the likelihood of trust include the results of merging human and typographic definitions of "character." As this chapter points out about the texts that elocution attempts to manage, these characters become identical to each other at least insofar as neither escapes elaborate staging. Finally, modern and later metadiscourses appear to recognize purity, directness, clarity, transparency, and especially trust in those who share individual experiences that they portray as unique. But these pedagogic sites also remind us that those trusted qualities are now so rhetorically overlayered that they irremediably blur statement into expression, evidence into opinion. Thus, eighteenth-century moral philosophy, even as it is partially represented here, raises material issues that deeply involve its concepts in distributions of texts and in the identities that will be constructed from modern consciousness. Confidence in discourse simultaneously evolves and devolves, creating increasing apprehension about the isolation of the Enlightenment Orator whose tasteful texts will inevitably blur into their singular interpretative Readers.

Literature, "Literature," and Rhetorical Truths

Histories of textual forms, genres, and oratorical rhetoric do often note that before the Romantic installation of officially aesthetic measures of fine writing, all texts were included in "Literature." This wide-ranging definition apparently fades as different orders of text and author appear, to be retained only in describing "the literature" around a particular topic or field. But the implications for rhetoric studies of that changed connotation are rarely unpacked, if often reported with a sense of loss. This change implies a decline, especially a falling-off of an oratorical rhetoric that becomes less distinct. For instance, insofar as rhetorical handbooks and other style guides had used literary literature as examples to demonstrate legal and poetic devices, its discrete modernized aesthetic status elevates literary passages to reverse the order of precept/example. The new sense of "literature" portrays poets and poetry as special orders of creation, not only as writers of trans-historical "poesy," which had been debased by its Renaissance makers in Sir Philip Sidney's *Defense of Poesy* (1595). Establishing aesthetic discourse as a distinct ontology implies that those who produce and absorb literary literature have interiorized insight that is its own reward and burden. That is, they at least tacitly rely on themselves for inspiration, not on texts as instruments of cultural preservation that recognize circulated conventions and recirculate them. Trevor Ross's "The Emergence of 'Literature': Making and Reading the English Canon in the Eighteenth Century" describes this creation of a separate literary textuality as a shift in the phenomenology of discourse: "No longer considered rhetorical or didactic instruments, they [literary texts] became prized as autonomous creations" (397).

This autonomy divides formerly mutual discourse pedagogies, especially separating oratorical from aesthetic purposes to create literate readers, and writers, who construct themselves as *essentially* either sensitive and perceptive or functional, purpose-driven personalities. Yet on the earlier side of that demarcation, "the function of poetry was defined in terms of social instrumentality, and its value measured wholly by its utility within a moral order that was determined less by economic profit than *by symbolism, rhetoric and representation*" (Ross 399, emphasis added). That is, before people treat some texts as pure aesthetic constructions, their moral and preservative cultural work is readily admired. Their composition as functional poetry is privileged over formalist descriptions of genres and discursive purposes. Calling this pre-aesthetic culture "the totality of poet and audience," Ross characterizes it as a confluence of text, audience, and a source—a poet/orator/trusted maker of crafted language:

> The culture, the totality of poet and audience, was *the consumer and the producer,* and there was felt to be no problem as to the question of where value resided, whether in the poetic activity, in the poetic utterance, or in its reception. It *was the same value or symbolic capital that circulated all around. . . . Whatever immortalizing, expressive, educative or exhortative effects poetry was felt to produce were ascribed to the verbal powers of the poet, who, in turn, was at one with the interests of the community.* The poet was not a maker of commodities for an autonomous audience, but an agent of production working on behalf of established social relations. (400, emphasis added)

Of course, this capaciously defined textuality does not disappear. All makers of texts and their recipients, including poets, still knowingly engage shared community values they realize interchangeably in trusted language and an ethos derived from their community's exigent history. Education in any specific discursive practice continues to include its dedicated special topics and commonplaces, formal conventions, and appropriate emotional responses. That is, legible oratorical and literary communication preserves the force of these texts. That legibility is identical to the cohesion of region, place, and experience.

As Ross says, "Early evaluative standards were keyed explicitly to each new generation's requirements for cultural and ideological production" (401).

Well after a new literati narrow the definition of "literature," its readers/audiences still expect to treat texts, which include highly conventional oral exchanges, as products of cultural instruction. Those lessons of course include tropes and figures that demonstrate access to what everyone knows, which is to say that across eras of variously organized discourse pedagogies, shared paideia inculcates identities with access to distinctive commonplaces. The changed meaning of "literature" thus consequentially affects metadiscursive theories that assumed the community origin of shared experiences, not their derivation from separate sorts of reading.

Ross exemplifies that movement before and after this redefinition of cultural expectations. For instance, Richard Tottel's 1557 *Miscellany*, what might be called the earliest English literary textbook/anthology, explicitly asks readers to enact a confluence between source and reception, writer and reader: "I aske help of the learned to defend their learned frendes, the authors of this work: And I exhort the vnlearned, by reding to learne to be more skilful, and to purge that swinelike grossenesse, that maketh the swete maierome not to smell to their delight" (1.2, qtd. in Ross 403). Ross cites the progress of such statements, for instance, John Milton's desire for a "fit audience . . . though few," and playwright Ben Jonson's desired "Reader extraordinary," distinguished from the mere "Reader in Ordinairie," in the 1611 preface to *Catiline* (403).[5] But readers are treated differently as the community of the learned is diffused. By 1661, immediately following the English Restoration, Alexander Brome instead begs for reciprocity from readers of his *Songs and other Poems*: "Being taught by custome, to beg something of the Reader, it shall be this; that in reading and judging these Poems, he will consider his own frailty, and fallibility; and read with the same temper and apprehension, as if [he] himself had written, and I were to judge" (A7V). Readers are no longer expected to live up to the texts they read, as familiarly perfumed receptacles, but are begged to approve of the writer on the basis of empathy in the face of error.

As literary historian Bertrand Harris Bronson summarizes this movement in the eighteenth century, "Gradually but increasingly, there develops a race of authors who write to an indefinite body of readers, personally undifferentiated and unknown; who accept this separation as a primary condition of their creative activity and address their public invisibly, through the curtain, opaque and impersonal, of print" (302, qtd. in Ross 403).[6] In this dramatized cultural matrix, authors must still display oratorical acumen that cannot depend on shared experience. But a reader is differently equipped, first as a still-extraordinary, well-read member of an increasingly uneven vernacular audience, as Milton and Jonson indicate. However, that reader becomes a potential adversary, centuries before Roland Barthes's *S/Z* designs contemporary readers as a text's source, not only its canny or unskilled, cooperative or adversarial interpreters. Ross argues that this first adversarial relation to print results from two sources: an ambiguously celebrated spread of literacy and the 1774 defeat of the idea of "perpetual copyright" in favor of making enduring texts a "property of the people" (410). Those owning that property are themselves new members of a class of readers who well before William Wordsworth's *Lyrical Ballads* (1798) have available both de-politicized, elevated taste and the socially necessary postrevolutionary calm and distance from worldly participation that fit newly literary literature. Open access to literary texts renders them no longer only cooperative participants in elite schooled composition and moral development. They become available sources of support for a commercial realm of literary appreciation, and thus of emotional instruction.

As Samuel Johnson's preface to his 1765 edition of *Shakespeare* describes it, historical works that have been judged to have "pleased many and pleased long" set literary standards (7.61). This new emotional criterion puts a reader into the position of a judge whose soon to be interiorized taste interacts with extant texts to elevate or to demean both taste and texts. Slowly increasing literacy and the publications that respond to it hereby join in the cultural phenomenon that Ross calls "commercial humanism" (406). That is, new channels for print dissemination shape their object, who is not the Learned Reader but a newly literate "common reader." This reader may be independently schooled, not only trained by secretarial and conduct books that avoid essentialist moral instruction, as both Locke's 1706 *Of the Conduct of the Understanding* and Jean-Jacques Rousseau's *Emile* demonstrate.[7]

On good evidence, Ross thus asserts that the often privileged aesthetic realms of modern high culture, including literary literature, in fact result from naturalizing a new and separate category of texts into middle-class society, precisely on the basis of making that category a freely available and relatively inexpensive commodity. Despite his inference that commodified texts enforce the cultural privilege of an aesthetic value, that privilege is no longer shared among a Learned Elite and their originals in the noble aristocracies of church and state. Thus, by the time of the mid- to late eighteenth century, treatises like Hume's "Of the Standard of Taste" (1757) and Blair's *Lectures on Rhetoric and Belles Lettres* (1783) are hereby enabled to create the "human nature" that vexes logic ever after. This traditional construction is simultaneously essential in universal human biology, as it was from Mesopotamian medicine onward, and discretely placed in Anglo-European republican individuals who perceive and cultivate Enlightenment universals. For these theorists, human nature joins preference, emotion, and trust in disseminated texts, not in trusted "frendes" like Richard Tottel's, to be named as either insiders or outsiders among those who can read.

In this modified version of Ross's argument, earlier metadiscourses that supplied directions and models for composing letters, legal documents, and contracts from templates needed long after their medieval chancery uses also stimulate myriad home canons of poetry. Across classes (and thus not only in records of formal schooling), patrons' collections of manuscripts and print anthologies like Tottel's join published objects of literary approval. These canons collect examples no longer circulated primarily to illustrate styles for imitation, although enormous numbers of domestic compositions trace the ideal of the Renaissance gentleman's verse. However, this new and copious access to literary literature is also perceived to be dangerously feminized. For instance, James Greenwood's 1717 *The Virgin Muse* exemplifies this feminization, a gradual domestication of a literary/moral realm. It directs readers' appropriate responses to its canon, which Greenwood selects from pieces that had had immediate currency among elevated classes. Thus, it means to constitute a domestic culture that distributes class and gender identities beyond their customarily ranked applications. Such commodified literature obviously distributes an aesthetic of human emotion aimed directly at readers who have "no practical use for it" outside nascent social motives to create an aestheticized self. As cultural critic Ian Hunter also points out about effects of literary literature's commonplace narratives, these aestheticized selves problematize ordinary experience and, following that special middle-class instruction, "conduct themselves as subjects of a superior mode of being" ("Aesthetics" 358).[8]

Of course, marginal readers at the time include "woman," especially a newly abstract "Mother," a cultural identity that Friedrich A. Kittler's *Discourse Networks: 1800/1900* identifies as the voice of this newly aestheticized home-place in which the practical and the superior join in a new imaginary emotional space. Fear of relocating learned discourses in the realms of females of any sort is common, as Samuel Johnson exemplifies in a statement to James Boswell that in his self-education before and after attending Oxford, he had read only "manly" literature (Boswell 1:57, qtd. in Ross 405). Yet this anxiety is ambivalent: Edmund Burke, Johnson's friend and member of his Literary Club, honors feminized politics. In *Reflections on the French Revolution* (1790), Burke insists that "public sentiments, combined with manners, are required . . . as supplements, . . . as correctives, . . . as aids to law" (74, qtd. in Eagleton, *Ideology* 59). As he continues, "To make us love our country, our country ought to be lovely." Burke earlier preferred the sublime to the lovely, at least in his contribution to many other midcentury statements about human taste, *A Philosophical Inquiry into the Origin of Our Ideas of the Sublime and the Beautiful* (1757). But here he asserts that a newly articulated legal realm requires an emotional identity infused into its procedures, a feminine tenor, not another assignment of courage, virtue, and nobility to "manly" literature.

Clearly, oratorical theory finds ways through this historic realignment of spheres of influence. It is visible in simultaneous but not always parallel shifts in relations of production *and* reception. This new ambience is educational, as Kittler sees it, a manifestation of newly mediated systems of vernacular speech *and* writing. David Wellbery characterizes Kittler's views as "post-hermeneutic" because they emphasize determinate material conditions that end the international, pre-Romantic Republic of Scholars, Kittler's name for the failing Learned Readers of Ross's account. Wellbery's summary is worth considering:

> We are dealing here with the system of learning that developed . . . in the wake of printing, a system in which knowledge was defined in terms of authority and erudition, in which the doctrine of rhetoric governed discursive production, in which patterns of communication followed the lines of social stratification, in which books circulated in a process of limitless citation, variation, and translation, in which . . . the learned constituted a special (often itinerant) class with unique privileges, and in which the concept of literature embraced virtually all of what was written. The breakdown of this system occurred gradually, beginning with Descartes' rejection of erudition and rhetoric and his simultaneous grounding of the truth of discourse in the inwardness of the ego in the Discourse on Method; and it extended across the first three-quarters of the eighteenth century that are generally referred to as the Enlightenment. (xviii)

This history describes a movement from Desiderius Erasmus to Samuel Johnson. This seventy-five-year span encompasses an international presumption that shared elite education in doctrinal rhetorics controls discourse production, the advent of significant printing, social and political standing and various forms of patronage that provide privileges for secular authority and erudition, the circulation of books and manuscripts along its lines of social stratification—and the gradual but definitive attenuation of these relatively isolated activities by the Cartesian "grounding of the truth of discourse in the inwardness of the ego." In this time as well, the spread of new technologies, not their invention, expresses secular republican culture. Notably, the "truth of discourse" moves inward, from its schooled testing against Divine Muses by Lollianus (see chapter 1) to a new human interiority. But after that latter identity's authority also fades, as science and Mind turn out to be severely limited resources for solving emotionally motivated global problems that have earlier also been classified as deadly sins, Wellberry's summary finds contemporary applicability.

That is, both theorists imply that conditions for trust, if any remain, create nineteenth-century and later separations of style from the messages that privilege style. Of course, the problematics of stylization, seemingly taken on straightforwardly by various eighteenth-century treatments of taste (see below) rarely appear precisely as the major point of those treatises. Nonetheless, the pedagogic conditions around post-Learned credibility for these eighteenth-century academic theorists include the different circumstances of reception that will dominate after formerly inscribed, recited, acted, and print texts additionally become "publications" in any medium.

This view that a realm of publication materializes a *pedagogic* shift may be counterintuitive, but publication obviously changes standards for successful articulation that will be codified and taught. As Michael Douglas Heumann stresses in "The Ghost in the Machine: Sound and Technology in Twentieth-Century Literature," the material conditions of textual reception come to include Kittler's "sweeping changes in the fields of education, grammar, and spelling which standardized how words were written, how they were spoken, and the values to which they were ascribed" (39–40). This realm makes it necessary to establish standard language systems like the "official" English that was the primary goal of Johnson's 1755 *Dictionary* (below). New language standards, systematic vernacular grammars, and standardized orthography together create an opportunity to determine a text's membership in the emerging category of "published" writing and thus to know whether its writer is standardized by publishing. That is, attitudes toward nonstandard dialects, "'minor languages,' newly possible spelling errors, animal sounds, marked accents and dialects, and other sounds, marks, or gestures that do not conform to prescribed rules" (Heumann 39–40) become diffused exclusionary practices that follow the privileging and slow standardization of London English. In addition, the sequestered nurturing continental Mother who teaches early language lessons and enforces shifts in schooled attention from Latin to, for instance, standardized German at least partially undermines the "spirit" or feminized Romantic ideal of poetry (Heumann 44). This pedagogue embodies textuality, representing "the institutionalization of authorship, the emergence of a pragmatics of universal poetic address, the monopoly of writing as a medium for the storage and transfer of kinaesthetic data" (Hartmann). These outcomes of combined Romantic philosophies and economically driven publication would logically recognize "thought" as always mediated, not as pure statements but "scripts" (Hartmann).

Together, these propositions portray the end of a Republic of Scholars and a significant attenuation of metadiscursive infrastructures whose logos or "thought" is no longer perceptible primarily *as* "thought" but as *media*. Persuasive intellectual coherence becomes a product of novel standardized language made *visible* in its spelling and orthography. Thus, persuasion is readily taken to be a function of human style, a result of neither reason nor good reasons, when both ancient character and material texts are twice removed from their composition and represented instead as functions of individual (authorial) development. In still later support of individual growth toward self-realization, that style, a "personality," garners trust. It displays its secular pilgrimage toward a salvation of fulfillment. But this style does not accept that its result in "person-ality" is precisely that, an example of historically successful self-representations within conglomerate situated interests and community values. DeQuincey's nineteenth-century precept follows logically from that space: style "has an absolute value . . . , quite distinct from the value of the subject about which it is employed, and irrelatively to the subject" (260).

Rhetorical Rhetoric and Literary Truth

Samuel Butler's *Hudibras* (1663) characterizes lessons in rhetoric as rules that teach nothing but tools. This anti-Protestant satire in some measure supports my earlier claim that theorized explanations of rhetoric are thin on the ground before the twentieth century. But readers of eighteenth-century moral philosophy, written in the form of lectures to be read aloud and later followed by many successful rhetoric textbooks, introduce a rhetorical theory that unfolds psychological consciousness in post-Cartesian guides to socialized preferences and more. Ross's "commodity humanism" thus identifies many of the prominent tensions in treatises by Hume, Campbell, Blair, and others who unfold and polish a human interior a century after it is discovered as another, at least partially autonomous, self-creation. Scottish moral philosophy pragmatically values the faith in tasteful lives that consciousness performs, for its simultaneous solidification of Scottish identity and entrée to British identity. But consciousness also promotes detachment from worldly concerns. Thus, with the exception of Whately's ties to organized religion, especially after he is named Anglican Archbishop of Dublin in 1831, these philosophers and their peers theorize emerging secular capitalism. Writing in innocence of modern disciplinary categories, they organize interacting cultural subsystems on a new model of secular pedagogies that convey religion, nationalism, the standards and international scholarship of the overthrown Scholarly Republic, devotion to establishing a regularized English language, and a recently published literary canon—all in the name of a new writerly character whose nobility rests on discernment.

However, each of these subsystems carries into traditional metadiscursive theory at least a limb of the Trojan horse of interpretation. As these philosophers tacitly acknowledge circumstances in which their pedagogy might privilege the consumption of published print discourse over performances of language—the living reader's needs and desires over a dead orator's skillful texts—they suggest that timely *kairos* itself diminishes. The rhetorical "moment" has passed, unless it represents an exigency of analysis or judgment of a ritual performance as more or less fulfilling. Simply by acknowledging readers, metadiscourses introduce lessons about how their performances will be read against an abstract standard of quality. Paradoxically, that standard, described as a matter of universal taste, imagines readers to be individuals, not members of communities.

With others, both Hume's essay "Of the Standard of Taste" and Blair's later uses of Hume's foundation make this move. They subtly detach composition from its situated motives to endow *any* composition with qualities that evoke interpretation. Hume's 1757 essay specifically fits taste to an appropriately tuned emotional disposition: "The sentiments of men often differ with regard to beauty and deformity of all kinds, even while their general discourse is the same.... Those who found morality on sentiment, more than on reason, are inclined to comprehend ethics under the former observation [that when terms are defined, "critics" will share the same judgments]" (par. 2).

But more than adjudicated terminology fosters agreement among critics. Hume additionally emphasizes the importance of accurately judgmental *feelings* and their proper content:

> The difference, it is said, is very wide between judgment and sentiment. *All sentiment is right; because sentiment is a reference to nothing beyond itself, and is always real,* wherever a man is conscious of it. But all determinations of the understanding [judgments] are not right; because they have a reference to something beyond themselves, to wit, real matter of fact; and are not always conformable to that standard. Among a thousand different opinions . . . there is . . . but one, that is just and true; and the only difficulty is to fix and ascertain it. *On the contrary, a thousand different sentiments, excited by the same object, are all right: Because no sentiment represents what is really in the object. It only marks a certain conformity or relation between the object and the organs or faculties of the mind.* ("Standard" par. 7, emphasis added)

But Hume's argument, which might be taken to exclude feelings from inconsequential decision-making, instantly unsettles connections among sentiment, objects of judgment, and organs of the mind—an easily accomplished feat in light of his added insistence that there are "good" critics and "bad" ones whose sentiments are not to be trusted. Yet his solution to possible losses of absolute values is, perhaps surprisingly, to value emotional responses over the rationalizing that had subsumed feelings since Plato, Seneca, Chrysippus, and Plutarch.[9] That is, he is bent on *practicing* desire, not on demeaning it: "Nothing tends further to encrease and improve this talent [delicate taste in wit or beauty], than *practice* in a particular art, and the frequent survey or contemplation of a particular species of beauty" ("Standard" par. 18, emphasis added). A newly interiorized agenda for guided reading and interpretation of words, works, and worlds is hereby drawn.

It is also significant that Hume compares the situation of an orator to that of "a critic of a different age or nation" (par. 20). An orator "addresses . . . a particular audience, and must have a regard for their particular genius, interest, opinions, passions, and prejudices" (par. 21). But the critic who succeeds the orator "must have all those circumstances in his eye, and must place himself in the same situation as the audience, to form a true judgment of the oration" (par. 21). Hume quickly instructs those critics in the elements of argument—"They must produce the best arguments, that their invention suggests . . . they must acknowledge a true and decisive standard to exist somewhere, to wit, real existence and matter of fact" (par. 25). Hume's critics are thus to produce discourse derived from delicacy of taste, which elevates them "by the soundness of their understanding and the superiority of their faculties," not by "persuasive successes of their critical opinions" (par. 25).

Blair opens his *Lectures on Rhetoric and Belles Lettres* with copious praise for excellence in speaking *and* writing. He adds that the always central study of composition "has acquired additional importance from the taste and manners of the present age" (par. 4–5).[10] For Blair, this is to say that writing and reading improve through identical instruction, a view held by many ever since: "Rhetoric is not so much a practical art as a speculative science, and the same instructions which assist others in composing will assist them in discerning, and relishing, the beauties of composition." But the virtues of criticism depend on knowledge nuanced a bit differently than Socrates' "know thyself." Blair says, "Such disquisitions are very intimately connected with *the knowledge of ourselves*. They necessarily lead us to reflect on the *operations of the imagination*, and the movements of the heart; and increase our acquaintance with some of *the most refined feelings which belong to our frame*" (par. 13, emphasis added). Thus, twenty-six years later, Blair appears to move Hume's emphasis on the critic's place in history to a still more deeply interiorized manifesto in which criticism is linked to reflection, imagination, and the heart, but not so emphatically to matters of fact. He further announces that "refined feelings" are a project for moral philosophy.

Blair's opening also separates orators from readers: those who "may have the view of being employed in composition, or in public speaking" and "others [who] may wish only to improve their taste with respect to writing and discourse, and to acquire principles which will enable them to judge for themselves in that part of literature called the *Belles Lettres*" (par.14). Unlike Hume's belief that comparisons among works teach discernment, Blair forecasts that improvement of taste will result from a canonical and specifically English literature. This course of study will extend early modern and earlier exercises in *narratio* and the schemes, tropes, and figures into skillful reading and contemporary creative writing projects that make up the culture of the middle class, whom Ross believes such activities also create.

By identifying as part of his audience those who may want to undertake composition *and* oratory, Blair suggests that belles lettres is a subspecies of the inclusively defined "literature," which had included oratory. His work is on a cusp that Ross describes, a moment at which guidance for reading crowds out both oratorical and writing instruction (406). In postrevolutionary societies, reading and taste mark "nationalism" as a country for readers. As such, it is governed by participatory observations, not by participatory writing by readers of politics. Productive oratory is thus gradually separated from increasingly aestheticized composition, as it was not for Cicero, who in *De Oratore* names poets *and* orators as creators of civil society.[11]

Campbell's *Philosophy of Rhetoric*, published the year of Hume's death in 1776, also links oratorical power to emotion. With Aristotle, it directs orators to evoke or to calm feelings to further a specific purpose, if with a different spin: "These [the pathetic and the argumentative] incorporated together . . . constitute that *vehemence of contention*, to which the greatest exploits of eloquence [should be] ascribed" (4, emphasis added). That is, this subtly "new" rhetoric frames "vehemence" and "greatest exploits" in a history Aristotle rarely told and did not characterize in these ways, even in the *Poetics*. This approach also takes up "Consciousness," which Campbell identifies as a man's Cartesian "assurance that he hath of . . . existence" (37). Book I of this different *Philosophy* calls sources of moral and intellectual evidence "sense and memory," defining *sense* as external and internal "original inlets of perception" (47). Yet despite introducing sensibility issues, as classical oratory would not, Campbell is emphatically writing rhetoric. He characterizes it as diminishing the "civic scope" of its origins in favor of a re-theorized guide to origins in the mind. He also takes up "intuitive evidence" (35) *before* he addresses traditionally honored deduction. Thus, Campbell recalls the oracular and religious access of ancient prophets and diviners to secret knowledge. For instance, he claims that a synonym for intuition may be "instinct," which is "not other than *the oracles of eternal wisdom* . . . axioms . . . essential to moral reasoning" (42, emphasis added). And moral reasoning—an interior process of correct interpretation, not a community deliberation—is "the proper province of rhetoric" (43).

Campbell hereby helps create the simultaneously natural and nationalist horizon of a Lockean hermeneutic understanding. Instead of separating Sir Francis Bacon's human faculties, he connects the "Imagination" (elsewhere "Fancy") to the purpose of pleasing and its object, or form: Beauty. As Carol Poster points out in "Being, Time, and Definition: Toward a Semiotics of Figural Rhetoric," Campbell hereby obliquely forecasts modern interest in the relation of figural language to thought, a linguistic manifestation of an unseen assumption (122–23, 130). He treats schemes and tropes not as the classical ornaments later criticized as bombastic, nor as the vernacular system early modern handbooks construct. Here, they stand in for feeling and thus are "natural" processes of language. Poster also notes that Campbell, like Joseph Priestley, looks to the past, following Quintilian and Donatus "insofar as figures are treated as part of a general theory of deviation from ordinary language" (123). But Campbell extends his treatment to the psychological impact of figures that the *Ad Herennium* describes. (Priestley, who Poster says "dwells upon the affective component of figures of thought," also undertakes "extensive psychological inquiries into how specific figures attain their effects" [123].) Both Campbell's *Philosophy* and Priestley's *Course of Lectures on Oratory and Criticism* (1777) treat figuration in ways that demonstrate "growing interest in the affective, belletristic, psychological, and argumentative aspects of rhetoric" (Poster, "Being" 123).

Ross takes up this turn to the affective dimension of rhetoric as a direct result of an imported aesthetics: "Eighteenth-century British aesthetics answered the undecidability of intellect and sensibility, or text and affect, with the theories of taste, judgment, imagination and *je ne sais quoi*" (407). Yet moral philosophy worries over that undecidability a bit differently, promoting it to the status of a cultural given. For instance, Campbell's *Philosophy* flirts with the possibility that commonsense perceptions and inferences may not remain in touch with ultimate Truth (51). This possibility suggests we should formalize the human interior whose Baconian and Cartesian parts—reason, imagination, will—may be put in contest with each other, as they were in antiquity. Whately's later *Elements of Rhetoric* calls such appeals within one individual focal points of self-persuasion. He explicitly hopes that ongoing interior argumentation will stimulate *emotions*—not principles—of which "reason will approve," in the interest of "informing faith with rational *and* intuitive processes" (183, qtd. in Nienkamp 73–74).

Thus, insofar as Whately and his predecessors search for a conventional emotional subjectivity to take them through such topics as the justification of religious choices, they raise at least a possibility of erroneous judgments and dire consequences for those making them, as Hume also does in closing "Of the Standard of Taste." Through the early and mid-eighteenth century, a major result of rhetorical instruction is to shore up the legitimacy of decisions made by individuals, yet still to withhold absolute authority from a translucent, self-involved interior.

Christiana Lupton summarizes the effect of this differently theorized personal rhetoric, pointing to its uncertain histories in her applications of Hume's "Standard" to the narratives of sensibility that constitute Laurence Sterne's *Tristram Shandy*:

> Even as the sociability of [fiction] soothes down and compensates for many forms of empirical doubt, it also produces a new object—*the reality of fiction*—that remains *subject to all the problems of experience. The concrete nature of words continues to generate the problem of subjective response which Hume has contained by . . . subsuming language under the aegis of socially defined tastes and passions and by suggesting a settled relation between a preexisting republic of readers and their objects of taste.* While Hume's emphasis on rhetorical presentation works as the answer to his own skeptical doubts, effecting this resolution within a space that we recognize as "philosophy," Sterne's emphasis on the figurative and interpretive freedoms that come with language aggravates these problems dialectically, *albeit in a movement which will be institutionalized as a playful mode called "literature."* (110, emphasis added)

The illogic of universal standards capable of adjudication by individual taste is irresolvable once it is centered in language, as Lupton says of Hume's tacit turn to a philosophical resolution. This difficulty is further complicated in light of the shift across the century from imitations of the oratorical vehemence of classical oratory to adopting the calm, Addisonian prose style suitable to "a republic of readers and their objects of taste." For example, Hume's support of the early century's Horatian and Ciceronian volubility turns in just this way. He first associates neoclassical eloquence with liberty and speaking out, making fun of Oliver Cromwell's "homely" style as "tedious, obscure, and embarrassed" (*History* 6.57, qtd. in Potkay 41). Adam Potkay explains that later, in his *Of Eloquence* (1742), Hume favors the temperate, polite style that midcentury politics associates with evolved aristocracy. With

Campbell, who criticizes "fantastic ornaments" in the *Philosophy*, he then favors "prose examples, neither from living authors, nor those who wrote before the Revolution" (150). Across that brief time, mannerly, quasi-aristocratic calm precisely expresses Enlightenment: "It ought to be observed," Campbell also says, "that the less enlightened a nation is, their language will of necessity the more abound in tropes" (299). Hume also claims that outside this same period, language has been and will be "too rhetorical." In his narrative of civilized language, he links the figurative language he had praised before to lower classes, primitives, and the unevolved. Foreshadowing Edmund Burke's later approval of feminized discourse, he assigns control of conversation, if not of the state, to the "Fair Sex." Hume argues what few would oppose—that men should not expose women to classical figuration, which is "too priapic . . . too 'swelling, monstrous, and gigantic'—to be admitted" ("Standard" 49).

For Hume and Blair, figuration is a function of the consciousness that attends Associationism. Campbell obviously agrees, calling figuration an argument that trusts mental links, not only a way to illustrate sentiment. Its devices, especially metaphor, "are also arguments from analogy in support of it" (*Philosophy* 294). A cooperative parallel between figural language and human feeling defines language as itself an argument that supports sentiment. In this conversation, figuration is not the stylistic domain among four other oratorical domains but the movement language embodies as it leaves one sort of community for another. It is too simple to say that Hume's view is communal while Blair's transfers the stakes in shared conventional language to the cultivated perspicuity of individuals; linguistic conventions may become equivalent to a gaze of disapprobation in some contexts, as elocutionary rhetoric demonstrates. Instead, at least at this stage of its articulation, consciousness re-informs community standards. Two overlapped communities emerge in commonplaces and discursive habits that signal shared education and experiential knowledge. But that knowledge is now to be interpreted through emotional conventions whose source is in the consciousness of those we trust, not the inherited voices of noble ancient characters. Thus, both versions of community test a message against its messenger's charisma, but their historical joining adds perception as an access to trustworthiness.

Of course, imitation of the ancients, the supposed source of the early century's energetic ornamentation of poetic and civil argument, is not uncomplicated. If Aristotle bears witness, the ancients were aware of the difference between the formal sequence of oratorical rhetoric's domains and the actual recursive simultaneity of their uses. That is, eighteenth-century concerns about figuration have much to do with the shifting politics of oratory, which, as Potkay points out, connects attitudes toward figuration to eighteenth-century standardizing of both written and spoken English, to colonizations of language pedagogies outside England,[12] and to new English republicanism, the civil result of unruly democracy. His fine-grained analysis of oratory's varying standing during British and American revolutions rejects the commonplace in rhetoric studies that revolutionary societies require rousing political oratory as later republican stability does not. For instance, Adam Smith sardonically derides the high style of the third Earl of Shaftesbury because it is divorced from common language, the easily recognized way of saying things among polite and by definition restrained members of a new upper-middle class. Historian J. G. A. Pocock calls this style a new norm between the ancients and democratically inclined rabble, an "ideology of manners." It fits an increasingly "transactional universe" that he says rejects classical warrior-farmer expectations in favor of the tasteful mildness that becomes another version of what everyone knows. At the end of this process, republican contractual and then bureaucratic governance mediate restraints that published textuality supports (48–49).

But the devaluation of eloquence is not entirely transactional, at least insofar as it affects both civic and personal expressions of feeling. Burke stresses the need for public *sentiments* that he immediately assigns to a feminized spirit. Female gender emerges in this era encrusted with the finer feelings rarely attributed to it by, for instance, Geoffrey Chaucer or Shakespeare, whose women are like Aristotle's: "weak" but not necessarily soft. Earlier sexual definitions of females involved promiscuity, the rank of their sexual partners, and motherhood (or its absence in Elizabeth I). But the feminization and isolation of the "passion" that once marked masculine public oratory gradually domesticates the emotional displays expected of women, in Burke's view as a patriotic project. And whatever their content or energy, expressions of feeling become the "tone" of limited, nurturing domestic space, making it not only socially and economically separate but also discursively removed from its freshly characterized, publicly "reasoned" opposite. For instance, the education in desire provided by novels instills in females this nuanced gender, then informs it with histrionics that polite men do not use publicly. Over time, oratorical figuration is mistrusted. Those who express it are monitored for relative inappropriate manliness elsewhere.

That process also definitively ranks emotion according to class. The "new kind of woman" that Nancy Armstrong's theory of eighteenth-century fiction describes is valued not for socio-sexual status but for "the more subtle nuances of behavior" (4). Written by Addisonian nicety, middle-class women might be said to result from the demise of passionate rhetorical eloquence. Armstrong claims that eighteenth-century male heroes "clearly declared themselves anomalous when they inverted the model and, as males, experienced life as a sequence of events that elicited sentimental responses" (4). But male expressions of sentimental response result as well from this later formation in gendered psychologies for male and female, "men" and "women," characters. Ultimately, norms of public discourse place authenticity, or its display as early modern "sincerity," in the ethically persuasive values of speakers who thoughtfully inspect their feelings about policy and appear to act on them.

The word "expressive" is implicated in none of these possibilities, neither as the nature of figures nor of emotions distributed according to gender in unofficial but constitutive domesticity. Expression is obviously involved in the pressing out of breath that elocutionary rhetorics take literally to heart in hands-to-chest gestures. But it otherwise awaits application by a more autonomous subject whose confidence in the social effects of any language register has lessened. That is, the feelings this moral philosophy portrays emanate from a still socialized interior whose consciousness recharacterizes this paideia. Self-practices that cultivate interiority do not yet replace earlier ways of defining human nature within shared community identities but remain in tension with them.[13] Thus, a socially certified education in refined middle-class emotion retains familiar, if recent, tropes: the self-interest attended to by new economic contracts and Locke's philosophical view of property rights and ownership, the religious fervor of individuals and congregations unmoored from a centralized iconography in a sea of sects, and the insight attributed to frequent, often self-declared, romantic originals.

Even without detailed examples of how each of these and other feelings are written on religions, bureaucracies, and other institutions, it is clear that literate classes are cultural sites of differentially organized assignments of feeling. These characterizations appear to disperse to individuals the emotions of stock personalities. But in the name of taste, they also create a lesser life script: "eccentric." Of course, recently constructed republican citizens learn perforce of this subtext in seemingly only procedural, bureaucratic, and constitutionally appropriate public encounters, as they do from interactions in the new social imaginary of private domestic scripts. The potential for desire to introduce diversity—wishes beyond a pale—is mooted by these shared lessons. They teach that there are secreted social meanings that individuals must unpack through their own always self-scrutinized hermeneutic understanding, not through access to hidden knowledge of orator, poet, prophet, or even physician. In sum, by insisting that this pervasive new pedagogy only perceives the essences of various social types, these lessons not only differentiate capacities for desire and their results but also assure that difference will register as opposition to a norm.

In this view, it is particularly unfortunate to treat eighteenth-century rhetorical treatises as offshoots of one classical rhetoric, as works that unevenly enact or fail to meet criteria set by a privileged totality. These treatises do not take up various emphases within that whole. They differently accomplish precisely the pedagogic shifts that cultural exigencies demand of metadiscourses, here the cultural project of realigning in support of secular capitalism the relations among desire, sanctioned discursive purposes, and subject formation. They thereby provide templates for modernist selves who learn conventional affective responses through certified literary canons that result from publishers' projects but become devices for winnowing and sifting more than taste when they become curricula. In the name of individualism, they challenge all but expected feelings. Personal independence, individual responsibility, reputed credibility, Locke's literal version of self-possession, and the visible results of discernment all constitute assumptions about character that rewrite single readers as cultural interlocutors.

Lupton's view of the interplay of fiction and philosophy restates this sketch of how trust is relocated in eighteenth-century metadiscourses. It occupies a precisely conscious interpretation, which privileges readers and empirical sensationalism. Her analysis suggests how unlikely it is that pedagogic unity or continuity attaches to any but the most formalist qualities of the oratorical template. Its domains, appeals, discourse types, parts and arrangement in argumentation, and stylistic devices all remain vehicles that transport a new cultural tenor. That new consciousness of individual taste, ultimately equated with many forms of "personal opinion" unhampered by evidence, sustains Butler's seventeenth-century dismissal of rules and tools, but not these formal parts of speeches.

The Communicative Essence of Language: Pure British Tongues

These inferences about eighteenth-century moral philosophy might all be falsified by a reminder that traditional histories of rhetoric accurately identify elocution as its most popular teaching in the mid- to late eighteenth century. But that preference alternatively gives great credibility to formalist analyses of the parts of discourse across this time—from mind to mouth, invention to delivery. Canonical histories note that English elocutionary lessons remain devoted to public speaking, yet do not take up the cross-continental linguistic issues that help explain their cultural impact as more than practical ways to elevate one's class or to monitor the relative status and thus the power of others. Nonetheless, elocution reconstitutes oratory's persuasive characters in unpredictable movements across its appeals and realizes moral philosophy's emphasis on meeting interpretative responsibilities to increasingly aesthetic/literary forms of reality that consciousness itself creates.

This history invites re-theorization of the coincidence of British elocution-ary rhetoric's eighteenth-century heyday and the continental enculturation of Romanticism through a silenced Mother's control of the child's mouth. For instance, in *Gramophone, Film, Typewriter*, Kittler again joins these signifi-cant moments. Just as the Republic of Scholars fades, the emergent discourse network of 1800 juxtaposes the education of children by a speaking mother against publicly approved methods of language education and emerging hermeneutic literary criticism (Winthrop-Young and Wutz xxxv). Those topics are explicit in the early-nineteenth-century "expression" movement founded by S. S. Curry. Julia Walker's *Expressionism and Modernism in the American Theatre: Bodies, Voices, Words* sees this attempt to overlay the body on the voice, acting onto oratory, as "based upon a moral-philosophical un-derstanding of human character and a Romantic belief in mystical sources of inspiration." But it also was "at once feminized within the cultural imaginary and deemed unworthy of serious scholarly attention, . . . despite its legacy in New Critical formalism and methods of oral interpretation" (6). Nonetheless, these highlighted pedagogic emphases offer a theoretical opportunity—to imagine British metadiscourses with others at this time as differing markedly from their own past and from modern and contemporary philosophy.[14] This is to say that elocutionary pedagogies that train both voice and body may absorb normal anxieties about both vocalization and identity that blend in the mouth. That physical space literally enables the expression absent from moral philosophies. Its expulsion of breath joins Romantic inspiration, a not entirely separate intake of air.

However, the harmony produced by the mouths of Mother and elocution-ist goes unnoticed in light of other common opinions, summarized by J. E. Congleton's 1954 comment that "when a school of rhetoricians who are greatly interested in the effectiveness of expression is dominant, one copies, refines, and *weakens another in succession until some such art . . . may spring tangent-like from the main tradition*" (144, emphasis added). Even apart from ques-tions about a "main tradition," common slurs like Congleton's on elocution's new energies in the mid- to late eighteenth century assert that its revived prominence is equivalent to inattention to the philosophical end of rhetorical domains, invention. Some may still avoid the topic in well-grounded appre-hension about the lowered standing attached to supposedly remedial speech courses. But the feminization Walker notes reduces any of its lessons to a marginal curriculum for class elevation and evaluation. Motives for Scot-tish attention to taste, moral philosophy, and elocution supply the humor of Boswell's famous knowledge of Johnson's prejudice against the Scots: "Mr. Johnson, [said I] I do indeed come from Scotland, but I cannot help it" (1.277).[15] All are emblems of obviously successful investments of language with more than nationalist fervor: an often overlooked yet decisively poetic, aestheticized literary purpose. But neither extension of chauvinism loses the ineffable processes of rhetorical composition.

No one denies that a powerful voice and strenuously enacted speech were emphasized throughout oratorical traditions that, despite electricity, extend into our new media situations. But this earlier elocutionary revival is characterized as a rejection of "ideas" and "thought" on the model of unified singular rhetoric. Nonetheless, as I have noted, ancient oratorical rhetoric was itself less likely than its formalist descendants to miss the recursive interdependence of the five domains. Demosthenes' concern for delivery ("delivery, delivery") involved both the trained oratorical voice and its result in energetic expressions of meaning on the model of successful acting. Adele C. Scafuro's *Forensic Stage* stresses that ancient speechwriters emphasized self-presentation through the voice, their represented character, more than they worried about "niceties" of law and legal systems. Juries would thereby recognize them as members of the local community, if not necessarily of their own local community. Again, she points out that *"the (original) orations were, in a very real sense, performance texts,* punctuated with entrances and exits, marked for the display of laws and contracts, witnesses and suppliants, and not infrequently, the speaker's own theatrical gesture" (57, emphasis added).[16] Thus, we might note as well that Aristotle's disappointment about the need for emotional appeals and the stylizations that conform speakers to what "everyone knows" (*Rhetoric*, Book III) does not preclude making visible the privileged moral characters of Book II, who display expected conventional emotion. Cicero in fact equates delivery with the "composition" now praised as thought and character. *De Oratore* claims that "the better the orator, the more profoundly is he frightened of the difficulty of speaking" (I.26): "The man who can do nothing in composition and delivery that is worthy of the occasion . . . seems to me to be without shame" (I.26). In *Brutus* (278), he suggests that the *manner* of making a case is in fact entirely identical to its speaker's feelings: "If, Marcus Callidius, you were not making that up, would you bring your case forward like this? . . . Where is that grief, where is that burning indignation, which stirs even men quite incapable of eloquence to loud outbursts of complaint? . . . *You did not even stamp your feet*" (qtd. in Wisse 264). Wisse's *Ethos and Pathos* also points out that Quintilian's *Institutes* appears to have had no difficulty with such associations of gestures to represented (rather than the later "real") selves. He references appropriate delivery to a speaker's ability "to adapt his action to every variant of complexion in which he utters" (2.12.9). G. H. Bantock's "Educating the Emotions: An Historical Perspective" extends such honors for delivery from ancient canons to Erasmus, for whom "'style' . . . was no supernumerary additional element for the delectation of idle minds, but absolutely central to the effectiveness of what was being maintained" (123). Erasmus himself supports Cicero's attention to delivery as an interchange between gesture and stylized language:

> Who could possibly regret an enthusiasm for this subject [*copia*] after observing that Cicero . . . was so dedicated to this kind of exercise that he used to vie with his friend, the actor, Roscius, to see whether Roscius could express the same material more often using different gestures, or Cicero himself applying the resources of eloquence and using different language? (qtd. in Bantock 124)

Bantock interprets this linking of language to gesture as "language challenging bodily movement" (125). This confrontation, he says, "alerts [us] to an historical fact—the important role played by bodily training and refinement of movement in the production of the renaissance *uomo universale*" (125). That is, extended ancient fashioning of selves embodies rank and aristocratic status in the historic continuity of elocutionary training in deportment, not its dismissal. Relative standing and physical training are at the core of attention to delivery, just as eighteenth-century elocution thrives in Lord Chesterfield's 1736–78 letters to his son Philip Stanhope. Chesterfield insists that he be "pleasing" in the highly nuanced uses of the body, which is also a standard topic in conduct manuals that write classed displays of emotion, and their masking, as equal to a character's actual status.[17]

Thus, by dismissing elocution as a disconnected, tangential embarrassment to eighteenth-century British rhetoric, we set aside our common and disciplinary knowledge that *sound* produces persuasion, not distinct words, which are received separately only when written and read. It is possible that in precisely this context, we mishear the ancient quarrel over whether orators can persuade without actually experiencing the feelings to be engendered in audiences. That is, modern readers treat the extensive Peripatetic debate about this issue as a matter of modern consciousness, in which feelings are hidden, or may be, in an inaccessible interiority that can be misrepresented in "acting," if not the later "acting out." This projection of post-Enlightenment psychology into a time long before this duality was an evocative emotional "problem" suggests that the ancient disagreement may as easily have assumed that whether to *display* genuine feeling—to stamp our feet—is at issue. As Cicero implies in his complaint to Marcus Callidius, outside intentions to deceive, we cannot avoid showing responses we feel.

One important loss that results from this trivializing attitude toward elocution is that it divorces many rhetoric histories from language scholarship. That research might explain elocution as a way to revive the materiality of *spoken* language that is, if paradoxically, encouraged by the increased dominance of print culture that is later folded into a credibility of publication. At the least, this logic suggests that more has been at stake in dismissing the enormously popular realization of eighteenth-century elocutionary teaching, and in ignoring its analogues to publicized domestic methods of training pronunciation, than has been noted. Beyond the questionable view that training the body and voice for expression can interfere with forming ideas, as though speech or thought may be zero-sum games, we might reexamine shifting cultural relations to spoken and written texts to note the inevitable effects of these shifts on perceptions of how spoken language distinctly achieves persuasion.

Reformed direct instruction in speaking standardized English takes part in a concurrent eighteenth-century move to normalize linguistic meanings and their spelled representations. Dictionaries that focus on etymology and/or pronunciation and treatises on language and its history tacitly enact a narrative of cultural development, but one that only verges on debating the relative advancement represented by either writing or nationally certified speech. These applied linguistic criteria for propriety eventually replace birth, rank, religious affiliations, and old school ties—paideia—as audible markers of shared belonging. The emergent literate middle-class recognizes itself, over time, in its diction, its stable accents, and the persuasive acuity of its class-marked emotional gestures.[18] Thus, this particular elocutionary moment manifests a potentially detached access to foundational views of character, of Truth reached through dialogue, and of other signs of stable, always already realized trust in discourse. In this case, discourse is trustworthy insofar as its readers—those speaking and those listening—accept as genuine the available surfaces of its *media* over its sources and content.

Philippa Spoel's "Rereading the Elocutionists" points out that almost all positive attention to elocution in the twentieth century occurs in America in the 1950s through the 1970s.[19] That span includes novel institutional adjustments in postsecondary education for newly admitted veterans and formerly excluded underprepared students. Institutions often perceived those students through prejudices similar to those against eighteenth-century Scots, among whom are authors of the responsive treatises that privilege interior qualities—perceptivity and consciousness. Thomas Sheridan, the notable Irish friend of Samuel Johnson and father of Richard Sheridan, the popular London actor, sets out to retrieve elocution for similar work within the limits of students' mental endowments and work ethic. In both historical settings, elocutionary rhetoric breaks down barriers to education by inculcating the skill of proper articulation, not public speech. It comes to attention when new populations encroach on traditionally elevated lessons and require the verbal signs of belonging to a new paideia.

However, the complaint about elocution within rhetoric studies focuses on its symbolic urging of a unified rhetoric to abandon invention in favor of what Wilbur Samuel Howell calls "declaiming a speech by rote, without regard to whether the thoughts uttered were trivial or false or dangerous" (713). Of course, this same charge might logically apply to a supposed mindlessness of editing texts for print consistency, a process that realizes Socrates' complaint in the *Phaedrus* that all writing can do is repeat itself. And the turn to textuality that elocution joins does include many new eighteenth-century editions of Shakespeare published between 1725 and 1785. Their editors praise and vilify each other, assist each other, plagiarize from each other, and generally form a collective authorship. This enclosed corrective discourse is undertaken by Alexander Pope (1725), Lewis Theobald (1726), Sir Thomas Hanmer (1743), William Warburton (1747), Samuel Johnson (1765), George Steevens (1773 and later), John Nicholas (1776), and Isaac Reed (1785). In addition, Johnson's edition of poems by fifty-two English poets was published in 1779, in fifty-eight volumes, including four volumes of prefaces that Johnson imagined as guides to reading. That purpose is opaque to our textual criticism, but these projects all involve producing texts for elocuted reading aloud within a stable textuality.

Thus, compiled dictionaries are better examples of texts that divorce meaning from a language that is still conceived of as a human production, not as a static physical object of interpretation. These compilations, given internal coherence only by their alphabetical ordering of words, gather linguistic, anthropological, and political interests in language. Yet they are lists without meaning that appear to "speak" only peripherally.[20] Were one eager to support Howell's complaint against elocution, its relation to dictionaries is perhaps the best evidence of a loss of interest in ideas.

These language-conscious interests share the purpose of re-theorizing and standardizing the vernacular, as I have said. Elocutionary rhetoric contributes to the first theoretical goal by exploring the implications of language in spoken sounds, not written words. This rhetoric realizes the identity between sounds and language systems to suggest that controlled articulation contains the identity of a moral agent of insight who is trusted for having access to shared perspicacity, the product of a shared disposition, not for predictably expressed emotional responses to community issues. In this view, to separate metadiscursive history from its literary realizations misses an important historical place-marker within metadiscourses: Mother Teacher's attention to forming the mouth to produce proper sounds *that fit words* imitates the elocutionary model, which reverses that priority by emphasizing that discrete words more or less fit communicative sounds.

The Turn to Words

The London/Edinburgh projects of lexicographer and editor Samuel Johnson and Thomas Sheridan join what we now see as separate literary and rhetorical attention to the growing eighteenth-century persuasiveness of linguistic surfaces. Sheridan theorizes that English language should be held to a standard of pronunciation that can stand the test of time, not only tests of inclusion or exclusion from London ranks. With others, both Sheridan and Johnson also want to erase the provincialism attributed to English, relative to classical languages and their Latinate continental vernaculars. Beyond their nationalism, both also want to preserve and elevate English literature and thought. Usually, however, these commonalities between them and their projects are ignored in the name of applying dual, and ranked, orality/literacy analyses to their work, thereby making these sometime friends only competitors who contest the privileges of one or the other medium. Nonetheless, their works—Johnson's standardizing historical *Dictionary* and Sheridan's *Course of Lectures on Elocution* (1762) and *General (Pronouncing) Dictionary of the English Language* (1780)—revise foundations of oratory and textuality.[21] Together they inadvertently point out that their era's texts are composed not to be delivered but to be *read*, and to be read at great distances from the authority, even the question, of origins. The written/print forms of words are not speech, that is, not elided sounds, so their boundaries make it possible if not necessary to perceive language as a discrete, quasi-autonomous player in singular and shared occasions for reading, which are quickly absorbed by the consciousness that midcentury and later treatises create.

Some characterize this historical moment in terms of its dedicated attention to spelling, assuming that orthography can be identical to speech, or that it cannot. Lexicographers additionally describe etymology, explaining accumulated changes in the forms of words and their dated uses, partially to justify eventually standard yet not homophonic English spellings. Of course, an ideal standardized spoken or spelled vernacular is impossible insofar as local dialects and historic sound changes will always occur. Therefore, the two supposedly competing camps, oral and literate, elocution and dictionary-making, differently address spelling as either homophonic or standardized for print, yet equally as access to a purified ideal (below). Spelling "correctly" becomes a way to recreate the new charisma of trusted language. But this correctness also attaches to purified pronunciation, in dictionary glosses establishing conventional guides to imitating sanctioned sounds. Of course, that dual project is not easily accomplished, as the 1747 *Plan* of Johnson's *Dictionary* acknowledges: "Many words written alike are differently pronounced" (*Works*, vol. 8). Spellings also affect both reading and writing, first as a way to represent spoken words, later as the only medium trusted to repeat them precisely to readers.

This topic's analyses involve other such fine distinctions. For instance, in modern media, Thomas Edison will explain his invention of the phonograph in the same terms, saying its recordings will easily have the advantage of print, since they *"preserve more than the mental emanations of the brain of the author*; and, as a bequest to future generations, they would be unequaled" (534, emphasis added). In "Early Talking Books: Spoken Recordings and Recitation Anthologies, 1880–1920," Jason Camlot argues that this late-nineteenth-century technology responds to a general observation that reading has become *too* divorced from sources. It is an antidote to a specific response to emerging cultures of publication:

> [It was a] Victorian yearning for a technology that would make the reading experience more immediate, [to] capture the character and subjectivity of an author without the mediation of the printed page. . . . [A] variety of practices . . . involve the manipulation or interpretation of written scripts or printed texts and identify . . . this desire to move beyond text toward an indexical trace of character. Interpretive techniques like graphology (the analysis of handwriting) looked at signatures for "selfhood epitomized." (148)[22]

This nineteenth-century desire to reanimate texts, something like a desire to reanimate the dead in séances, demonstrates how elocutionary rhetoric contributes to transforming the ways print culture can convey directly intended messages. "What is said" thus attracts a new media anxiety that "yearns" for the increasingly repressed oratorical character, as Marshall McLuhan and Jean Baudrillard do later.[23]

These diverging ideas about print and publication expose the stakes in the larger and obviously overdetermined historical certification of a credible vernacular English. That is, differences among abilities to ~~hear~~ (a silent) sound for the purpose of reading aloud, to write that same sound/silence, and ultimately to overlay a recorded voice on an absent, unknown, never-to-be encountered body all illuminate elocutionary rhetoric's attempts to situate the primacy of purified oratorical speech in a larger metadiscursive theory. But these processes also help explain the consequences of English language practices—for instance, anxiety about Scottish accents that Campbell and Whately circulate as concern about "correct" language. A Republic of Dictionaries is realized in the kitchen-table prescriptive uses of these print authorities, but such uses of homely guides also symbolize the end of the privileges of Kittler's Scholars.

Thomas P. Miller's *The Formation of College English: Rhetoric and Belles Lettres in the British Cultural Provinces* verifies the scope of these concerns. It counts "over four hundred editions of English grammars and some two hundred and fifteen editions of English dictionaries [that] were published in the eighteenth century, with five times more new dictionaries and grammars appearing after 1750 than had been published in the first half of the century" (1). Obviously, homeland conversations about origins, propriety, and orthography that occur just as travelers report imperial encounters with new Others contribute to a significant reconception of language. In this project, the classical paideia that taught letters, syllables, words, and spoken recitation is traced in language education in which letters must be sounded out for accurate reading *and* writing, for instance to deal with the *o* in "people." But the new paideia also includes reaching for pronouncing dictionaries like Sheridan's, which allow that word's spelling as "peepl." That is, if we make less of this historic turn to language than is warranted by its effective reduction of opportunities to theorize rhetoric as an always occasional, situated process, its histories may righteously avoid elocution and the educational practices it involves. We thus lose the import of John Walker's reminder in his *Elements of Elocution* that *grammar* is "the basis of rhetoric and oratory" (1:4, qtd. in Spoel 73), a view that ties rhetoric and oratory more closely to elocutionary pedagogies than to how we form sentences that constitute written texts. Lessons in gestures and demeanor that fit a text's meanings, not word-by-word but conceptually, also constitute an elocuted Standard English discourse. It transforms provincial accents into imitations of printed handbooks, pronouncing dictionaries, and the visual markings of sounds that fit specific texts. But it also teaches a metaphorically unaccented way of thinking and speaking as an insider.

These guides also put a consequential spin on the more favored spoken language that they equate with meanings. That is, the irony of meticulous visual guides depicting body, mouth, and expressions to standardize regional pronunciations is not primarily that they tacitly contradict claims by Sheridan and other elocutionists that speech is more "natural" than print. Nor is it that this approach expresses a paradoxical self-demeaning but forceful London-centrism among Scots, Irish, and others who will wait two centuries to celebrate their home identities. Instead, the primary contradiction of elocution within oratorical rhetoric is that it accesses a *standardized* London dialect in printed guides whose London users may never occupy the actual space of that standard, even in London itself. Yet Sheridan's purifying exercises for the English *tongue* portray these guides as embodied descriptors of in-the-flesh access to status, stability, and moral correctness. Here, "tongue" is not a metaphor for language. Sheridan's *British Education: Or, the Source of the Disorders of Great Britain* (1756) claims that the embodied voice of pure oratorical pronunciation accustoms audiences to "hearing such as spoke in the most pure and perfect manner, [and who] would immediately be sensible of the least deviation from what was right, and be offended at any improper tone, or use of words in their public speakers" (193, qtd. in Beach 123). Nonetheless, at the time, hearing implies proximity and embedment in the abstract London speech rarely heard anywhere.

My point is that this misfit of generalized London standards to actual locations where they are to be applied is itself a place-marker in theories of rhetoric. It also requires attention, to account for the *timely* opportunities that motivate the speeches that Sheridan would purify. He articulates a specific rhetoric-hope, portraying correct pronunciation, intended meaning, and correct written grammar as a combined, newly articulated production of trust in equally new published textuality. Thus, his *Lectures on the Art of Reading* (1775) joins "reason" and "emotion" in a recursively interactive, linguistically packaged persuasion. Sheridan establishes this equality as a matter of first principles:

> Now, as the end of . . . communication is not merely to lay open the ideas, but also all the different feelings which they excite in him who utters them, there must be some other marks, besides words, to manifest these; as words uttered in a monotonous state can only represent a similar state of mind, perfectly free from all activity or emotion. . . . [T]here is not an act of the mind, an exertion of the fancy, or an emotion of the heart, which have not their peculiar tone, or note of the voice, by which they are to be expressed, all suited to the exactest proportion, to the several degrees of internal feeling. (qtd. in Hudson 107)

In the service of identifying a message with its nuanced emotional spin, this argument forecasts a certain positivism: it insists on exactly proportionate tenor and vehicle—on specific, peculiar tones attached to each thought, imagination, and feeling. It also exactly balances empty "words uttered in a monotonous state" against precise degrees of "*internal* feeling," a fit of utterance to emotion that accurate elocutionary articulation means to realize. But Sheridan hereby also implies, however inadvertently, that speech *follows* (from) a new multiplicity of print texts. By collapsing the human faculties into proportions that suit communicative ends, he blends them into a single site of expression that cannot be accurately portrayed as "the body," nor as the Cartesian Mind, nor its Thought. That is, written language has appropriated an embodied "voice" that is not the physical instrument of oratory but is the only available access to a text's intentions. Here, elocution pursues the ideal of precise reading to infuse signs that constitute print with an absent source, its authorial written or spoken origins, a task that published texts make urgent. In this view, we look to pure *pronunciation* to find their recited force *in* that medium, not in obviously impossible direct communication. Publication reinstates their ancient rhetorical *enargia*, or zest, if only through guided articulation.

Of course, the displacement of an absent speaker into a trained reader's body is to take place in language: "[T]he mere language of ideas," Sheridan writes, "whether written or spoken can of itself have no . . . power but that of conveying knowledge and improving the understanding. *To touch the heart and agitate the fancy* . . . the language of emotions should be joined with it" (qtd. in Hudson 107, emphasis added). As parallel treatises witness, this amalgamation of language and the faculties—reason, sympathy, imagination, action—also underlies eighteenth-century language theories that deconstruct the rationalist mind/action binary. In addition, this blurring makes sense of Sheridan's desire to create correct, standardized pronunciation that never becomes entirely equivalent to newly standardized written spellings. In that regard, he joins prominent (often French) author/philosophers like Rousseau, who with Claude Buffier, Charles Pinot Duclos, and Voltaire promoted homophonic spellings that, as Nicholas Hudson notes in *Writing and European Thought: 1600–1830*, set aside the conventional hand of the French Academy. They instead "adopted a personal style of spelling, commonly dropping double consonants and changing letters" (121). But the different standardized print whose malleability elocutionary recitations create even as they attempt to control it may project any speaker across regions and times as equal to any other authorized reader.

I should stress that the phenomena I have been naming as ironies and paradoxes are so only in relation to this particular Anglo-American moment; they comprise the content of a shift to a transactional culture that Pocock describes (above). In that culture of interested interactions, elocution is a twofold medium yet (again, paradoxically) one that is nonverbal in both of its versions. That is, elocution unmoored from ancient delivery organizes a long history of gestures—silent language—into an eighteenth-century "somatic tradition," which involves the entire body (Hudson 107). James Burgh's *The Art of Speaking* (1761) exemplifies this restatement of directions to actors into rhetoric's domains in his exemplary description of how a speaker shall embody "desire" in combined gestures and facial movements. In his description, "desire" involves "*bending* the *body* forward, and *stretching* the *arms* toward the object, as to grasp it. The *countenance smiling*, but *eager* and *wishful*; the *eyes wide open*, and *eyebrows raised*; the *mouth open*; the tone of voice *suppliant*, but *lively* and *cheerful*" (qtd. in Hudson 106).

This body language also incorporates the artificiality of written signs and the rules of grammar—while overcoming them. It relies on intonations named as proper and precisely scripted gestures that realize a word. But the somatic tradition also declares that the ontology of "real" communication recapitulates a phylogeny of articulation, a progress across the spaces in which voice becomes print. That is, like Blair's pedagogy and others that combine speculative history with speculative anthropology,[24] Burgh's guidance explains that the sounds of primitives—the uncivilized and babies—have developed into highly nuanced emotional codes. He implies that if we do not know a concept's correct original tones, we cannot use, and especially cannot understand, writing.

Thus, a second form of nonverbal body language is the carefully articulated, marked body of the elocutionist's text. Here again, "body" is not a metaphor. The elocutionist's graphically enlivened written transcript participates actively in Sheridan's essence of communication. Clearly directed moods, emphases, and feelings are attached to the text as words are read, whether alone or reciting for others. Sterne's *Tristram Shandy* realizes these implications of commodified, published texts for readers in its send-up of such marks. Its punctuation translates meaningless signs into signs of meaning: dashes indicate the length of pauses, darkened pages witness the (temporary) death of its authorial Parson Yorick, and asterisks and wandering lines indicate omissions, transitions, and a reader's best clues to what is reported as "said." This literary elocution expresses its own textual anxieties, not only those of a rhetoric that is at the time newly separated from "literature." Unlike Ben Jonson's embodied playwright standing in for relations among publisher, author, and audience in *Bartholomew Fair* (see chapter 2), *Shandy* is a textual closed circuit between a later reader and a narration. Its author's and fictionalized narrator's voices constitute a text so layered with meaning/marks that it is difficult to read aloud. A text without such marks is thus tacitly dis-embodied, its gestures, tones, and emotional essence left uncommunicative. Unlike the animated ancient scroll under Socrates' cloak in Plato's *Phaedrus*, its neatly packaged rectangle makes little contact with an interlocutory reader.

Through both a reader's explicit gestures and the body/text marked with feeling, elocutionary rhetoric's corpus produces a final contradiction: nonverbal signs constitute speech-privileged texts. These silent agents of communicative exchanges are themselves at least as important as their meaning and authorship. In this final obvious duality, Sheridan's concerns with predominantly *accurate* sounds and Johnson's *Dictionary*'s embodiment of the Republic of Scholars cooperate. Together, they standardize a vernacular as a Royal Society or Academy cannot—from within its correct speakers, those who "talk like books."

The Ends of Trust

The different view of rhetoric's history presented here is often asserted, hinted at, or suggested and quickly dismissed in all but a few sources like Daniel Gross's *The Secret History of Emotion* and James L. Kastley's *Rethinking the Rhetorical Tradition*. But from perspectives created by recent discourse archaeology uncovering both antique literacies and modern publishing trade routes, defining oratory as one among many sites of metadiscursive practices and theories across Western history makes sense. For example, as François Zabbal says in *Ancestor of the West: Writing, Reasoning, and Religion in Mesopotamia, Elam, and Greece*, Athens was not a cradle of either literacy or political discussion:

> The unexpected result of archeological excavation was to push the past back several millennia, upsetting the myth of the two ultimate origins of the West: Greece and the Bible.... The positive reasoning of the Greeks was formed not *ex nihilo* but out of cosmogonic myths borrowed from Mesopotamia.... It is not certain, however, that [this revised history] will triumph as long as the ideology of origins remains impervious to the facts that have been established by historical knowledge. (x)

This view accounts for discourse beyond imposing one abstract model on many historic sites we take to be offshoots, fragments, or perversions of Athenian public speaking. And in the literate proficiencies of antique Mesopotamia, the overdetermined authorship of Shakespeare's earliest printed plays, the equally multiple editorships of eighteenth-century editions of Shakespeare, and still other, active codex-to-volume publications that historian of the book Roger Chartier has argued create readers as coauthors of novels (49), we have definitive material evidence that ranked essences of cultural practices, with more and less developed social cognition, may be convenient expressions of chauvinism.

If that evidence might urge rhetoric studies to review its usual historiography, it might also encourage writing studies to collect its balkanized emphases on various purposes and genres of writing under a less leaky theoretical umbrella than reapplied oratorical categories offer. Formalist descriptions of the parts of composing, argumentation, and appeals to audiences that stretch toward difficult-to-locate "public spheres" in a twenty-first century are worn ways to account for making contemporary texts. If we were to renew theories of discourse production to account for the interested cultural projects of various metadiscursive pedagogies, we might also return attention to language, the linguistic surfaces that Paolo Valesio's treatment of commonplaces says are "interesting enough." My argument on these grounds suggests that emotions that are identical to conviction have been historically re-articulated in specific situations that now include the possibilities for conviction and its limits in regard to published textual styles and authorities, which are thereby always at once under erasure and in quotation marks.

Of course, Sheridan's hope that elocutionary rhetoric could contain publication in normalized vernacular communities now seems a halcyon dream of revivification. But as I have argued, the elocutionary moment was enormously significant precisely for that reason: single-minded speakers and their voices, deploying recognized conventions that create the illusion of that control and of its predictable outcomes, have collapsed into ad hoc yet almost universally available performances. We witness them in disorganized settings as their occasional audiences. The emotions taught and evoked in this delivery system and their relation to actions to follow remain undertheorized, in fact largely ignored, by those who somewhat naively focus on the fortunes of rational decision-making.

That last point suggests that trust among contemporary groups and individuals still depends on identities they derive from shared pedagogies, but that recognition of this sharing is impossible to predict and difficult to perceive *as* shared. Yet we rarely apply that difficulty in analyses of persuasion, except in conceptual abstractions that nostalgically portray it as a now-fragmented whole. Videophones and other satellite technologies evidently cannot repair gaps among communities that never held each other in common. Their failure is evident in their commercial reassurance that they keep everyone always "in touch." Thus, we might easily infer from experience and anxiety that no one trusts anyone or anyone's discourse. This is to say that nostalgia for stable linguistic referents and reliable cultural commonplaces overrides possible enjoyment of unsettled possibilities.

John Bender and David E. Wellbery's introduction to *The Ends of Rhetoric: History, Theory, Practice* makes these points in terms of the demise of a singular rhetoric in the face of new social organizations:

> The cultural hegemony of rhetoric, as a practice of discourse, as a doctrine of codifying that practice, and as a vehicle of cultural memory, is grounded in the social structures of a premodern world. Conceived in its broadest terms, . . . the demise of rhetoric coincides with the long and arduous historical process that is often termed modernization: the replacement of a symbolic-religious organization of social and cultural life by rationalized forms, the gradual shift from a stratificational differentiation of society to one that operates along functional axes. (7)

This view also implies that the shared content of contemporary education is threefold; it includes traditional information, time-honored processes, and an awareness of its own "spin." Thus, it is equally arguable that trusted discourse is now, much like its audiences, often ad hoc rather than framed or canonical and usually volunteered with direct references to its possible inaccuracy, self-interest, and constrained moments of statement. A new *kairos* of overdetermined circumstance trusts personally narrated texts that, by definition, will transmit formative uncertainties.

Of course, the oratorical scene remains plausible itself and may be reenacted, if not acted originally, in increasingly limited settings. Eighteenth-century elocutionary rhetoric demands a newly configured "text itself," the well-marked, well-read, and more than casually proofread vernacular artifact that projects the possibility of texts that are media templates. These material results of patriotic, moral-philosophical consciousness formation trace and thereby blur an earlier cultural matrix in which all texts are active agents, members of the "literature" that is not limited to performance scripts of drama, epic, ancient lyric, oratory, and other literary set-pieces. Thus, texts that had been locally consequential—inscribed or printed tracts, letters, sermons, pamphlets, and broadsides—also lose the protection of moral exigencies that determined their delivery and reception. Instead, emerging modernist occasions situate a contemporary text that produces its own exigent moments, if as shadows in increasingly fabled, merely imitated exigencies of a "commodity *kairos*." That is, the impersonal commodified status of textuality that constitutes our inevitable ignorance about its unknown destinies and suddenly encountered intentions also frustrates our sense of receiving direct knowledge from any source, the sense formerly implied by oratorical rhetoric's synergy of exposed character, defended reasoning, and receptive audience.

Signs of this dissolution of the credibility of the oratorical situation often appear without explanation. For instance, the purity of published language sought through standardized dictionaries and elocutionary rhetoric resulted in burgeoning reference industries. We use their omnipresent resources to find "correct" meanings, usages, pronunciations, commonplace sayings, and appropriate tones. Their status as repositories of that accumulated linguistic authority, its own medium made from disembodied ghosts of immediacy, does not lessen the power of schooled bonding. Yet they become that power itself, an affiliative authority connecting instantly evoked scholars who cannot verify each other's tuition. They simultaneously disrupt and maintain bonding that no longer reflects personal "place."[25] This reversal, in which ad hoc affiliations precede group identification, and in which entitlement precedes class access to it, also makes reference works the sources of practices, not their result.

In the twentieth century, in an unknowing and oblique tribute to Sheridan and Burgh, brain sciences create further evidence that while persuasion occurs on already established grounds of trust, the oratorical situation is lost on contemporary inferential processes. Neuroscientists interested in locating precise synaptic sources of emotions have appropriated photographs of staged emotional expressions, pictures first used to study how people respond to the expressions that once constituted acting and elocution lessons in emotional display. But now, those models for demonstrating feeling inform "an entire research program designed to localize emotion to particular structures of the human brain" (Watson 30). The subjects of the experiment physically imitate photographs; experimenters then pinpoint their neurological responses and infer from this data that they have located the physiological *source* of a displayed emotion, not a response to it. McClain Watson's "From Interpretation to Identification: A History of Facial Images in the Sciences of Emotion" argues that this experiment sets aside the "experimental value of affective disposition, personal history, and other situational variables that influenced interpretation of a facial expression" (29). These photographs are hereby *identical to* emotion. Researchers are evidently unaware of their first uses to teach how to match expression to conventional iconographic displays and so do not equate the physical response of the brain to interpretative pedagogies in acting and oratory, to their subjects' personal histories, or to individual brain chemistry. Neuroscientists assume all are identical, just as a hammer might be seen to be equivalent to a knee-jerk response to its tap. In this view, the medium is its own self-trusting tautology, not Marshall McLuhan and Lewis H. Lapham's "extensions of man," not a highlighted container for sense, but its remainder.

This example at the least shows that the diffusion of a text's sources and perceived content onto an unmoored photographic publication and its unpredictable reception is a distinct historical event. Publishing does not represent power relations as abstract, negative social forces, nor does it only create a disastrous cultural teleology. It is a material circumstance trusted more than any of its content. We may deliver ourselves to an actor or a film director without knowing the title, plot, or genre of a production. That is, we trust the media of publication itself, a contemporary charismatic pull, without reference to a specific result from the attraction.

This re-theorized historiography thus notices the progress of attitudes toward media, specifically toward printed texts, over the eighteenth and nineteenth centuries. For instance, despite Jacques Derrida's reading of Rousseau, the earlier philosopher did not see writing as Europe's greatness, nor as a sign of the rationality it was equated with by many. But he did think writing served purposes other than those that speech fulfills, which may explain Derrida's oversight about his position.[26] Sheridan and others thought that writing is useful for some purposes, yet they obviously assign the ideological foundations of any country to speech, as does sensational-ist Scottish philosopher Thomas Reid. Reid speculates about illiteracy in his *Inquiry into the Human Mind on the Principles of Common Sense* (1764), where he claims that a century *without* writing would happily produce many painters, musicians, and actors (Hudson 101). Henry Home, Lord Kames's *Elements of Criticism* (1762) distinguishes writers and readers on the basis of separate skills: "The chief talent of a fine writer, is a ready command of the expressions that nature dictates to every man when *any vivid emotion* struggles for utterance; and the chief talent of a fine reader, is a ready com-mand of the tones suited to those expressions" (2:119–20, qtd. in Hudson 112, emphasis added). Obviously, Kames assumes he is discussing a reader who reads aloud, whose elocutionary schooling would also include mastery of gestures like those of Burgh's *Art of Speaking*. Expression and tone, not meaning and interpretation, are at issue. But Joseph Priestley also points out that it is almost impossible for a reader *not* to invest a text with feelings if the stated sentiments are already known to that reader: "We *unavoidably* do give the language the assistance we can from pronunciation" (*Course of Lectures*, qtd. in Hudson 112, emphasis added).

Others in this era begin to stress the value of writing: John Rice argues that the meaning of speech depends on the precision of a written grammar and observable language (Hudson 113), a position he forms as a critic interested in visual poetry and thus in the effects of graphic texts on meaning. William Cockin's *The Art of Delivering Written Language* (1775) also privileges graphic texts. It proposes that reading a printed text should *not* reenact a speech's original energy. This reading should be more "faint," properly dignified and restrained (Hudson 114). And Hudson notes that Sterne's *Tristram Shandy* enacts a visible satire on elocution that makes it impossible to forget that you are reading a book, that writing cannot be transparent speech (116).

These comments attempt to process changes in a cultural situation that includes available literacy, schooling, published texts, and resources to ac-quire them. Later, William Hazlitt's 1825 essay "On the Difference between Writing and Speaking" echoes the views of Sheridan and Rousseau about the separate uses of each medium. But it also categorizes them only on the psychological basis of the spontaneous "faculties" that an individual's internal talents and predispositions must deploy to make either text. In fact, Hazlitt's writing and speech differ only in reference to time spent, perhaps their only meaningful separation:

> The great leading distinction between writing and speaking is, that more time is allowed for the one than the other; and hence different faculties are required for, and different objects attained by[,] each. He is properly the best speaker who can collect together the greatest

number of apposite ideas *at a moment's warning*: he is properly the best writer who can give utterance to the greatest quantity of valuable knowledge *in the course of his whole life*. The chief requisite for the one, then, appears to be quickness and facility of perception—for the other, patience of soul, and a power increasing with the difficulties it has to master. (par. 2, emphasis added)

By emphasizing the processes of one "writer" and one "speaker" over "writing" and "speech," Hazlitt places writing closer to individual "thought." He asserts that "the writer was far more likely than the speaker to aim at nothing but the expression of truth in a language selected with the greatest care and sensitivity" (qtd. in Hudson 154).

None of these statements about media is a claim that must necessarily disappear in light of alternative explanations.[27] In that sense, these views credit the mediocrity theory with which this study began considering how we trust discourses. That is, my inferences acknowledge, formatively, that there are many other worlds much like the one I am mapping and that they are not necessarily in competition with mine. But this dispersed metadiscursive criticism tacitly transforms the formal categories applied to one oratorical rhetoric, especially its domain of delivery, into another, more static theory. In it, publication becomes its own *kairos*. It is only an exigency of time, or timeliness, without reference to the conceptual definition of "occasions" as opportune moments. These common topics reappear often in contemporary analogues to Sterne's lampooning visual criticism of texts, outside one rhetorical tradition whose history might be opened to many other investigations that follow Kittler's project in another key. A "shift in focus from a totalizing concept of society to an analysis of specific subsystems" brings with it what Wellbery calls a "gain in . . . concreteness" (xviii). This study's displayed examples of that concreteness allow us to accept the mobility of trust as a cultural fact. Its interest disputes Thomas Miller's warning that "the rhetorical tradition is a fiction that has just about outlasted its usefulness" ("Reinventing" 26).

Conclusion: Centering Rhetoric—The Psychology of Anxious Moments and Solemn Occasions

Paul Bénichou closes *The Consecration of the Writer: 1750–1830* by pointing out that the secular spiritual power he has been describing only begins in the mid-nineteenth century; his book unfolds the prehistory of that power and engages a point of view whose full narration might begin where his ends and continue to the current moment. He identifies this power as "critical in its essence," saying that when organized religion (or any social "ministry of lofty edification") no longer holds cultural authority, a "law of examination and debate" takes over. Claiming with many that literature replaces religion as its secular counterpart in this authority,[1] he concludes that trust in all such discourses dissipates: "Our age knows where the real priests are and no longer counts much on them for its salvation, [so it] is not ready to grant to newcomers a kind of authority that it denies to their predecessors." After the world no longer works in old commonplaces or even knows those who once announced a certain kind of mediating character—priests and analogous icons—any continuing sign of pedagogic or literary self-privileging insults its audiences. Certified authorities are no longer identical to charismatic discourse: "As soon as such a pretension takes too peremptory or too precise form, it can appear absurd to the average person" (341–42).

Bénichou's point has a great deal to do with my recurring critiques of formalist approaches to metadiscourses. Certainly the foundational claim of that approach is that stable Truth about any phenomenon emerges from naming its parts and describing their relationships. That dour confidence may have inspired the late-twentieth-century reaction to it, the then apparently obvious naming of *jouissance* as the center of poststructuralism. The play of signs endorsed a rather serious notification that language is a self-referential system to be taken in the spirit of its infinite play. But neither of those turns—neither to meaning nor to self-referential stylizations of language—has bothered rhetoric studies in significant ways. The argument that language is never so controllable as oratorical rhetoric claims appears not to affect its belief that we *can* (much less should) "mean what we say," nor the conviction that no matter how obviously crafted a text is, its reader/audience can discern its intentions. Instead, rhetoric studies continues to rely on formalism to convey the spirit of its cultural work, projects whose exemplifications are more interesting than Bénichou's "too peremptory or too precise." Thus, in the interest of another sort of truth, my point has been that continuing to ignore the authority of many forms of precedent trust over any discursive persuasion, and the partiality of any persuasion no matter how it is effected, retains a formalist history that cleanses rhetoric of feelings that actually constitute its importance. In such histories, Hudibrasian "rules and tools" yield little to sources and forces, human and supposedly "philosophical," that become historical objects of study. Ignoring the still unremarked essence of persuasion—willingness to cooperate—allows historians to ignore how formalist categories offer false substitutes for the diffused "spirit" of many rhetorics.

The generative problematic that my choice has involved is typical in post-structuralist histories. That is, they must simultaneously turn to specific examples, as New History does, but without re-turning to totalizing explanations of them, to a retained religious spirit that makes Hegelian histories cohere around organized canonical authorities. In this case, however, if understanding persuasion depends on reviving pre-Cartesian acceptance of emotion as always at its center, even if for some quite regrettably, it further requires recharacterizing trust, our emotional consent. We have taken many forms of comfort from antique Mediterranean cultures, and more, insofar as new findings about them suggest that some centers have held. That is, the word "civilization" might become descriptive rather than evaluative were we to forgo origin stories that have begun much later than they should, to extend a Western history that includes all of its Mesopotamian precedents. That beginning also might remind us of another obvious starting-place for rhetorical analyses, in the identity between persuasion and emotionally invested interaction. Of course, to make that emotional point as we recast rhetoric as multiple metadiscursive sites produces a less detailed analysis than is warranted. Rhetoric history that enlarges its view of the sites and nature of persuasion to include multiple, equally active pedagogies requires many close readings of alternative canons and intriguing examples.

These limits of course make this study a starting-point, an encouragement to reconceptualize discourse history along lines many have already drawn.

In it, I have inevitably situated my points around the figure of a persuasive character, the abstraction across discursive fields who is trusted as sharing a class entitlement to paideia, or who with increasing frequency is trusted by any ad hoc audience on the basis of imitative access to that character. That equally abstracted audience is always present to discourse, insofar as it recognizes conventional language as a sign of a relevant, preserved body of texts. That is, the persuasive character deploys conventions that indicate being aware of what is conventional, a motive not precisely identical to un-selfconsciously displaying offhand allusions to a body of literary, historical, and other social texts. On this basis, a particular trusted character mediates between tentative, emerging knowledge and a particular situation in multiple ways. It brings to bear differential means of persuasion. In oratory, these means may be allusions like those that Aristotle's *Rhetoric* and *Poetics* take to be commonplace versions of critical proof by example. In philosophy and sophistry, these means may be in the use of the dialogic genre. In poetry and drama, the inspired are trusted because, like orators, they think through familiar figuration, stock characters, mythic cultural plots, and ultimately in and through Western consciousness. In medicine, physicians are trusted as interlocutors, not as technicians. They know exactly what their patients know: traditional symptoms of specific diseases, the infamous mother's milk as a sign of recent pregnancy, and that illness may be a punishment or some other displaced reality. The oratorical requirement of reputation is necessary but insufficient without such shared, culturally specific values.

A retreat from rationalist oratory toward a sense of the orphic implies a specific belief in things unseen. Hidden realities, or "hidden" "realities," emerge from these mediators, insightful characters of seer, prophet, diviner, or magician that this study has traced through the publication of texts that we now trust only after unseen forces present them to Bénichou's "law of examination and debate." But from seer to paperback, these powers of mediated trust are identical to a metaphysical truth. They appear neither after nor before its realization, a proposition that obviously cannot be verified by observation.

Thus, trusted interpretation itself has no origin yet demands many originals, in the gods, "nature," science, and commodities, all of which are simultaneously invoked from the earliest examples and records of their separate methods of persuasion. To focus on what appears most obvious, we find a well-developed mythology around the gods at least from Hesiod's *Theogony* on and assume that similar stories of participation in human mysteries antedate his.[2] But no organized religion may be said to begin in ancient Greece, nor do we find an antique precedent for one that allusively threads its way toward a named religion in the serial works of magic, omens, oracles, and prophecies. All of these signs operate through ritual incantatory language that will be preserved in the method of Gorgias and in other highly stylized examples. But *a* religion is missing. No one source is seen to characterize oratorical propositions with insights from poetry, drama, or other forms of mesmerizing speech. As Carol Poster points out, just as rhetorical practices preexist the word *rhêtorikê* (as the elements preexist their organizing periodic table), it is obvious that "Hesiod and Pherecydes systematize knowledge of the gods without any single term corresponding to our English 'religion' or even the Platonic *'theologia'*" ("Being" 119).

Nonetheless, missing icons and organizations do not excuse us from explaining "the religious," a sense of ineffable, unspeakable presence that evokes enormous verbal efforts to simultaneously articulate "Truth" and maintain that it is available only in always ambiguous encounters with a particular character and in constitutive critical laws of examination and critique, if not in the most evident facts.

The Motive to Act

I belabor this point because, as Poster hints, a finer exposition of trust attached to specifically characterized voices is not found in definitions of rhetoric. Jacqueline de Romilly criticizes mistaken nominalist attempts to encompass this emotional process in definitions of characters around "rhetoric" as a concept: "When Protagoras . . . says that the poets and seers were the first sophists . . . what he means is that they were educators, as were the sophists" (93n13). That is, she identifies rhetoric as a pedagogy, a way of educating and being educated that distinguishes trust as the shared epistemology among these cultural figures. George Kennedy's 1997 definition of rhetoric also alludes to that pedagogic ambience insofar as he defines rhetoric as "a form of mental and emotional energy" (*Comparative* 3). Were we to find a center to which dispersed discursive practices that participate in one cultural function return, it might be in Kennedy's conception of antique human energies.

The standard treatments of this force unfortunately still divide feeling from thought to examine the "irrational," a negative term that implies the missing positive valence in which binary completions of a human whole need not efface each other. In this case, rational and irrational oppositions give way to the different antique idea of a human spirit placed in individuals, the relatively familiar Greek *thumos*. Insofar as this spirit operates apart from reason, not necessarily in contradiction to it, to express energy, it must be explained through the assumption that an (also vaguely placed) mind is separate from the body that houses it. In this configuration of human faculties, emotion is not an action but the tenor of separated "frames of mind." Across its history, thumos appears in various body parts and ultimately in "good" and "evil" forces acting through those locations. For instance, the word is often (if not in the earliest uses we have) simply equated with "anger."

E. R. Dodds's classic description in *The Greeks and the Irrational* takes up such physiognomies of a human imagined to have a psychic self and spirit:

> The *psyche* is the living self, and, more specifically, the appetitive self; it has taken over the functions of Homeric *thumos*, not those of Homeric *nous* [mind]. Between psyche in this sense and *soma* [body] *there is no fundamental antagonism*; psyche is just the mental correlate of *soma*. . . .
>
> In fifth-century Attic writers, as in their Ionian predecessors, *the "self"* which is *denoted by the word* psyche *is normally the emotional rather than the rational self.* The *psyche* is spoken of as the seat of courage, of passion, of pity, of anxiety, of animal appetite, but before Plato seldom if ever as the seat of reason; its range is broadly that of the Homeric *thumos*. (138–39, emphasis added)

This Homeric version of thumos, Dodds says, is not a psychic self's precedent "life-soul" or "breath-soul" but "an organ of feeling" in a very simple sense. It is the part of a person that desires to eat, "drink, or slay an enemy" (16). In Homer, however, as is witnessed when Odysseus "plans in his *thumos*" to kill the Cyclops (Dodds 16), this seat of motivated action is restrained by still other forces. It may appear as a conversant in a two-part internal conversation, to reappear in *Hamlet* and even later in Whately's interior arguments (see chapter 3). Thumos is not imagined apart from the body but as "dwelling somewhere in the depths of the organism, and out of those depths it can speak to its owner *with a voice of its own*. In most of these respects it is again a successor to the Homeric *thumos*" (Dodds 139, emphasis added). Moreover, this soul is near *nous*, the reasoning part of the self, and "was not a reluctant prisoner of the body; it was the life or spirit of the body, and perfectly at home there" (139).

But Dodds distinguishes the classical rationalism of fourth-century Athens, which depicts thumos as Homer did not, that is, not as a force that occupies the human as part of the supernatural demonic world. In classical treatments, that force had withdrawn to leave in its place significant interiorized anger and wickedness. As Medea says, "The *thumos* is stronger than my purposes, *thumos,* the root of man's worst acts" (Euripides, *Medea,* ln. 1079, qtd. in Dodds 186). Certainly the dangers of this doubly motivated thumos explain Peripatetic philosophy's emphasis on educating the soul by supplying it with culturally conventional feelings appropriate to specific situations. Its motives also explain a number of traditional Christian assumptions about the nature of redemption from sin. Therefore, it is important to emphasize that the Homeric conscious spirit was a vehicle of thought *and* feeling. It was in the chest, usually associated with the diaphragm and breath (and thus with ex-pression), as opposed to the *epithumia* in Plato, then a literally lower desiring faculty in the belly.

This different spirit of the classical soul is taken up in recent philosophy, political science, and theater studies, each of which seeks a "persuasive [re]definition"[3] of how persuasion operates in and on the ancient self. For instance, Angela Hobbs in *Plato and the Hero: Courage, Manliness and the Impersonal Good* emphasizes that the self-worth attached to thumos is an ally of reason, an energy working in concert with the reasoning *nous*, or mind. However, as she defines it, thumos, the individual's spirit, does not question appearances unless they are relevant to forming "an ideal image of oneself in accordance with one's conception of the fine and noble" (30). Hobbs here defines thumos in relation to Plato's attempts in the dialogues to hone "courage" into a soul-enriching combination of reason and desire, so she emphasizes "self-image." But if we focus instead on character as the source of discursive practices, we see that either emphasis intends to persuade the self to act in line with public approval and to seek self-satisfaction as a consequence of admired language, not to seek battlefield honors. As Hobbs also says, thumos, the spiritedness of this desired appearance, is "the need to believe that one counts for something" (30).

Barbara Koziak's *Retrieving Political Emotion: Thumos, Aristotle, and Gender* portrays this liminal spiritedness differently. She reviews conspicuous precedent treatments of thumos, citing Jan Bremmer in *The Early Greek Concept of the Soul* and James Redfield in *Nature and Culture in the* Iliad*: The Tragedy of Hector*, who see thumos as an "organ of emotion," its source and the "heart of the affective life."[4] However, Koziak herself reads thumos as "one formulation of the place of emotion in the soul that the ancient Greeks envisioned," that is, as Aristotle suggests the functions of emotion in the *Rhetoric* (33). This view of thumos is that it participates in deliberation, "a feature so strange to modern readers that they have launched a contentious debate about whether Homeric characters can be said to make decisions or even to reason" (38). Nonetheless, in her view, this energy accomplishes persuasion as "the source of impulses themselves that constitute a person's active being in the world. It combines emotion and action, revealing [how] emotion is always implicated in action, and even in the activity of thought" (53).

Koziak's new history of emotion concepts also takes up Aristotle's many statements about emotion as a social force. She notes that the *Rhetoric* itself deploys emotion rhetorically "to correct [the elitism of] Plato's *Republic*, to elaborate the benefits of the regime called polity, to define the character of the best regime, *to understand the impact of political speech*, to judge the possibilities of political cooperation" (99, emphasis added). She also in part follows W. W. Fortenbaugh's *Aristotle on Emotion*, which argues that emotion in the *Rhetoric* "grounds an improved educational theory that consists primarily of a young child's habituation into *'proper loves and hates through enjoyment of good characters and noble deeds in musical education'*" (Koziak 30, emphasis added). Plato sees thumos still differently, as a balance between light and dark urges. He names it one of three parts of the soul in the *Republic* (439e6–440a6). But Koziak's problematized view of thumos allows it openly to receive the training provided by artful dramatic narrative and other cultural productions. It is not fixed as an interiorized energy that one has, or not, nor found only in one or another sort of person. Thus, Aristotle's developmental view of education assigns the paideia taught in dramatic performances to fostering pity in a communal identity, which Koziak calls a source of overriding kinship with strangers (150).

In both views, thumos is precisely the basis of a social system of emotional trust. As in the *Politics* (VII.6.1327b–39ff), this result is twofold: "*Thymos* is the faculty of our souls which issues in love and friendship. . . . It is also the source . . . of any power of commanding and any feeling for freedom."

The Motivator

These interpretative formulations of classical emotions and their recent extensions across disciplines support parallel claims that a theory of education joins politics, theater, oratory, and other discourses insofar as all must persuade their audiences not only toward a course of action but concomitantly to accept and act from specific *emotional* reasons for that action. In this world, the spirit wants what the spirit wants. These discourses embody precisely the educative process undertaken and circulated among Sophists, poets, and seers, as de Romilly says. Yet the issue remains: can we know how a liminal yet situated space of trust results from shared educational processes, teachings that become conventional perceptions of actions, personalities, and styles? Given the symbolic receptivity of actual attendees and others who project themselves into the immediacy of any of these discursive sites, how do both language and audience join a character perceived to be separate from both: a creature of performance who stylizes insight itself?

Perhaps a plausible answer to these and other questions about trust is available in the familiarity of the terms applied to thumos, even now. As Paolo Valesio puts it in *Novantiqua: Rhetorics as a Contemporary Theory*, "It is misleading to suggest that the 'real connection' (with others, the self, death) can be expressed by going against the commonplaces; as if they were not really *common*, as if there were—somewhere—a more edifying, more 'beautiful'

language" (36). [from a]
shared educati[precisely equiv[means among a[[n 'mon" is] [ttement] [eparate,]
as they have so definitively, trusted language is equivalent to feeling and thought, not separate from them. And in that equivalence, commonplaces are thereby more often shared across differences.

(handwritten margin note: Miller claim: trust derives from a shared education in the commonplace! Trusted language = equal to feeling and thought)

If it is impossible to describe trust outside rationalist assumptions that still constitute the idioms of body and spirit, or soul, or Mind, and their separation within one aptly named human being, we can trace those separations to a specific difference between Ionian and later definitions of the psychic self. As Dodds explains, seventh-century trade across the Black Sea exported to Ionian culture a northern European shaman tradition. It demanded mastery of the body through its purification, a complex interaction that Dodds calls an ancient "puritanism." He speculates that this tradition of a mind and a spirit that can each be split from the body to act on it takes hold in Greek philosophy and elsewhere not from Asiatic influences but from applying principles of shamanism to another simple and readily available perception. Whatever its geographic source, many agree that the shaman's defining act is to cross the *axis mundi*, to bring back to earth from heaven the special knowledge of the healer whose staff is the medical caduceus, the tree of life.

In this narrative, the psyche Dodds associates with thumos is assumed to be most active when the body is asleep, since dreams and intimations of death then appear to be the spirit's only activity. Dodds reasons that it follows that the body awake and the mind/spirit asleep begin to be conceived of as opposites, and further as in conflict. The comfortably housed thumos, or spirit within the body, is hereby attached to impulses and the activity of dreams, inexplicably vivid desires and fantasies that come from outside a unified soul. Their interpretations are based in symbols, not direct relations between a self and a vision, and thus can be attributed to insight, magic, and access to divinity—as they were and often still are. In sleep, we cross over, if not the *axis mundi*, a division within ourselves; we expect that "sleep on it" tells us more than an order to "rest before deciding." Thus, histories of rhetorics include this concept of access to special interpretative power insofar as poets, orators, doctors, diviners, philosophers, and other meditative icons partake of widespread shamanist origins. But most descriptions based on classical culture follow a history of diverse meanings of "thumos" that include its inaccessible origins.

David Galin's "Rehabilitating the Concept 'Spirit' for the Non-Religious and the Scientifically-Minded" extends this connection between ancient spirit and now commonly catalogued interpretive recognitions of repetitions, patterns, and form. He argues, however, that "the experience of spirit is a special case of our capacity to experience implicit organization, part of our specialization for detecting patterns" (1). That reversed order of causality, in which spirited perceptions are within the category of patterns, not their source, places the burden of insight on modern criticism. It also helps explain the ease with which nineteenth-century Anglo-Europe accepted that schooled interpretation of literature is equivalent to biblical hermeneutics and thus to a surrogate religion. That is, if a sense of spirit and spirituality results from pattern recognition, interpretation of texts in any setting becomes a holy task.

To bring the spirit and the character who invokes it home to rhetorical traditions, we might follow the argument of Juha Sihvola and Troels Engberg-Pedersen's introduction to *The Emotions in Hellenistic Philosophy*, which points out that "the basic meaning of the term *pathos* is not 'emotion'; *pathos* stands for a much more general notion which covers all accidental and contingent changes that happen to somebody in contrast to what he or she actively does" (viii). They note that "*pathos*" appears in Aristotle's *Categories* and *Metaphysics* and is translated multiply as "'affection,' 'experience,' 'undergoing' or 'attribute,' as opposed to 'emotion' or even 'passion'" (viii). That is, appeals to reason and character, to logic and to trust—the closely guarded logos and ethos positioned to succeed—are appeals to allow argument to work on already known cultural and individual narratives. Affections, experiences, and attributes are conventional and easily accessed among framed Athenian audiences.

Thus, Aristotle's treatment of "emotion" in Book II of the *Rhetoric* is not what many name it, "the first psychology book," unless we equate psychology with a thorough cultural education in feeling, as we easily might do. The *Rhetoric*'s references to predictable responses among ages and stations of men describe conventional displays that can be trusted among those conventionally educated to display them and those who thereby trust them to be appropriate to the situation at hand, who only much later in history will describe these displays as the experience/result of individual consciousness. As many definitions of thumos also suggest, the "pathetic" appeal reinvigorates experience and experiencing with a specified energy, thumos, or *Geist*. Arguments that will carry a case will manipulate already available responses by appealing to the spirit or energy of those who display those responses. They will not succeed if they merely elaborate the correct choices on an abstract list of positive and negative feelings, no matter how skillfully they do so.

Of course, specific pedagogies determine how these responses become differentially available and how the ethical and logical arguments that evoke them are perceived to "fit" specific rhetorical performances. But even this partial introduction of the many implications of thumos for discussions of the workings of rhetorical appeals uncovers a familiar and discernible energy, a feeling that persuades others, and ourselves. That energy is clearly not separate from reason, if separate categories are thought as more than artifacts of the *axis mundi*. Nor are we unfamiliar with its human sources.

Notes

Works Cited

Index

Notes

Introduction: Rhetoric, Emotion, and Places of Persuasion

1. See Clanchy, ch. 9, "Trusting and Writing."

2. See Butler:

> For rhetoric, he could not ope
> His mouth, but out there flew a trope. . . .
> Else, when with greatest art he spoke,
> You'd think he talk'd like other folk,
> For all a rhetorician's rules
> Teach nothing but to name his tools. (*Hudibras* 11.81–82, 87–90)

3. See Worsham, "Eating History," 145.

4. The articles on which the book is based are the following: "Aristotle: Emotion and Moral Virtue," "Aristotle's Rhetoric on Emotions," "Aristotle: Animals, Emotion and Moral Virtue," and "On the Antecedents of Aristotle's Bipartite Psychology."

5. See the project outline at <http://www.rhetoricculture.org/conpast.htm>, n.d.

6. In the first instance, Micciche, in "Emotion, Ethics, and Rhetorical Action," cites Nelson, Megill, and McCloskey, *Rhetoric of the Human Sciences*, ix; in the second, she quotes from Simons, *Rhetorical Turn*, 17. Micciche's essay focuses on recent treatments of emotion in composition studies (161–84). See also Bouson, "True Confessions," for a study of professional "emotional troubles" (625).

7. See LeDoux, *Emotional Brain*, "Emotion and the Amygdala," "Emotional Memory Systems in the Brain," and "Emotion, Memory and the Brain"; and Aggleton and Mishkin, "Amygdala."

8. Kerford attributes the pedagogic method of question and answer to the Sophists and locates its source in Socrates (*Sophistic Movement*). See also Beck, *Greek Education*, 197.

9. Said's *Orientalism* names Western representations of Asian and mid-Eastern cultures that justify Western dominance as "Orientalism," a highly contested term.

10. See Aristotle, *Nicomachean Ethics*, 1155a10–1172a15.

11. Citation of Gorgias, *Encomium of Helen* (MacDowell translation and cited by his line numbers), in Register, "Logic and Validity."

12. See also Swanson, *Public and the Private*.

13. The tenor of many antique examples of envy catalogued in Walcot's *Envy and the Greeks* also identifies this emotion as a political force; for instance, a funeral speech by Lysias sees envy and jealousy as direct causes of war among the Greeks.

14. See Gill, "Did Galen Understand Platonic and Stoic Thinking on Emotions?," 126–29.

15. See Bataille, *Accursed Share*; and Clement, *Lives and Legends of Jacques Lacan,* 134: "The same goes for women as for madmen: in a *manifest* position of exclusion, they keep the system together, *latently,* by virtue of their very exclusion" (emphasis in original).

16. Peter Green's full translation of the poem retains its sense of simultaneous feelings, not the "approach/avoidance" imposed on it by some: "I hate and love. You wonder, perhaps, why I'd do that? / I have no idea. I just feel it. I am crucified" (Catullus, *Poems of Catullus* 191).

1. Decentering Rhetoric

1. See Murphy, *Three Medieval Rhetorical Arts*, xiv–xv.

2. See Poster, "Pedagogy and Bibliography." See also Brandes, *History of Aristotle's* Rhetoric.

3. See also John Guillory, "Canon," 237.

4. For instance, Ringvej cites deliberations of the Argives in Aeschylus's *Suppliants* as evidence of a full-fledged democracy as early as 508 BCE in "Interpretation of a Political Idea," 239–61. Cited by Pernot, review, 12–14.

5. Nonetheless, this information is successfully retrieved in many cases by those reading papyrological evidence; see, e.g., Bagnall, *Reading Papyri.*

6. See also K. Robb, *Literacy and Paideia in Ancient Greece*, "The Greek Alphabet."

7. For the commonality of handbooks, see Kennedy, *Classical Rhetoric*, 19. For the thought processes attached to the alphabet, see Havelock, *Literate Revolution*, esp. 8: the alphabet "converted the Greek spoken tongue into an artifact,

thereby separating it from the speaker and making it into a 'language,' that is, an object available for inspection, reflection, analysis."

8. Arguments on both sides include Fox, "Ancient Egyptian Rhetoric"; Cole, "Who Was Corax?"; and Grimaldi, "How Do We Get from Corax–Tisias to Plato–Aristotle in Greek Rhetorical Theory?" Cicero refers to the Sicilian origin of rhetoric in *Brutus.*

9. This oversimplified logic is not far from Hugo Rabe's 1931 updating of Christianus Walz's *Rhetores Graeci,* which describes the return of democracy to Syracuse: "The people had produced an unsteady and disorderly state of affairs, and he [Corax] thought that it was speech by which the course of human events was brought to order. He then contemplated turning the people toward and away from the proper course of action through speech" (Rabe, *Prolegomena* 270 qtd. in Schiappa, 43).

10. See Koziak, *Retrieving Political Emotion,* 30.

11. See Wisse, *Ethos and Pathos,* 7.

12. See Griswold, "Plato on Rhetoric and Poetry."

13. See also Ledbetter, *Poetics before Plato.*

14. See Kennedy, *Art of Persuasion,* 54–57, and *New History,* 48–49; and Quintilian, *Institutes,* 3.1.14; all cited by Kirby, review.

15. I cite the first edition of Corbett to identify the revival of interest in rhetoric within English studies in the last quarter of the twentieth century.

16. See the last chapter of Oliensis's *Horace and the Rhetoric of Authority* for a detailed argument that Horace agrees with Cicero (*De Officiis*) in *Ars Poetica* about crafting character and for Horace's adoption of the "mad poet" creative identity simultaneously to efface and face down audiences.

17. See Robinson, *Contrasting Arguments,* 34–41, for a discussion of this dating and proposals that it was written much earlier. The point, however, is that the binary quality of its exchanges circulated throughout early Greek history in many forms.

18. Arieti is referring to classical analyses by Werner Jaeger and W. K. C. Guthrie.

19. See S. Miller, *Rescuing the Subject,* 104–24.

20. Qtd. in Andrew Gregory, handout for course HPSC 325, the History of Science, lecture 3.1, "Babylonian Astrology and Medicine, 1. The Babylonian Achievements," <www.ucl.ac.uk/sts/gregory/325/handouts/h03_bab.doc>.

21. See Kerby, *Narrative and the Self,* 4–6.

22. E.g., Jarratt, *Rereading the Sophists;* Neel, *Plato, Derrida, and Writing;* and Vitanza, *Writing Histories of Rhetoric.* Relevant sources that are not referenced to composition studies are multitudinous, but especially helpful are Poster, "Persuasion in an Empty Ontology"; and Poulakos, "Early Changes."

23. His exclusion of women from thinking this way is legendary. See Aristotle, *Politics,* 1260a12–14.

24. "Words spoken are symbols or signs of affections or impressions of the soul, written words are the signs of words spoken. As writing, so also is speech not the same for all races of men. But the mental affections themselves, of which these words are primarily signs, are the same for the whole of mankind, as are also the objects of which these affections are representations or likenesses, images, copies" (Aristotle, *On Interpretation* I.16a).

25. See L. Green, "Aristotle's Enthymeme"; and Jeffrey Walker, "Body of Persuasion" and "*Pathos* and *Katharsis*," esp. 84–85.

26. See Bobzien, "Determinism and Freedom."

27. See Hoskin, "Technologies of Learning."

28. See Vlastos, *Socrates*; and Plato, *Ion*.

29. See Derrida, "Plato's Pharmacy."

30. See Manetti, *Theories of the Sign*, 3–5.

31. See also Covino, *Art of Wondering* and *Magic, Rhetoric, and Literacy*.

2. Trusting Texts

1. See Krueger, *Reader's Repentance*; and Donawerth, "Poaching on Men's Philosophies."

2. See Rosenwein, *Anger's Past*, 5; and Justice, *Writing and Rebellion*, 16–26. Justice describes the writing of the petitions as "acts of assertive literacy" guided by the processes of epistolary instruction (24).

3. See Jardine, "Humanism and the Teaching of Logic," 805–6.

4. Jones, in *Triumph of the English Language,* 211, dates the acceptance of the vernacular as precisely between 1575 and 1580, a turn he attributes to poets.

5. See Meyers, "Method and Civic Education."

6. See Rodd, "Before the Flood," 64.

7. See Love, *Scribal Publications*, 15; and North, *Anonymous Renaissance*, ch. 6.

8. See Lowenstein, "Script in the Marketplace," 101–3.

9. See Stern, "'Small-Beer Health,'" 187. For a slightly different interpretation, see Preiss, "Natural Authorship."

10. See Day, *English Secretorie*, table of contents. See also Richard Rambuss, "Secretary's Study," for an exposition of the secrecy attached to both secretaries and their "cabinets," writing places.

11. See Hexter, "Education of the Aristocracy," 54.

12. See McKeon, "Politics of Discourses," 44.

13. See Morson, "Misanthropology," 60.

14. See Norton, "Sir Francis Bacon."

15. See Kahn and Hutson's introduction to their anthology *Rhetoric and Law in Early Modern Europe*, 19; and Hirschman, *Passions and Interests*.

16. See T. Miller, *Selected Writings of John Witherspoon*, and *Formation of College English*.

17. See Westlake's review of Albrecht Dihle, *Studien zur griechischen Biographie*, for reference to Ion, Herodotus, and Sophocles' pre-Platonic characters; Osley, "Greek Biographies," for Isocrates; and Isocrates, *Evagoras*, 9.

18. Many exceptions to this assertion fortunately take up women speakers, as do K. Campbell's *Women Public Speakers*, Royster's *Traces of a Stream*, and Glenn's *Rhetoric Retold* and *Unspoken*, among many others. Spofford's "First Steps in Literacy" and Vincent's *Literacy and Popular Culture*, with many of their other works, detail literate practices and autodidacticism among working-class English men. Cushman's study of the rhetorical acumen of African American welfare recipients, *Struggle and the Tools*, and Moss's analyses of spoken exchanges and sermons in African American churches, *A Community Text Arises*, are among many rhetorically oriented studies of minorities, as is Gonzalez's *I Am My Language*. My point is that such work is only rarely referenced to, or by, centrist studies of a unified, classically oriented "rhetoric."

19. See Poster, "Conversation Halved."

20. See Foucault, "What Is an Author?"; and Woodmansee, "Genius and the Copyright."

21. See Henderson, "Humanist Letter Writing," 27.

22. See P. Burke, *Art of Conversation*, for a sociolinguistic historical approach to these guides.

23. E.g., Perelman, "The Medieval Art of Letter Writing," 116. Camargo says in his introduction to the *Rhetorica* issue on epistolary rhetoric that a small chapter on letter writing in the fourth-century *Ars rhetorica* of Julius Victor is singular in including this material in a textbook (135–36). See also McNabb.

24. See S. Miller, *Assuming the Positions,* 205.

25. Evidence of this decline is substantial, but many note the persistence of letter-writing manuals.

26. See Perelman, "Medieval Art of Letter Writing," 99, 102. Perelman cites Murphy, *Rhetoric in the Middle Ages,* 202.

27. Seventeenth-century France and nineteenth-century California attempted to outlaw dueling; neither was successful.

3. The Mobility of Trust

1. See Scott, *Only Paradoxes to Offer,* for the gendering and classing of the subjectivity of republican citizenry.

2. See McKeon, "Politics of Discourse," 46–47.

3. The *Oxford English Dictionary* (1979 ed.) cites definitions of "medium" as "a means or channel of communication" as early as Bacon's 1605 *Advancement*

of Learning. The word also applies to "a species of musical recitation forming the medium between air and rhetorical declamation" in 1786. But the *OED*'s earliest citation of "media" as "means of mass communication" is G. Snow in N. T. Praigg, *Advertising & Selling* (1923): "Mass media represents the most economical way of getting the story over the new and wider market in the least time."

4. See Bakhtin, *Dialogic Imagination.*

5. See Milton, *Paradise Lost*, 7.31; and Jonson, *Works*, 5:432.

6. Ross also notes Jane Tompkins's similar statement in her "Reader in History," 211–16.

7. See Newton, "Sociogenesis of Emotion"; Armstrong and Tennenhouse, *Ideology of Conduct*; and Goldberg, *Sex and Enlightenment.*

8. See Ross, "Emergence of 'Literature,'"407.

9. Recall Aristotle's attention to pity and fear in the *Poetics*, and other treatises that directly address separate feelings in forms of ancient psychology. Seneca (4 BCE–65 CE), for instance, treats anger, an agitation combined with will and judgment, as a developmental symptom. He recasts Aristotle's ages of feeling as the child's sharp, unfocused expressions and the "irritability" of old age. Many also, of course, elaborate on Socrates' and Plato's opposition of body to reason, tellingly using "diseased mind" to connect emotion to various forms of judgment. Both Chrysippus (280–209 BCE), who evidently wrote a lost work on rhetoric, and Plutarch (46?–120? CE), whose *Lives of the Ten Orators* verifies his attention, believe emotion to be evidence of ailing reason in erroneous and hasty, but potentially "reasonable," evaluations. That category is also traced in the later Cartesian link between emotion and cognition, the dominant paradigm within which modern philosophy addresses feelings, treating them as more and less rational processes. Posidonius (130–46 BCE) maintains the evaluative category but undertakes intertextual emotion critique in his refutation of Chrysippus. Passions cannot, he responds, be erroneous judgments since, again following Plato, emotions are irrational from the start, not an oxymoronic "unreasonable reason."

10. See Ross, "Emergence of 'Literature,'"407.

11. Ross cites Cicero, *Of Oratory*, 1.8.33, as attributing to both poets and orators the power to "gather scattered humanity into one place, or to lead it out of its brutish existence in the wilderness up to our present condition of civilization as men and as citizens, or, after the establishment of social communities, to give shape to laws, tribunals, and civic rights." As chapter 2 argues, many rhetorics attribute these contributions to ancient civilizing influences.

12. See, e.g., Rajeswari, *Lie of the Land*, for the East Indian example of critical pedagogy.

13. See Foucault, *History of Sexuality*, 67.

14. See Berlin, "Postmodernism, Politics, and the Histories of Rhetoric," cited in Graff and Leff, "Revisionist Historiography and Rhetorical Tradition(s)," 25.

15. See T. Miller, *Formation of College English*. Miller discusses standards for English usage and taste, calling the elocutionists "the best example of how early English teachers worked to unify the nation by eradicating the dialectical differences that distinguished provincials" (18).

16. Scafuro also cites Graf, "Gestures and Conventions."

17. Cited in Bantock: Stanhope, *Lord Chesterfield's Letters*, 102. See McClish, "Is Manner in Everything, All?"

18. See Feather, *Provincial Book Trade*, 33; and Ulman, *Things, Thoughts, Words, and Actions*, 48.

19. Spoel cites in this regard Gray, "What Was Elocution?"; Grover, "John Walker"; Guthrie, "Elocution Movement"; Haberman, "English Sources of American Elocution"; Mohrmann, "Language of Nature"; Parrish, "Concept of 'Naturalness'" and "Elocution"; M. Robb, *Oral Interpretation of Literature*; and Vandraegen, "Thomas Sheridan and the Natural School."

20. See Ulman, *Things, Thoughts, Words, and Actions*, 26.

21. See Beal, *English Pronunciation*, for the connection between such projects and land reform, which motivated Spence's many educational projects for the illiterate poor.

22. See Matthews, "Psychological Crystal Palace?," 127.

23. E.g., in McLuhan and Lapham, *Understanding Media*.

24. Compare Blair, *Lectures on Rhetoric and Belles Lettres*, 1:124: "The Progress of Language, in this respect, resembles the progress of age in man."

25. See Bataille, *Accursed Share*, 21.

26. See Hudson, *Writing and European Thought*, 141.

27. See Trowbridge, "Scattered Atoms of Probability."

Conclusion: Centering Rhetoric—The Psychology of Anxious Moments and Solemn Occasions

1. E.g., Eagleton, *Literary Theory*, ch. 1, and "Subject of Literature"; and Hunter, *Culture and Government*, 4, 67.

2. Hesiod is sometimes thought a contemporary of Homer; the best estimate of his date is sometime between the second half of the eighth century BCE and the first quarter of the seventh.

3. See Stevenson, *Ethics and Language*.

4. See Koziak, *Retrieving Political Emotion*, 53; Bremmer, *Early Greek Concept of the Soul*, 55; and Redfield, *Nature and Culture*, 173.

Works Cited

Adkins, Arthur. "Orality and Philosophy." *Language and Thought in Early Greek Philosophy*. Ed. Kevin Robb. La Salle: Hegeler Institute, 1983. 206–27.

Aeschylus. *Aeschylus: The Suppliants*. Trans. Peter Burian. Princeton: Princeton UP, 1991.

Aggleton, J. P., and M. Mishkin. "The Amygdala: Sensory Gateway to the Emotions." *Emotion: Theory, Research, and Experience*. Ed. R. Plutchik and H. Kellerman. Orlando: Academic, 1986. 281–99.

Alberic of Monte Cassino. *Flowers of Rhetoric*. Trans. Joseph M. Miller. *Readings in Medieval Rhetoric*. Ed. Thomas W. Benson, Joseph M. Miller, and Michael H. Prosser. Bloomington: U of Indiana P, 1973.

Albrecht-Crane, Christa. "An Affirmative Theory of Desire." *Journal of Advanced Composition* 23.3 (2003): 563–98.

Althusser, Louis. "Ideology and Ideological State Apparatuses (Notes towards an Investigation)." *Lenin and Philosophy and Other Essays*. Trans. Ben Brewster. London: New Left, 1971. 127–86.

Arieti, James A. *Interpreting Plato: The Dialogues as Drama*. Savage, Md.: Rowman and Littlefield, 1991.

Aristotle. *The Nicomachean Ethics*. Trans. W. D. Ross. *Digireads.com*. 2005.

———. *On Interpretation*. Trans. E.M. Edghill. Loeb Classical Library. Cambridge: Harvard UP, 1938.

———. *Poetics*. Trans. Ingram Bywater. New York: Modern Library, 1954.

———. *Politics*. Trans. H. Rackam. <http://www.perseus.tufts.edu>.

———. *Rhetoric: A Theory of Civic Discourse*. Trans. George Kennedy. New York: Oxford UP, 1991.

Armstrong, Nancy. *Desire and Domestic Fiction: A Political History of the Novel*. New York: Oxford UP, 1987.

Armstrong, Nancy, and Leonard Tennenhouse, eds. *The Ideology of Conduct: Essays on Literature and the History of Sexuality*. New York: Methuen, 1987.

Arnold, Magna B. *Feelings and Emotions: The Loyola Symposium*. New York: Academic, 1970.

Arranz, José María Gutiérrez, and Ricardo J. Sola Buil. Rev. of "The Late Medieval Epistle," *Disputatio: An International Transdisciplinary Journal of the Late Middle Ages*. Ed. Carol Poster and Richard J. Utz. *Prolepsis: The Tuebingen Review of English Studies*. 4 Nov. 1998. <http://www.uni-tuebingen.de/uni/nes/prolepsis/98_9_arr.html>.

Bacon, Sir Francis. *De Augmentis*. London: Longman's, 1901. Vol. 4 of *The Works*. Ed. J. Spedding, R. L. Ellis, and D. D. Heath.

Bagnall, Roger S. *Reading Papyri, Writing Ancient History*. New York: Routledge, 1995.

Bakhtin, M. M. *The Dialogic Imagination: Four Essays*. Austin: U of Texas P, 1981.

Baldwin, T. W. *Shakespeare's Five-Act Structure*. Urbana: U of Illinois P, 1947.

Bantock, G. H. "Educating the Emotions: An Historical Perspective." *British Journal of Educational Studies* 34.2 (June 1986): 122–41.

Barthes, Roland. *S/Z*. Trans. Richard Miller. New York: Hill and Wang, 1974.

Bataille, George. *The Accursed Share*. Trans. Robert Hurley. New York: Zone, 1988.

Beach, Adam R. "The Creation of a Classical Language in the Eighteenth Century: Standardizing English, Cultural Imperialism, and the Future of the Literary Canon." *Texas Studies in Literature and Language* 43.2 (2001): 117–41.

Beal, Joan. *English Pronunciation in the Eighteenth Century: Thomas Spence's "Grand Repository of the English Language."* Oxford: Oxford UP, 1999.

Beals, Peter. *In Praise of Scribes: Manuscripts and Their Makers in Seventeenth-Century England*. The Lyell Lectures: 1995–1996. Oxford: Clarendon, 1998.

Beck, Frederick A. G. *Greek Education: 450–350 B.C.* New York: Barnes and Noble, 1970.

Belfiore, Elizabeth. *Tragic Pleasures: Aristotle on Plot and Emotion*. Princeton: Princeton UP, 1992.

Bender, John, and David E. Wellbery. "Rhetoricality: On the Modernist Return of Rhetoric." *The Ends of Rhetoric: History, Theory, Practice*. Ed. John Bender and David E. Wellbery. Stanford: Stanford UP, 1990. 3–39.

Bénichou, Paul. *The Consecration of the Writer: 1750–1830*. Trans. Mark K. Jensen. Lincoln: U of Nebraska P, 1999.

Berchman, Robert M., ed. *Mediators of the Divine: Horizons of Prophecy, Divination, Dreams and Theurgy in Mediterranean Antiquity*. Atlanta: Scholar, 1998.

Berlin, James. "Postmodernism, Politics, and Histories of Rhetoric." *Pre/Text* 11.3–4 (1990): 169–87.

————. "A Revisionary History: The Dialectic Method." *Pre/Text* 8.1–2 (1987): 47–61.

Bettini, Maurizio. Preface. *Poet, Public, and Performance in Ancient Greece: From Homer to the Fifth Century.* Ed. Lowell Edmunds and Robert W. Wallace. Baltimore: Johns Hopkins UP, 1997. vii–xiii.

Blair, Hugh. *Lectures on Rhetoric and Belles Lettres.* 2 vols. London, 1783.

Bobzien, Susanne. "Determinism and Freedom in Stoic Philosophy." *Oxford University Press Oxford Scholarship Online.* Oxford: Oxford UP, 2001. <http://www.oxfordscholarship.com/oso/public/content/philosophy/0199247676/toc.html>.

Bonanno, Maria Grazia. "All the (Greek) World's a Stage: Notes on (Not Just Dramatic) Greek Staging." *Poet, Public, and Performance in Ancient Greek: From Homer to the Fifth Century.* Ed. Lowell Edmunds and Robert W. Wallace. Baltimore: Johns Hopkins UP, 1997. 112–23.

Boswell, Grant. "Language and Emotion in 17th-Century Rhetorics." Paper presented at the annual meeting of the International Society for the History of Rhetoric. U of Saskatchewan, Saskatoon. 22 July 1997.

Boswell, James. *The Life of Samuel Johnson.* Ed. G. B. Hill, rev. L. F. Powell. 6 vols. Oxford: Clarendon, 1964.

Boucher, Warren. "Literature, Thought or Fact? Past and Present Directions in the Study of the Early Modern Letter." *Self-Presentation and Social Identification: The Rhetoric and Pragmatics of Letter Writing in Early Modern Times.* Ed. Constant Matheussen, Jan Papy, Gilbert Tourney, and Toon Van Houdt. Leuven, Belgium: Leuven UP, 2002. 137–63.

Bouson, J. Brooks. "True Confessions: Uncovering the Hidden Culture of Shame in English Studies." *Journal of Advanced Composition* 25.4 (2005): 625–50.

Branch, Lori. "Rituals of Spontaneity: Novelty, Repetition, and the Quandaries of Resistance in Eighteenth-Century Britain." Diss. Indiana U, 2000.

Brand, Alice G. "Social Cognition, Emotions, and the Psychology of Writing." *Journal of Advanced Composition* 11.2 (1991): 395–407.

————. "The Why of Cognition: Emotion and the Writing Process." *College Composition and Communication* 38.4 (1987): 436–43.

Brandes, Paul D. *A History of Aristotle's* Rhetoric*, with a Bibliography of Early Printings.* Metuchen: Scarecrow, 1989.

Bremmer, Jan. *The Early Greek Concept of the Soul.* Princeton: Princeton UP, 1987.

Bristol, Michael D., and Arthur F. Marotti, eds. Introduction. *Print, Manuscript, Performance: The Changing Relations of the Media in Early Modern England.* Columbus: Ohio State UP, 2000. 1–32.

Brome, Alexander. *Songs and other Poems.* London, 1661.

Bronson, Bertrand Harris. *Facets of the Enlightenment.* Berkeley: U of California P, 1968.

Brown, Peter Robert Lamont. *Power and Persuasion in Late Antiquity: Towards a Christian Empire.* Madison: U of Wisconsin P, 1992.

Bryant, Donald. "Rhetoric: Its Functions and Its Scope." *Quarterly Journal of Speech* 39 (Dec. 1953): 401–24.

Burckhardt, Jacob. *The Civilization of the Renaissance in Italy.* Trans. S. G. C. Middlemore. New York: Penguin, 1990.

Burke, Edmund. *Reflections on the French Revolution.* London: Dent, 1955.

Burke, Kenneth. *Language as Symbolic Action: Essays on Life, Literature, and Method.* Berkeley: U of California P, 1966.

———. *A Rhetoric of Motives.* Berkeley: U of California P, 1969.

Burke, Peter. *The Art of Conversation.* Ithaca: Cornell UP, 1993.

Bury, J. B., and Russell Meiggs. *A History of Greece to the Death of Alexander the Great.* 4th ed. London: Macmillan, 1975.

Butler, Samuel. *Hudibras. The Norton Anthology of English Literature.* 3rd ed. 2 vols. New York: Norton, 1974. 1:1865–72.

Camargo, Martin. "The Waning of Medieval *Ars Dictaminis.*" *Rhetorica* 19.2 (2001): 135–40.

Camlot, Jason. "Early Talking Books: Spoken Recordings and Recitation Anthologies, 1880–1920." *Book History* 6 (2003): 147–73.

Campbell, George. *The Philosophy of Rhetoric.* Ed. Lloyd F. Bitzer. Carbondale: Southern Illinois UP, 1963.

Campbell, Karlyn Kohrs. *Women Public Speakers in the United States, 1925–1933: A Bio-Critical Sourcebook.* Westport, CT: Greenwood, 1993.

Carr, Jean Ferguson, Stephen L. Carr, and Lucille M. Schultz. *Archives of Instruction: Nineteenth-Century Rhetorics, Readers, and Composition Books in the United States.* Studies in Writing and Rhetoric. Carbondale: Southern Illinois UP, 2005.

Catullus, Gaius Valerius. *The Poems of Catullus: A Bilingual Edition.* Ed. and trans. Peter Green. Berkeley: U of California P, 2005.

Chartier, Roger. *Forms and Meanings: Texts, Performances, and Audiences from Codex to Computer.* New Cultural Studies Series. Philadelphia: U of Pennsylvania P, 1995.

Cicero, Marcus Tullius. *Brutus, Orator.* Trans. G. L. Hendrickson and H. M. Hubbell. Ed. G. P. Goold. Loeb Classical Library 342. Cambridge: Harvard UP, 1988.

———. *Cicero: On Old Age, On Friendship, On Divination.* Trans. William Armistead Falconer. Loeb Classical Library 154. Cambridge: Harvard UP, 1979.

———. *De Oratore: De fato, Paradoxia Stoicorum, De partitione oratoria.* Trans. H. Rackham. Loeb Classical Library 349. Cambridge: Harvard UP, 1942.

————. *On Oratory.* Trans. E. W. Sutton and H. Rackham. *The Rhetorical Tradition: Readings from Classical Times to the Present.* Ed. Patricia Bizzell and Bruce Herzberg. Boston: St. Martin's, 1990. 195–292.

Clanchy, M. T. *From Memory to Written Record: England 1066–1307.* Rev. ed. London: Basil Blackwell, 1993.

Classen, Albrecht. "Female Explorations of Literacy: Epistolary Challenges to the Literary Canon in the Late Middle Ages." *Eighteenth-Century Studies* 17.4 (Summer 1984): 89–121.

Clément, Catherine. *The Lives and Legends of Jacques Lacan.* Trans. Arthur Goldhammer. New York: Columbia UP, 1983.

Cole, A. Thomas. Introduction. *Poetry and Its Public in Ancient Greece: From Homer to the Fifth Century.* By Bruno Gentili. Trans. A. Thomas Cole. Baltimore: Johns Hopkins UP, 1988. v–xv.

————. "Who Was Corax?" *Illinois Classical Studies* 16 (1991): 65–84.

Congleton, J. E. "Historical Development of the Concept of Rhetorical Properties." *College Composition and Communication* 5.4 (1954): 140–45.

Cooper, John M. "Posidonius on Emotions." *The Emotions in Hellenistic Philosophy.* Ed. Juha Sihvola and Troels Engberg-Pedersen. New Synthese Historical Library 46. Heidelberg and New York: Springer, 1998. 72–112.

Corbett, Edward P. J. *Classical Rhetoric for the Modern Student.* New York: Oxford UP, 1971.

Covino, William. *The Art of Wondering: A Revisionist Return to the History of Rhetoric.* Portsmouth, NH: Heinemann–Boynton/Cook, 1988.

————. *Magic, Rhetoric, and Literacy: An Eccentric History of the Composing Imagination.* Albany: SUNY P, 1994.

Craig-McFeely, Julia. "Lute Scribes and Handwriting." *English Lute Manuscripts and Scribes 1530–1630.* Thesis. U of Edinburgh, 1994. <http://www.craigmcfeely.force9.co.uk/thesis/html>.

Cushman, Ellen. *The Struggle and the Tools: Oral and Literate Strategies in an Inner City Community.* Albany: SUNY P, 1998.

Day, Angel. *English Secretorie.* London: C. Burbie, 1586.

Dear, Peter. "*Totius in verba*: Rhetoric and Authority in the Early Royal Society." *Isis* 76 (1985): 144–61.

DeQuincey, Thomas. "Language." *Collected Writings.* Vol. 10. Ed. David Masson. Edinburgh, 1890. 260–61.

de Romilly, Jacqueline. *The Great Sophists in Periclean Athens.* Trans. Janet Lloyd. Oxford: Clarendon, 1992.

————. *Magic and Rhetoric in Ancient Greece.* Cambridge: Cambridge UP, 1975.

Derrida, Jacques. "Plato's Pharmacy." *Dissemination.* Trans. Barbara Johnson. Chicago: U of Chicago P, 1981. 61–172.

Descartes, René. *The Passions of the Soul.* Trans. Stephen Voss. Indianapolis: Hackett, 1989.

Dodds, E. R. *The Greeks and the Irrational.* Berkeley: U of California P, 1956.

Donawerth, Jane. "Poaching on Men's Philosophies of Rhetoric: Eighteenth- and Nineteenth-Century Rhetorical Theory by Women." *Philosophy and Rhetoric* 33.3 (2000): 243–58.

Dougherty, Carol. *The Poetics of Colonization: From City to Text in Archaic Greece.* New York: Oxford UP, 1993.

Eagleton, Terry. *The Ideology of the Aesthetic.* Oxford: Basil Blackwell, 1990.

———. *Literary Theory: An Introduction.* Minneapolis: U of Minnesota P, 1983.

———. "The Subject of Literature." *Cultural Critique* 2 (1985): 95–104.

Edbauer, Jennifer. "(Meta)Physical Graffiti: 'Getting Up' as Affective Writing Model." *Journal of Advanced Composition* 25.1 (2005): 131–60.

Edison, Thomas A. "The Phonograph and Its Future." *North American Review* 126 (May 1878): 527–37.

Edmunds, Lowell, and Robert W. Wallace, eds. *Poet, Public, and Performance in Ancient Greece.* Baltimore: Johns Hopkins UP, 1997.

Ehninger, Douglas. "On Rhetoric and Rhetorics." *Western Speech* 31 (1967): 242–49.

———. "The Promise of Rhetoric." *H TEXNH: Proceedings of the Speech Communication Association 1978.* Ed. Richard Leo Enos and William E. Weithoff. Falls Church, Va.: Speech Communication Association, 1978. 1–9.

Eisenstein, E. L. *The Printing Press as an Agent of Change: Communication and Cultural Transformations in Early Modern Europe.* Chicago: U of Chicago P, 1979.

Erasmus, Desiderius. *The Collected Works of Erasmus.* Toronto: U of Toronto P, 1974.

Euripides. *Medea and Other Plays.* Trans. James Marwood. Oxford World Classics. Oxford: Oxford UP, 1998.

Feather, John. *The Provincial Book Trade in Eighteenth-Century England.* Cambridge: Cambridge UP, 1986.

Finely, J. H. "Aristophanes and the Art of Rhetoric." *Harvard Studies in Classical Philology* 49 (1938): 69–113.

———. "Euripides and Thucydides." *Harvard Studies in Classical Philology* 49 (1938): 23–68.

———. "The Origins of Thucydides' Style." *Harvard Studies in Classical Philology* 50 (1939): 35–84.

Fliegelman, Jay. *Declaring Independence: Jefferson, Natural Language, and the Culture of Performance.* Stanford: Stanford UP, 1993.

Fortenbaugh, W. W. "Aristotle: Animals, Emotion and Moral Virtue." *Arethusa* 4 (1971): 137–65. Rpt. in *Articles on Aristotle.* Ed. J. Barnes. London: Duckworth, 1976. 4:133–53.

——. "Aristotle: Emotion and Moral Virtue." *Arethusa* 2 (1969): 163–85.

——. *Aristotle on Emotion: A Contribution to Philosophical Psychology, Rhetoric, Poetics, and Ethics.* New York: Barnes and Noble, 1975.

——. "Aristotle's Rhetoric on Emotions." *Archiv fuer die Geschichte der Philosophie* 52 (1970): 40–70. Rpt. in *Aristotle: The Classical Heritage of Rhetoric.* Ed. K. Erickson. Metuchen, N.J.: Scarecrow, 1974. 204–34.

——. "Cicero as a Reporter of Aristotelian and Theophrastean Rhetorical Doctrine." *Rhetorica* 23.1 (Feb. 2005): 37–64.

——. "On the Antecedents of Aristotle's Bipartite Psychology." *Greek, Roman, and Byzantine Studies* 11 (1970): 233–50. Rpt. in *Essays in Ancient Greek Philosophy.* Ed. J. P. Anton and A. Preus. Vol. 2. Albany: SUNY P, 2001. 303–20.

Foucault, Michel. *The History of Sexuality: The Care of the Self.* New York: Random House, 1986, rpt. Vintage Books, 1988.

——. "What Is an Author?" *Language, Countermemory, Practice: Selected Essays and Interviews.* Ed. Donald F. Bouchard and Sherry Simon. Ithaca: Cornell UP, 1977. 113–38.

Fox, Michael V. "Ancient Egyptian Rhetoric." *Rhetorica* 1.1 (Spring 1983): 9–22.

Foxhall, Lin. "The Politics of Affection: Emotional Attachments in Athenian Society." *Kosmos: Essays in Order, Conflict and Community in Classical Athens.* Ed. Paul Cartledge, Paul Millett, and Sitta von Reden. Cambridge: Cambridge UP, 2002. 52–68.

Frede, Dorothea. "Plato's Ethics: An Overview." *The Stanford Encyclopedia of Philosophy.* Fall 2003 ed. Ed. Edward N. Zalta. <http://plato.stanford.edu/archives/fall2004/entries/plato-ethics//>.

Freedman, Joseph S. "The Diffusion of the Writing of Petrus Ramus in Central Europe, c. 1570–c. 1630." *Renaissance Quarterly* 46.1 (1993): 98–152.

Galin, David. "Rehabilitating the Concept 'Spirit' for the Non-Religious and the Scientifically-Minded." Abstract. San Francisco: Publication of Langley Porter Neuropsychiatric Institute, University of California, 2004.

Gentili, Bruno. *Poetry and Its Public in Ancient Greece: From Homer to the Fifth Century.* Trans. A. Thomas Cole. Baltimore: John Hopkins UP, 1988.

Gibbs, Anna. "Contagious Feelings: Pauline Hanson and the Epidemiology of Affect." *Australian Humanities Review* (Dec. 2001). <http://www.lib.latrobe.edu.au/AHR/archives/Issues-December-2001/gibbs.html>.

Gill, Christopher. "Did Galen Understand Platonic and Stoic Thinking on Emotions?" *The Emotions in Hellenistic Philosophy.* Ed. Juha Sihvola and Troels Engberg-Pedersen. New Synthese Historical Libraries 46. Heidelberg and New York: Springer, 1998. 113–48.

Gillingham, John. "From *Civilitas* to Civility: Codes and Manners in Medieval and Early Modern England." *Transactions of the Royal Historical Society* 12 (2002): 267–89.

Gleason, Maud. "The Semiotics of Gender: Physiognomy and Self-Fashioning in the Second Century B.C." *Before Sexuality: The Construction of Erotic Experience in the Ancient Greek World.* Ed. D. M. Halpern, J. J. Winkler, and F. Zenithin. Princeton: Princeton UP, 1991. 389–415.

Glenn, Cheryl. *Rhetoric Retold: Regendering the Tradition from Antiquity through the Renaissance.* Carbondale: Southern Illinois UP, 1997.

———. *Unspoken: A Rhetoric of Silence.* Carbondale: Southern Illinois UP, 2004.

Goldberg, Rita. *Sex and Enlightenment.* Cambridge: Cambridge UP, 1984.

Goldhill, Simon, and Robin Osborne, eds. *Performance Culture and Athenian Democracy.* Cambridge: Cambridge UP, 1999.

Gonzalez, Norma. *I Am My Language: Discourses of Women and Children in the Borderlands.* Tucson: U of Arizona P, 2001.

Graf, Fritz. "Gestures and Conventions: The Gestures of Roman Actors and Orators." *A Cultural History of Gestures.* Ed. J. Bremmer and H. Roodenburg. Ithaca: Cornell UP, 1994. 36–58.

Graff, Richard, and Michael Leff. "Revisionist Historiography and Rhetorical Tradition(s)." *The Viability of the Rhetorical Tradition.* Ed. Richard Graff, Arthur E. Walzer, and Janet M. Atwill. Albany: SUNY P, 2005. 11–30.

Gray, Giles Wilkenson. "What Was Elocution?" *Quarterly Journal of Speech* 46.1 (Feb. 1960): 1–7.

Green, Lawrence D. "Aristotle's Enthymeme and the Imperfect Syllogism." *Rhetoric and Pedagogy: Its History, Philosophy, and Practices, Essays in Honor of James J. Murphy.* Ed. Winifred Bryan Horner and Michael Leff. Mahwah, N.J.: Lawrence Erlbaum, 1995. 19–41.

———. "Aristotle's *Rhetoric* and Renaissance Views of the Emotions." *Renaissance Rhetoric.* Ed. Peter Mack. New York: St. Martin's, 1994. 1–26.

Green, Ronald Walter. "Rhetoric and Capitalisms: Rhetorical Agency as Communicative Labor." *Philosophy and Rhetoric* 37.3 (2002): 188–206.

Greenblatt, Stephen. *Renaissance Self-Fashioning: From More to Shakespeare.* Chicago: U Chicago P, 1980.

Greg, W. W. *The Shakespeare First Folio: Its Bibliographical and Textual History.* Oxford: Clarendon, 1955.

Griffiths, Paul E. *What Emotions Really Are: The Problem of Psychological Categories.* Chicago: U of Chicago P, 1997.

Grimaldi, William. *Aristotle, Rhetoric II: A Commentary.* New York: Fordham UP, 1988.

———. "How Do We Get from Corax–Tisias to Plato–Aristotle in Greek Rhetorical Theory?" *Theory, Text, Context: Issues in Greek Rhetoric and Oratory.* Ed. Christopher Lyle Johnstone. Albany: SUNY P, 1996. 19–43.

Griswold, Charles. "Plato on Rhetoric and Poetry." *The Stanford Encyclopedia of Philosophy.* Spring 2004 ed. Ed. Edward N. Zalta. <http://plato.stanford.edu/archives/spr2004/entries/plato-rhetoric/>.

Gross, Daniel. *The Secret History of Emotion: From Aristotle's* Rhetoric *to Modern Brain Science.* Chicago: U of Chicago P, 2006.

Grossberg, Lawrence. *We Gotta Get Out of This Place: Popular Conservatism and Postmodern Culture.* New York: Routledge, 1992.

Grover, David H. "John Walker: The 'Mechanical' Man Revisited." *Southern Speech Journal* 34 (Summer 1969): 288–97.

Guillory, John. "Canon." *Critical Terms for Literary Study.* Ed. Frank Lentricchia and Thomas McLaughlin. Chicago: U of Chicago P, 1990. 233–49.

Guthrie, Warren. "The Elocution Movement—England." *Speech Monographs* 18 (Mar. 1951): 17–30.

Haberman, Frederick W. "English Sources of American Elocution." *Histories of Speech Education in America: Background Series.* Ed. Karl M. Wallace. New York: Appleton-Century-Crofts, 1954. 105–25.

Hamilton, David. "From Dialectic to Didactic." Nov. 2001. Working Papers from the Textbook Colloquium, no. 4. <http://facultyedu.uiuc.edu/westburg/textcol/HAMILTON.html>.

———. "Instructions in the Making: Peter Ramus and the Beginning of Modern Schooling." Paper presented at the Annual Convention of the American Educational Research Association. Chicago. 21–25 Apr. 2003.

Hamilton, Mary. "Expanding the New Literacy Studies." *Situated Literacies: Readings and Writing in Context.* Ed. David Barton, Mary Hamilton, and Roz Ivaic. New York: Routledge, 1999. 16–34.

Hansen, Morgens Herman. *The Athenian Assembly in the Age of Democritus.* Oxford: Basil Blackwell, 1987.

Hartmann, Frank. "nettime: Communication Material/on the position of F. A. Kittler." 5 Mar. 1997. <http://www.nettime.org/Lists-Archives/nettimes-1-9703/msg00016.html>.

Haugen, Kristine Louise. "Death of an Author: Constructions of Pseudonymity in the Battle of the Books." *The Faces of Anonymity: Anonymous and Pseudonymous Publication from the Sixteenth to the Twentieth Century.* Ed. Robert J. Griffin. New York: Basingstoke, 2003. 39–62.

Havelock, Eric. "The Linguistic Task of the Presocratics." *Language and Thought in Early Greek Philosophy.* Ed. Kevin Robb. La Salle, Ill.: Hegeler Institute, 1983. 7–82.

———. *The Literate Revolution in Greece and Its Cultural Consequences.* Princeton: Princeton UP, 1982.

Haynes, Cynthia. "pathos@play.prosthetic.emotion." *Works and Days: Essays in Socio-Historical Dimensions of Literature and the Arts* 13.1–2 (1995): 261–76.

Hazlitt, William. "On the Difference between Writing and Speaking." *Selected Essays*. Ed. Geoffrey Keynes. London: Nonesuch, 1930. <http://www.blupete. com/Literature/Essays/Hazlitt/DiffWritSpeak.htm>.

Heil, John. "The 'Appearance' of Emotions in *Republic*." Fourth Annual Arizona Colloquium in Ancient Philosophy. University of Arizona, Tucson. 21 Feb. 1999.

Henderson, Judith Rice. "Humanist Letter Writing: Private Conversations or Public Forum?" *Self-Presentation and Social Identification: The Rhetoric and Pragmatics of Letter Writing in Early Modern Times*. Ed. Constant Matheussen, Jan Papy, Gilbert Tourney, and Toon Van Houdt. Leuven, Belgium: Leuven UP, 2002. 17–38.

———. "Valla's *Elegantiae* and the Humanist Attack on the *Ars dictaminis*." *Rhetorica* 19.2 (2001): 249–68.

Heumann, Michael Douglas. "The Ghost in the Machine: Sound and Technology in Twentieth-Century Literature." Diss. U of California, Riverside, 1998.

Hexter, J. H. "The Education of the Aristocracy in the Renaissance." *Reappraisals in History: New Views on History and Society in Early Modern Europe*. 2nd ed. Chicago: U of Chicago P, 1979. 45–70.

Hillman, James. *Emotion: A Comprehensive Phenomenology of Theories and Their Meaning for Therapy*. Evanston: Northwestern UP, 1960.

Hinman, Charlton. *The Printing and Proof-Reading of the First Folio of Shakespeare*. 2 vols. Oxford: Clarendon, 1963.

Hirschman, Albert O. *The Passions and Interests: Political Arguments for Capitalism before Its Triumph*. Princeton: Princeton UP, 1977.

Hobbs, Angela. *Plato and the Hero: Courage, Manliness and the Impersonal Good*. Cambridge: Cambridge UP, 2000.

The Holy Bible: Revised Standard Edition. New York: New American Library, 1962.

Hoskin, Keith. "Technologies of Learning and Alphabetic Culture: The History of Writing as the History of Education." *The Insistence of the Letter: Literacy Studies and Curriculum Theorizing*. Ed. Bill Green. Pittsburgh: U of Pittsburgh P, 1993. 27–45.

Howell, Wilbur Samuel. *Eighteenth-Century British Logic and Rhetoric*. Princeton: Princeton UP, 1971.

Hudson, Nicholas. *Writing and European Thought: 1600–1830*. Cambridge: Cambridge UP, 1994.

Hume, David. *The History of England: From the Invasion of Julius Caesar to the Revolution in 1688*. Ed. William B. Todd. 6 vols. Indianapolis: Liberty Classics, 1983.

———. "Of the Standard of Taste." *Four Dissertations*. London, 1757. <http://fordham.edu/halsal/mod/1760hume-taste-html>.

Hunter, Ian. "Aesthetics and Cultural Studies." *Cultural Studies*. Ed. Lawrence Grossberg, Cary Nelson, and Paula Treichler. New York: Routledge, 1992. 347–72.

———. *Culture and Government*. London: Macmillan, 1988.

Hutson, Lorna, and Victoria Kahn. Introduction. *Rhetoric and Law in Early Modern Europe*. Ed. Victoria Kahn and Lorna Hutson. New Haven: Yale UP, 2001. 10–29.

Rev. of *An Introduction to the Art of Reading*, by John Rice. *Monthly Review* 32 (1965): 445–46.

Irvine, T. "A Sociolinguistic Approach to Emotion Concepts in a Senegalese Community." *Everyday Conceptions of Emotion: An Introduction to the Psychology, Anthropology, and Linguistics of Emotion*. Ed. J. A. Russell, José-Miguel Fernández-Dols, Anthony S. R. Manstead, and Jane C. Wellenkamp. Nato Science Series D. Heidelberg and New York: Springer, 1995. 251–89.

Isocrates. *Evagoras. Isocrates III*. Trans. La Roe Van Hook. Loeb Classical Library. Cambridge: Harvard UP, 1945.

Jaeger, Werner. *Paideia: The Ideals of Greek Culture*. Trans. Gilbert Highet. New York: Oxford UP, 1963. Vol. 2 of *In Search of Divine Centre*. 3 vols. 1943–45.

Jardine, Lisa. *Erasmus, Man of Letters: The Construction of Charisma in Print*. Princeton: Princeton UP, 1993.

———. "Humanism and the Teaching of Logic." *Cambridge History of Later Medieval Philosophy*. New York: Cambridge UP, 1982. 797–807.

Jarratt, Susan C. *Rereading the Sophists: Classical Rhetoric Refigured*. Carbondale: Southern Illinois UP, 1998.

Johns, Adrian. "Identity, Practice, and Trust in Early Modern Natural Philosophy." *Historical Journal* 42.4 (Dec. 1999): 1125–45.

Johnson, Samuel. *Johnson on Shakespeare*. Ed. Arthur Sherbo. New Haven: Yale UP, 1968. Vols. 7 and 8 of the *Yale Edition of the Works of Samuel Johnson*.

———. *The Works of Samuel Johnson, L.L.D.* 10 vols. Oxford, 1825. New York: AMS, 1970.

Johnston, Victor S. *Why We Feel: The Science of Human Emotion*. Reading, Pa.: Perseus, 1999.

Johnstone, Christopher. "The Origins of the Rhetorical in Archaic Greek." *Theory, Text, Context: Issues in Greek Rhetoric and Oratory*. Ed. Christopher Johnstone. Albany: SUNY P, 1997. 4–18.

Jones, Richard Foster. *The Triumph of the English Language: A Survey of Opinions Concerning the Vernacular from the Introduction of Print to the Restoration*. Stanford: Stanford UP, 1953.

Jonson, Ben. "Newes from the new world, discover'd in the Moone." *The Works of Ben Jonson*. Ed. C. H. Hereford and Percy and Evelyn Simpson. 11 vols. Oxford: Clarendon, 1925–52. 7:513–25.

———. *The Works of Ben Jonson*. Ed. C. H. Herford and Percy and Evelyn Simpson. 11 vols. Oxford: Clarendon, 1925–52.

Jowett, Benjamin. Introduction. *Laws*. By Plato. <http://isis.library.adelaide.edu/au/cgi-bin/pg/etext99/plaws1-/txt>.

Justice, Stephen. *Writing and Rebellion: England in 1381*. Berkeley: U of California P, 1994.

Kahn, Charles H. "Philosophy and the Written Word: Some Thoughts on Heraclitus and the Early Greek Uses of Prose." *Language and Thought in Early Greek Philosophy*. Ed. Kevin Robb. La Salle, Ill.: Hegeler Institute, 1983. 110–24.

Karp, Andrew. "Prophecy and Divination in Archaic Greek Literature." *Mediators of the Divine: Horizons of Prophecy and Divination in Mediterranean Antiquity*. Ed. Robert M. Berchman. Atlanta: Scholars, 1998. 9–44.

Kastley, James L. *Rethinking the Rhetorical Tradition: From Plato to Postmodernism*. New Haven: Yale UP, 1997.

Kemp, Fred. "Re: Assessing the affective." Online posting. 12 Feb. 2005. WPA-L. <http://lists.asu.edu/cgi-bin/wa?A2=ind0502&l=wpa=I&D=D&F=&S=&P+41114>.

Kennedy, George. *Aristotle on Rhetoric: A Theory of Civic Discourse*. New York: Oxford UP, 1991.

———. *The Art of Persuasion in Greece*. Princeton: Princeton UP, 1963.

———. *The Art of Rhetoric in the Roman World, 300 B.C.–A.D.300*. Princeton: Princeton UP, 1972.

———. *Classical Rhetoric and Its Christian and Secular Tradition from Modern Times*. Chapel Hill: U of North Carolina P, 1980.

———. *Comparative Rhetoric: An Historical and Cross-Cultural Introduction*. New York: Oxford UP, 1998.

———. *A New History of Classical Rhetoric*. Princeton: Princeton UP, 1994.

Kerby, Anthony Paul. *Narrative and the Self*. Bloomington: U of Indiana P, 1991.

Kerford, G. B. *The Sophistic Movement*. Cambridge: Cambridge UP, 1981.

Kirby, John T. Rev. of *The Handbook of Classical Rhetoric in the Hellenistic Period, 330 B.C.–A.D. 400*. Ed. Stanley E. Porter. *Bryn Mawr Classical Review* 7.9 (1998). <http://ccat.sas.upenn.edu/bmcr/1998/1998-07-09.html>.

Kittler, Friedrich A. *Discourse Networks: 1800/1900*. Trans. Michael Metteer with Chris Cullens. Stanford: Stanford UP, 1990.

Koziak, Barbara. *Retrieving Political Emotion: Thumos, Aristotle, and Gender*. University Park: Pennsylvania State UP, 2000.

Krueger, Christine. *The Reader's Repentance: Women Preachers, Women Writers, and Nineteenth-Century Social Discourse*. Chicago: U of Chicago P, 1992.

Ledbetter, Grace M. *Poetics before Plato: Interpretation and Authority in Early Greek Theories of Poetry*. Princeton: Princeton UP, 2003.

LeDoux, Joseph. *The Emotional Brain: The Mysterious Underpinnings of Emotional Life*. New York: Simon and Schuster, 1996.

———. "Emotional Memory Systems in the Brain." *Behavioral Brain Research* 58 (1993): 69–79.

———. "Emotion and the Amygdala." *The Amygdala: Neurobiological Aspects of Emotion, Memory, and Mental Dysfunction*. Ed. J. P. Aggleton. New York: Willey–Liss, 1992. 339–51.

———. "Emotion, Memory and the Brain." *Scientific American* 6 (1994): 50–57.

Locke, John. *A New Method of Making Common-Place Books*. London: J. Greenwood, 1706.

Love, Harold. "Dryden's Rationale of Paradox." *ELH* 51.2 (Summer 1984): 297–313.

———. *Scribal Publications in Seventeenth-Century England*. Oxford: Oxford UP, 1993.

Lowenstein, Joseph. "The Script in the Marketplace." *Representations* 12 (Autumn 1985): 101–14.

Lupton, Christiana. "*Tristram Shandy*, David Hume, and Epistemological Fiction." *Philosophy and Literature* 27.1 (2003): 98–115.

Macfarlane, Alan. "Individualism and the Ideology of Romantic Love." *Rethinking the Subject: An Anthology of Contemporary European Social Thought*. Ed. James D. Faubion. Boulder: Westview, 1995. 125–37.

MacIntyre, Alasdair. *After Virtue: A Study in Moral Theory*. 2nd ed. Notre Dame: U of Notre Dame P, 1984.

Mack, Peter. *Elizabethan Rhetoric: Theory and Practice*. Cambridge: Cambridge UP, 2002.

Manetti, Giovanni. *Theories of the Sign in Classical Antiquity*. Trans. Christine Richardson. 2nd ed. Bloomington: U of Indiana P, 1993.

Marcus, Leah S. "From Oral Delivery to Print in the Speeches of Elizabeth I." *Print, Manuscript, Performance: The Changing Relations of the Media in Early Modern England*. Ed. Michael D. Bristol and Arthur F. Marotti. Columbus: Ohio State UP, 2000. 33–48.

Margolis, Joseph. "The Emergence of Philosophy." *Language and Thought in Early Greek Philosophy*. Ed. Kevin Robb. La Salle, Ill.: Hegeler Institute, 1983. 228–43.

Markus, Hazel Rose, and Shinobu Kitayama. "The Cultural Construction of Self and Emotion: Implications for Social Behavior." *Emotion and Culture: Empirical Studies of Mutual Influence*. Ed. Shinobu Kitayama and Hazel Rose Markus. Washington, D.C.: American Psychological Association, 1994. 89–130.

Martin, John. "Inventing Sincerity, Refreshing Prudence: The Discovery of the Individual in Renaissance Europe." *American Historical Review* 102.5 (Dec. 1997): 1309–42.

Matthews, Samantha. "Psychological Crystal Palace? Late Victorian Confession Albums." *Book Histories* 3 (2000): 125–54.

McClish, Glen. "Is Manner Everything, All? Reassessing Chesterfield's Art of Rhetoric." *Rhetoric Society Quarterly* 28.2 (Spring 1998): 5–24.

McGlew, James F. *Citizens on Stage: Comedy and Political Culture in Athenian Democracy.* Ann Arbor: U of Michigan P, 2002.

McKeon, Michael. "The Politics of Discourse and the Rise of the Aesthetic in Seventeenth-Century England." *Politics of Discourse: The Literature and History of Seventeenth-Century England.* Ed. Kevin Sharp and Steve N. Zwicker. Berkeley: U of California P, 1987. 35–51.

McLeod, Susan. *Notes on the Heart: Affective Issues in the Writing Classroom.* Carbondale: Southern Illinois UP, 1997.

McLuhan, Marshall, and Lewis H. Lapham. *Understanding Media: The Extension of Man.* Rpt. Cambridge: MIT Press, 1994.

McNabb, Richard. "Innovations and Complications: Juan Gil de Zamora's *Dictaminis Epithalamium.*" *Rhetorica* 21.4 (2003): 225–54.

McPhearson, Bruce, and Nancy Fowler. "Making Connections: Writing and Emotion." *The Writing Instructor* 12.1 (1992): 39–48.

Meyers, Peter Alexander. "Method and Civic Education." *Humanitas* 16.2 (2003): 4–47.

Micciche, Laura. "Emoting for a Change: Feminism and the Rhetoric of Anger." Second Biennial Feminism(s) and Rhetoric(s) Conference. University of Minnesota, Minneapolis. Oct. 1999.

———. "Emotions, Ethics, and Rhetorical Action." *Journal of Advanced Composition* 25.1 (2005). 161–85.

Micciche, Laura, and Dale Jacobs. *A Way to Move: Rhetorics of Emotion and Composition Studies.* Portsmouth, NH: Heinemann–Boynton/Cook, 2003.

Miller, Jacqueline. "The Passions Signified: Imitation and the Construction of Emotion in Sidney and Wroth." *Criticism* 43 (2001): 407–21.

Miller, Paul Allen. *Lyric Texts and Lyric Consciousness: The Birth of a Genre from Archaic Greece to Augustan Rome.* New York: Routledge, 1994.

Miller, Susan. *Assuming the Positions: Cultural Pedagogy and the Politics of Commonplace Writing.* Carbondale: Southern Illinois UP, 1998.

———. *Rescuing the Subject: A Critical Introduction to Rhetoric and the Writer.* Carbondale: Southern Illinois UP, 1989.

Miller, Thomas P. *The Formation of College English: Rhetoric and Belles Lettres in the British Cultural Provinces.* Pittsburgh: U of Pittsburgh P, 1997.

———. "Is Rhetoric American?" Listserve. H-Net History of Rhetoric Discussion List. 3 June 1997. <http://www.h-net.msu.edu/%&Erhrhetor/>.

———. "Reinventing Rhetorical Traditions." *Learning from the Histories of Rheto-*

ric: Essays in Honor of Winifred Bryan Horner. Ed. Theresa Enos. Carbondale: Southern Illinois UP, 1993. 26–41.

———, ed. *The Selected Writings of John Witherspoon.* Carbondale: Southern Illinois UP, 1990.

Milton, John. *Paradise Lost.* Ed. Merritt Y. Hughes. New York: Odyssey, 1935.

Mitchell, Lynette G. M. *Greeks Bearing Gifts: The Public Use of Private Relationships in the Greek World, 435–323 B.C.* Cambridge: Cambridge UP, 1998.

Mohrmann, G. R. "The Language of Nature and Elocutionary Theory." *Quarterly Journal of Speech* 52 (1966): 116–24.

Morsbach, H., and W. J. Tyler. "Some Japanese–Western Linguistic Differences Concerning Dependency Needs: The Case of 'Amae.'" *Life Sentences: Aspects of the Social Role of Language.* Ed. Rom Harre. New York: John Wiley, 1976. 129–45.

Morson, Gary Saul. "Misanthropology." *New Literary History* 27.1 (1996): 57–72.

Moss, Beverly. *A Community Text Arises: A Literate Text and a Literacy Tradition in African-American Churches.* Cresskill, N.J.: Hampton, 2003.

Mr. Smith Goes to Washington. Dir. Frank Capra. Perf. James Stewart. Columbia Pictures, 1939.

Murphy, James J. "The Origin and Early Development of Rhetoric." *A Synoptic History of Classical Rhetoric.* Ed. James J. Murphy. New York: Random House, 1972. 3–18.

———. *Rhetoric in the Middle Ages.* Berkeley: U of California P, 1974.

———. *Three Medieval Rhetorical Arts.* Berkeley: U of California P, 1971.

Neel, Jasper. *Plato, Derrida, and Writing.* Carbondale: Southern Illinois UP, 1988.

Nelson, John S., Allan Megill, and Donald M. McCloskey, eds. *The Rhetoric of the Human Sciences: Language and Argument in Scholarship and Public Affairs.* Madison: U of Wisconsin P, 1987.

Newton, Tim. "The Sociogenesis of Emotion: A Historical Sociology?" *Emotions in Social Life: Critical Themes and Contemporary Issues.* Ed. Gillian Bendelow and Simon J. Williams. New York: Routledge, 1998. 60–82.

Nienkamp, Jean. *Internal Rhetorics: Toward a History and Theory of Self-Persuasion.* Carbondale: Southern Illinois UP, 2001.

North, Marcy. *The Anonymous Renaissance: Cultures of Discretion in Tudor–Stuart England.* Chicago: U of Chicago P, 2003.

Norton, Rictor. "Sir Francis Bacon." *The Great Queens of History.* 8 Jan. 2000. <http: www.infopt.demon.co.uk/baconfra.html>.

Nussbaum, Martha C. *Love's Knowledge: Essays on Philosophy and Literature.* New York: Oxford UP, 1990.

———. *Poetic Justice: The Literary Imagination and Public Life*. Boston: Beacon, 1995.

———. *Therapy of Desire: Theory and Practice in Hellenistic Ethics*. Princeton: Princeton UP, 1994.

Ober, Josiah. *Mass and Elite in Democratic Athens: Rhetoric, Ideology, and the Power of the People*. Princeton: Princeton UP, 1989.

Oliensis, Ellen. *Horace and the Rhetoric of Authority*. Cambridge: Cambridge UP, 1988.

Ong, Walter. *Ramus, Method, and the Decay of Dialogue: From the Art of Discourse to the Art of Reason*. Cambridge, Mass.: Harvard UP, 1958.

Osley, A. S. "Greek Biographies before Plutarch." *Greece and Rome* 15.43 (Jan. 1946): 7–20.

Parrish, W. M. "The Concept of 'Naturalness.'" *Quarterly Journal of Speech* 37 (1951): 448–54.

———. "Elocution—A Definition and a Challenge." *Quarterly Journal of Speech* 43.1 (1957): 1–11.

Patkin, Terri Toles. "Explosive Baggage: Female Palestinian Suicide Bombers and the Rhetoric of Emotion." *Women and Language* 27.2 (Fall 2004): 79–89.

Perelman, Chaim, and Lucie Olbrechts-Tyteca. *The New Rhetoric: A Treatise on Argumentation*. Trans. John Wilkinson and Purcell Weaver. Notre Dame: U of Notre Dame P, 1969.

Perelman, Les. "The Medieval Art of Letter Writing: Rhetoric as Institutional Expression." *Textual Dynamics of the Professions: Historical and Contemporary Studies of Writing in Professional Communities*. Ed. Charles Bazerman and James Paradis. Madison: U of Wisconsin P, 1991. 97–119.

Pernot, Laurent. Rev. of *La Rhétorique dans l'Antiquité*. *Rhetorical Review* 3.1 (2005): 12–14.

Perreiah, Alan. "Humanistic Critique of Scholastic Dialectic." *Sixteenth Century Journal* 13.3 (Autumn 1982): 3–22.

Plato. *Gorgias*. Trans. W. D. Woodhead. *Plato: The Collected Dialogues*. Ed. Edith Hamilton and Huntington Cairns. Princeton: Princeton UP, 1961. 229–307.

———. *Ion*. <http://www.gutenberg.org/etext/1635>.

———. *Laws*. Trans. Benjamin Jowett. <http://isis.library.adelaide.edu.au/cgi/bin/pg/etext99/plaw10.txt>.

———. *Phaedrus*. Trans. R. Hackforth. *Plato: The Collected Dialogues*. Ed. Edith Hamilton and Huntington Cairns. Princeton: Princeton UP, 1961. 475–525.

———. *Protagoras*. Trans. W. K. C. Guthrie. *Plato: The Collected Dialogues*. Ed. Edith Hamilton and Huntington Cairns. Princeton: Princeton UP, 308–52.

———. *Republic*. Trans. Paul Shorey. *Plato: The Collected Dialogues*. Ed. Edith Hamilton and Huntington Cairns. Princeton: Princeton UP, 1961. 575–844.

————. *Timaeus.* Trans. Benjamin Jowett. *Plato: The Collected Dialogues.* Ed. Edith Hamilton and Huntington Cairns. Princeton: Princeton UP, 1961. 1151–211.

Pocock, J. G. A. *Virtue, Commerce, and History: Essays on Political Thought and History, Chiefly in the Eighteenth Century.* Cambridge: Cambridge UP, 1985.

Polanyi, Michael. *Personal Knowledge: Towards a Post-Critical Philosophy.* Chicago: U of Chicago P, 1958. Corr. ed. 1964.

Porter, Stanley E. *Handbook of Classical Rhetoric in the Hellenistic Period, 330 B.C.–A.D. 400.* Leiden: Brill, 1997.

Posner, David M. *The Performance of Nobility in Early Modern Literature.* Cambridge Studies in Renaissance Literature and Culture 33. Cambridge: Cambridge UP, 1999.

Poster, Carol. "Being, Time, and Definition: Toward a Semiotics of Figural Rhetoric." *Philosophy and Rhetoric* 33.2 (2001): 116–36.

————. "A Conversation Halved: Ancient Epistolary Theory." *Letter Writing Manuals and Instruction from Antiquity to the Present: Historical and Bibliographic Studies.* Ed. Linda Mitchell and Carol Poster. Columbia: U of South Carolina P, 2006. Chap. 3.

————. "Pedagogy and Bibliography: Aristotle's *Rhetoric* in Nineteenth-Century England." *Rhetoric Society Quarterly* 31.2 (2001): 5–36.

————. "Persuasion in an Empty Ontology: The Eleatic Synthesis of Philosophy, Poetry, and Rhetoric." *Philosophy and Rhetoric* 27 (1994): 277–99.

Potkay, Adam. "Classical Eloquence and Polite Style in the Age of Hume." *Eighteenth-Century Studies* 25.1 (Autumn 1991): 31–56.

Poulakos, John. "Early Changes in Rhetorical Practice and Understanding: From the Sophists to Socrates." *Texte* 8 (1989): 307–24.

————. *Sophistical Rhetoric in Classical Greece.* Columbia: U of South Carolina P, 1995.

Poulakos, Takis. "Human Agency in the History of Rhetoric: Gorgias's Encomium of Helen." *Writing Histories of Rhetoric.* Ed. Victor J. Vitanza. Carbondale: Southern Illinois UP, 1994. 59–80.

Preiss, Richard. "Natural Authorship." *Renaissance Drama* 34 (2005): 69–104.

Priestley, Joseph. *A Course of Lectures on Oratory and Criticism.* 1777. Ed. V. M. Bevilacqua and R. Murphy. Carbondale: Southern Illinois UP, 1965.

Quintilian. *Institutes (Institutio Oratoria).* Trans. H. E. Butler. Loeb Classical Library. Cambridge: Harvard UP, 1996.

Rabe, Hugo. *Prolegomena Sylloge: Rhetores Graeci.* Leipzig: Teubner, 1931.

Rajeswari, Sundar Rajan, ed. *The Lie of the Land: English Literary Studies in India.* Delhi: Oxford UP, 1992.

Rambuss, Richard. "The Secretary's Study: The Secret Designs of *The Shepheardes Calender.*" *ELH* 59 (1992): 313–35.

Rebhorn, Wayne A., ed. and trans. *Renaissance Debates on Rhetoric*. Ithaca: Cornell UP, 2000.

Redfield, James. *Nature and Culture in the* Iliad: *The Tragedy of Hector*. Chicago: U of Chicago P, 1975.

Register, Bryan. "The Logic and Validity of Emotional Appeal in Classical Greek Rhetorical Theory." Honors thesis. U of Texas, 1999. <http://englightenment. supersaturated.com/essays/text/bryanregister/thesis>.

Reynolds, Nedra. *Geographies of Writing: Inhabiting Places and Encountering Difference*. Carbondale: Southern Illinois UP, 2004.

Rhodes, Neil. *The Power of Eloquence and English Renaissance Literature*. New York: St. Martin's, 1992.

Richards, Jennifer. *Rhetoric and Courtliness in Early Modern Literature*. Cambridge: Cambridge UP, 2003.

Richardson, Malcolm. "The Fading Influence of the Medieval *Ars Dictaminis* in England after 1400." *Rhetorica* 19.2 (2001): 225–47.

Richmond, Kia Jane. "Repositioning Emotions in Composition Studies." *Composition Studies* 30.1 (2002): 67–82.

Ringvej, Mona Renate. "Interpretation of a Political Idea: The Radical Democracy of 508–462 Acta, humaniora." Diss. U of Oslo, 2004. 239–61.

Robb, Kevin, ed. *Literacy and Paideia in Ancient Greece*. New York: Oxford UP, 1994.

Robb, Mary Margaret. *Oral Interpretation of Literature in American Colleges and Universities: A Historical Study of Teaching Methods*. Rev. ed. New York: Johnson Reprint, 1968.

Robinson, T. M. *Contrasting Arguments: An Edition of the* Dissoi Logoi. New York: Arno, 1979.

Rodd, Thomas, Jr. "Before the Flood: Composition Teaching in America 1637–1900." *English Journal* 72.2 (Feb. 1983): 62–69.

Rogers, Lynne. "Close, Closed, Closure and the Settlers." *Al Jadid: A Review and Record of Arab Culture and Arts* 8.41 (Fall 2002): 4.

Rorty, Amélie Oksenberg, ed. *Essays on Aristotle's* Rhetoric. Berkeley: U of California P, 1996.

Rosenwein, Barbara H., ed. *Anger's Past: The Social Uses of an Emotion in the Middle Ages*. Ithaca: Cornell UP, 1998.

Ross, Trevor. "The Emergence of 'Literature': Making and Reading the English Canon in the Eighteenth Century." *ELH* 63.2 (1996): 397–422.

Royster, Jacqueline Jones. *Traces of a Stream: Literacy and Social Change among African American Women*. Pittsburgh: U of Pittsburgh P, 2000.

Russell, J. A., José-Miguel Fernández-Dols, Anthony S. R. Manstead, and Jane C. Wellenkamp, eds. *Everyday Conceptions of Emotion: An Introduction to the Psychology, Anthropology, and Linguistics of Emotion*. Nato Science Series D. Heidelberg and New York: Springer, 1995.

Russo, Joseph. "Prose Genres for the Performance of Traditional Wisdom in Ancient Greece: Proverb, Maxim, Apothegm." *Poet, Public, and Performance in Ancient Greece: From Homer to the Fifth Century.* Ed. Lowell Edmunds and Robert W. Wallace. Baltimore: Johns Hopkins UP, 1997. 49–64.

Said, Edward. *Orientalism.* New York: Vintage, 1979.

Samons, Loren J., II. *What's Wrong With Democracy? From Athenian Practice to American Worship.* Berkeley: U of California P, 2004.

Scafuro, Adele C. *The Forensic Stage: Settling Disputes in Graeco-Roman New Comedy.* Cambridge: Cambridge UP, 1997.

Schein, Seth L. "Cultural Studies and Classical: Contexts and Opportunities." *Contextualizing Classics: Ideology, Performance, Dialogue.* Ed. Thomas M. Falkner et al. Lanham, Md.: Rowman and Littlefield, 1999. 285–99.

Schiappa, Edward. *The Beginning of Rhetorical Theory in Classical Greece.* New Haven: Yale UP, 1999.

Schilb, John. "Review: Histories of Pedagogy." *College English* 61.3 (1999): 340–46.

Scott, Joan W. *Only Paradoxes to Offer: French Feminists and Rights of Men.* Cambridge: Harvard UP, 1997.

Scribner, Sylvia, and Michael Cole. "Unpacking Literacy." *Perspectives on Literacy.* Ed. E. R. Kitgen, B. M. Kroll, and M. Rose. Carbondale: Southern Illinois UP, 1988. 57–70.

Sedgwick, Eve. *Touching Feeling: Affect, Pedagogy, Performativity.* Series Q. Durham: Duke UP, 2003.

Sennett, Richard. *The Fall of Public Man.* London: Faber and Faber, 1986.

Sharma, Dinesh, and Kurt W. Fischer. "Socioemotional Development across Cultures: Context, Complexity, and Pathways." *Socioemotional Development across Cultures.* Ed. Dinesh Sharma and Kurt W. Fischer. New Directions for Child Development 82. San Francisco: Jossey-Bass, 1998. 3–20.

Sheridan, Thomas. *British Education: Or, the Source of the Disorders of Great Britain.* 1756. Menston, England: Scholar, 1971.

Sherman, Nancy. *The Fabric of Character: Aristotle's Theory of Virtue.* Oxford: Clarendon, 1989.

Sihvola, Juha, and Troels Engberg-Pedersen, eds. *The Emotions in Hellenistic Philosophy.* New Synthese Historical Library 46. Heidelberg and New York: Springer, 1998.

Simons, Herbert W. *The Rhetorical Turn: Invention and Persuasion in the Conduct of Inquiry.* Chicago: U of Chicago P, 1990.

Smith, C. Gregory. *Elizabethan Critical Essays.* 2 vols. Oxford: Oxford UP, 1946.

Solomon, Robert C. "The Politics of Emotion." *Midwest Studies in Philosophy: Philosophy of Emotions.* Midwest Studies in Philosophy 22. Ed. Peter E. French and Howard K. Wettstein. Notre Dame: U of Notre Dame P, 1999. 1–20.

Sperber, Dan, and Deirdre Wilson. "The Mapping between the Mental and the Public Lexicon." *Language and Thought: Interdisciplinary Themes.* Ed P. Carruthers and J. Boucher. Cambridge: Cambridge UP, 1998: 184–200.

Spoel, Philippa. "Rereading the Elocutionists: The Rhetoric of Thomas Sheridan's *A Course of Lectures on Elocution* and John Walker's *Elements of Elocution.*" *Rhetorica* 19.1 (Winter 2001): 49–91.

Spufford, Margaret. "First Steps in Literacy: The Reading and Writing Experiences of the Humblest Seventeenth-Century Spiritual Autobiographies." *Social History* 4 (1979): 407–35.

Stanhope, Philip Dormer, 4th Earl of Chesterfield. *Lord Chesterfield's Letters to His Son and Others.* London: Everyman's Library, 1969.

Stehle, Eva. *Performance and Gender in Ancient Greece: Nondramatic Poetry in Its Setting.* Princeton: Princeton UP, 1997.

Stern, Tiffany. "'A Small-Beer Health to His Second Day': Playwrights, Prologues and First Performances in the Early Modern Theater." *Studies in Philology* 101.2 (Spring 2004): 172–99.

Stevenson, Charles. *Ethics and Language.* New Haven: Yale UP, 1944.

Stewart, Alan. "The Early Modern Closet Discovered." *Representations* 50 (1995): 76–100.

Stockwell, Lance. "Appealing through Logic and Emotion: Logos, Pathos, and OJ [Simpson]." Paper presented at the annual meeting of the Southern States Communication Association, Memphis. 1996.

Stone, Lawrence. *The Crisis of the Aristocracy: 1558–1641.* Oxford: Oxford UP, 1965.

Struever, Nancy. "The Discourse of Cure: Rhetoric and Medicine in the Late Renaissance." *Rhetoric and Pedagogy: Its History, Philosophy, and Practice, Essays in Honor of James J. Murphy.* Ed. Winifred Bryan Horner and Michael Leff. Mahwah, N.J.: Lawrence Erlbaum, 1995. 277–94.

Swancutt, Diana. "The Paideia of Paul: Instructions, Identity, and the Scriptures of Israel in Pauline Christian Judaism." Unpublished monograph (work in progress). July 2004.

Swanson, Judith A. *The Public and the Private in Aristotle's Political Philosophy.* Ithaca: Cornell UP, 1992.

Tester, Keith. *Moral Culture.* London: Sage, 1997.

Thorne, Christian. "Thumbing Our Nose at the Public Sphere: Satire, the Market, and the Invention of Literature." *PMLA* 116.3 (May 2001): 531–44.

Tompkins, Jane P. "The Reader in History: The Changing Shape of Literary Response." *Reader-Response Criticism: From Formalism to Post-Structuralism.* Ed. Jane P. Tompkins. Baltimore: Johns Hopkins UP, 1980. 201–32.

Tottel, Richard. Preface. *Songes and Sonnettes, written by the ryght honourable Lorde Henry Haward late Earle of Surrey, and other.* London, 1557. Rpt. as

Miscellany. Ed. Hyder E. Rollins. 2nd ed. 2 vols. Cambridge: Harvard UP, 1965. 1:2.

Trowbridge, Hoyt. "Scattered Atoms of Probability." *Eighteenth-Century Studies* 5 (1971): 1–38.

Ulman, H. Lewis. *Things, Thoughts, Words, and Actions: The Problem of Language in Late Eighteenth-Century British Rhetorical Theory.* Carbondale: Southern Illinois UP, 1994.

Valesio, Paolo. *Novantiqua: Rhetorics as a Contemporary Theory.* Advances in Semiotics. Bloomington: Indiana UP, 1986.

Vandraegen, Daniel. "Thomas Sheridan and the Natural School." *Speech Monographs* 20 (Mar. 1953): 58–64.

van Liere, Katherine Elliot. "Humanism and Scholasticism in Sixteenth-Century Academe: Five Student Orations from the University of Salamanca." *Renaissance Quarterly* 53.1 (Spring 2000): 57–107.

Vickers, Brian. Introduction. *Rhetoric Revalued: Papers from the International Society for the History of Rhetoric.* Binghamton, N.Y.: Medieval and Renaissance Text and Studies, 1983. 13–39.

Vincent, David. *Literacy and Popular Culture: England 1750–1914.* Cambridge: Cambridge UP, 1992.

Vitanza, Victor J., ed. *Writing Histories of Rhetoric.* Carbondale: Southern Illinois UP, 1994.

Vlastos, Gregory. *Socrates: Ironist and Moral Philosopher.* Ithaca: Cornell UP, 1991.

Walcot, Peter. *Envy and the Greeks: A Study of Human Behaviour.* Warminster, England: Aris and Phillips, 1978.

Walker, Jeffrey. "The Body of Persuasion: A Theory of the Enthymeme." *College English* 56.1 (1994): 46–65.

———. "Michael Psellos on Rhetoric: A Translation and Commentary on Psellos' Synopsis of Hermogenes." *Rhetoric Studies Quarterly* 31.1 (Winter 2001): 5–39.

———. "*Pathos* and *Katharsis* in 'Aristotelian' Rhetoric: Some Implications." *Rereading Aristotle's* Rhetoric. Ed. Alan G. Gross and Arthur E. Walzer. Carbondale: Southern Illinois UP, 2000. 74–92.

———. *Rhetoric and Poetics in Antiquity.* Oxford: Oxford UP, 2000.

Walker, John. *Elements of Elocution.* 2 vols. London, 1781. Menston, England: Scholar, 1969.

Walker, Julia. *Expressionism and Modernism in the American Theatre: Bodies, Voices, Words.* Cambridge Studies in American Theatre and Drama 21. Cambridge: Cambridge UP, 2005.

Walton, Douglas N. *The Place of Emotion in Argument.* University Park: Pennsylvania State UP, 1992.

Walz, Christianus. *Rhetores Graeci*. Stuttgart: J. G. Cotta, 1835.

Ward, John O. "Rhetorical Theory and the Rise and Decline of *Dictamen* in the Middle Ages and Early Renaissance." *Rhetorica* 19.2 (2001): 175–223.

Watson, John McClain. "From Interpretation to Identification: A History of Facial Images in the Sciences of Emotion." *History of Human Sciences* 17.1 (2004): 29–51.

Watts, James W. "Story—List—Sanction: A Cross-Cultural Strategy of Ancient Persuasion." *Rhetoric Before and Beyond the Greeks*. Ed. Carol S. Lipton and Roberta A. Binkley. Albany: SUNY P, 2004. 197–212.

Webb, William. *A Discourse of English Poetrie*. 1586. Ed. Edward Arber. Freeport: Books for Libraries, 1970.

Wellberry, David. Foreword. *Discourse Networks: 1800/1900*. By Friedrich A. Kittler. Trans. Michael Metteer with Chris Cullens. Stanford: Stanford UP, 1990. vii–xxxiii.

Werstine, Paul. "Narratives about Printed Shakespeare Texts: 'Foul Papers' and 'Bad' Quartos." *Shakespeare Quarterly* 41.1 (Spring 1990): 65–86.

Westlake, H. D. Rev. of *Studien zur griechischen Biographie*, by Albrecht Dihle. *Classical Review* 7.2 (June 1957): 118–19.

Whately, Richard. *The Elements of Rhetoric: Comprising an Analysis of the Laws of Moral Evidence and of Persuasion, with Rules for Argumentative Composition and Elocution*. Ed. Douglas Ehninger. Carbondale: Southern Illinois UP, 1973.

Wierzbicka, Anna. "Everyday Conceptions of Emotion: A Semantic Perspective." *Everyday Conceptions of Emotion: An Introduction to the Psychology, Anthropology and Linguistics of Emotion*. Ed. J. A. Russell, José-Miguel Fernández-Dols, Anthony S. R. Manstead, and Jane C. Wellenkamp. Nato Science Series D. Heidelberg and New York: Springer, 1995. 17–47.

Wilcox, Stanley. "The Scope of Early Rhetorical Instruction." *Harvard Studies in Classical Philology* 53 (1942): 121–55.

Wilson, Thomas. *The Art of Rhetoric*. Ed. Peter E. Medline. University Park: Pennsylvania State UP, 1994.

Winthrop-Young, Geoffrey, and Michael Wutz. Translators' introduction. *Gramophone, Film, Typewriter*. By Friedrich A. Kittler. Stanford: Stanford UP, 1999. xi–xxxviii.

Wisse, Jakob. *Ethos and Pathos from Aristotle to Cicero*. Amsterdam: Hakkert, 1989.

Woodmansee, Martha. "The Genius and the Copyright: Economic and Legal Conditions of the Emergence of the 'Author.'" *Eighteenth-Century Studies* 17.4 (Summer 1984): 425–48.

Worsham, Lynn. "Eating History, Purging Memory, Killing Rhetoric." *Writing Histories of Rhetoric*. Ed. Victor J. Vitanza. Carbondale: Southern Illinois UP, 1994. 139–55.

———. "Going Postal: Pedagogic Violence and the Schooling of Emotion." *Journal of Advanced Composition* 18 (1998): 213–45.

Yunis, Harvey. "The Constraints of Democracy and the Rise of the Art of Rhetoric." *Democracy, Empire, and the Arts in Fifth-Century Athens.* Ed. Deborah Boedeker and Kurt A. Raabflaub. Cambridge: Harvard UP, 1998. 223–40.

Zabbal, François. Foreword. *Ancestor of the West: Writing, Reasoning, and Religion in Mesopotamia, Elam, and Greece.* By Jean Bottero, Clarice Herrenschmidt, and Jean-Pierre Vernant. Trans. Teresa Lavander Fagan. Chicago: U of Chicago P, 2000. vii–xi.

Zhu, Rui. "Distinguishing the Public from the Private: Aristotle's Solution to Plato's Paradox." *Histories of Political Thought* 25.2 (2004): 231–42.

Index

Bryant, Donald, 13
Buffier, Claude, 137
Buil, Ricard J. Sola, 98–100
Burckhardt, Jacob, 95, 97
Burgh, James, 137–38, 141; *Art of Speaking*, 137, 143
Burke, Edmund, 115, 124; gender and, 125
Bury, J. B., 44
Butler, Samuel, 118, 127

Calias, 61
Callidius, Marcus, 130
Calvin, John, 95
Calvinism, 5
Camargo, Martin, 100
Cambridge University, 78
Camlot, Jason, 134
Campbell, George, 16, 118, 134; *Philosophy of Rhetoric*, 121, 124
Carr, Jean Ferguson, 5
Cartesianism, 45, 65, 116, 118, 146; emotion and, 16, 18, 121–22; language and, 10, 107, 136
Castiglione, Baldesar, 80; secrecy and, 96
Categories (Aristotle), 153
Catholicism, 97
Catiline (Jonson), 113
Catullus, 32
Certain Notes of Instruction Concerning the Making of Verse in English (Gascoigne), 80
character, 11, 110; Aristotle and, 96; novels and, 94; prevailing types of, 26; *thumos* and, 150
Chartier, Roger, 139
Chaucer, Geoffrey, 125
Cheke, John, 80
Chesterfield, Philip Stanhope, 130
China, 19
Christianity, 18, 20, 22–23, 26–27, 39, 149; anger in, 48; martyrdom and, 21; modernism and, 73, 74; Neoplatonism and, 71; *paideia* and, 21; *phronesis* and, 96; poetry and, 57; pre-Reformation, 26; privacy and, 47; sermons and, 75

Chrysippus, 120
Cicero, 7, 13, 36, 130; commentaries on, 35; *De Oratore*, 121, 129; divinity and, 69; epistolary rhetoric and, 102, 103; *Epistulae ad Atticum*, 100; hermeneutics and, 34; letters of, 73; origin of, 79; *paideia* and, 101; precepts of, 82; print and, 80; Renaissance and, 76
citizens, 5, 11, 18, 27, 43–44; medicine and, 63; oratory and, 110, 126; trust and, 21, 25
city-states, 43–44, 55
Civilization of the Renaissance in Italy, The (Burckhardt), 95
Clanchy, M. T., 2
Clarissa (Richardson), 94
Classen, Albrecht, 99
Classical civilization, 72–73, 77–81, 83–84; Christianity and, 21; emotion and, 93, 97, 121–25, 149–52; epistolary rhetoric and, 98, 101–2; language and, 4, 8–10, 86, 89, 126, 133; oratory and, 37, 54, 91, 135; tradition and 28, 78. *See also* antiquity; Athenians; Greece
Classical Rhetoric for the Modern Student (Corbett), 54
Cockin, William, 143
Cole, A. Thomas, 58
Cole, Michael, 39
Colet, John, 77
Comenius, John, 80
community, 7, 8
compassion, 19, 26, 27
Congleton, J. E., 128
consciousness, 16–17, 30, 35, 118, 130–31, 141, 147; Aristotle on, 46; Associationism and, 124; cures and, 62; drama and, 59; Enlightenment era and, 94; 107–8; language and, 9, 10, 81, 111, 126–27, 133; individualism and, 97; *pathos* and, 109; poetry and, 56, 57; post-Freudian feelings and, 24; privacy and, 47; Scottish moral philosophy and, 118; trust and, 147, 153
Consecration of the Writer, The: 1750–1830 (Bénichou), 145

Susan Miller is a professor of English at the University of Utah. She is the author of *Rescuing the Subject: A Critical Introduction to Rhetoric and the Writer,* which received the W. Ross Winterowd Award and is in a paperback edition with a new introduction; *Textual Carnivals: The Politics of Composition,* which received the Mina P. Shaughnessy Prize from the MLA, the NCTE/CCCC Outstanding Book Award, and the W. Ross Winterowd Award; *Assuming the Positions: Cultural Pedagogy and the Politics of Commonplace Writing,* which received the NCTE/CCCC Outstanding Book Award and was named a Choice Outstanding Academic Title; *Writing: Process and Product*; and four other textbooks.